W9-BXX-734

Buying a Business That Makes You Rich

Toss Your Job Not the Dice

John Martinka

Book Publishers Network

Book Publishers Network
P.O. Box 2256
Bothell • WA • 98041
Ph • 425-483-3040
www.bookpublishersnetwork.com

Copyright © 2013 by John Martinka

All rights reserved. No part of this book may be reproduced, stored in, or introduced into a retrieval system, or transmitted in any form, or by any means (electronic, mechanical, photocopying, recording, or otherwise) without the prior written permission of the publisher.

10 9 8 7 6 5 4 3 2 1

Printed in the United States of America

LCCN   2012954732
ISBN   978-1-937454-72-2

Editor: Laurel Harmon
Cover Design: Laura Zugzda
Interior Design: Stephanie Martindale

Contents

PREFACE

This book is aimed at three target audiences:

1. Corporate executives who are fed up with the corporate world (or the corporate world is fed up with them) and want their own business. These people have honed their management and leadership skills, have capital and don't have an idea themselves for the next great rocket ship growth business.

2. Small business owners who are tired of slugging it out with the competition for pure organic growth and wants to buy market share, a product line, a geographic area or quality employees.

3. Managers of a small equity fund that has either pooled personal money or has raised money from outside investors, usually friends and family.

The characteristics of these three buyer types are quite close so the message to them is the same. While there is a lot of value for other audiences, the target audience is not the serial buyer, private equity groups or large corporate buyers.

To buy a business you need to meet a lot of sellers. Do that and analysis, financing, due diligence, deal structure and everything else will come together if it's a mature, profitable business. I tell my clients that we have three objectives as we search for companies and these should also be your objectives.

1. To see a wide variety of businesses from 100% of the market. This means you must access both the public and the hidden markets.

2. To get a good deal on a wonderful company, one where your skills can provide value to leverage growth.

3. Stay out of bad deals, as the only thing worse than no deal is a bad deal.

All business buyers (and business sellers) make a leap of faith when they consummate a transaction. With proper planning, a proven system and an experienced guide that leap of faith is off a chair not off the roof.

ACKNOWLEDGEMENTS

The writing of any book and especially a first book takes a lot of time. That's time that could have been spent with family, relaxing, doing things around the house or generating more clients. For that reason, I must first thank my wife Jan for putting up with this project and taking over many things in our personal life as I put time in on this book.

There are three other "thanks" I'd like to make, first and foremost to my good friend Ted Leverette. I got into this business by serendipity. Ted and I were back-to-back Rotary Club presidents in Kirkland, Washington and got to know each other pretty well. This led to my entering the consulting business, becoming a Business Buyer Advocate® and helping found "Partner" On-Call Network. Thanks Ted!

I thought of writing a book for years and then I attended Alan Weiss' Million Dollar Consulting College®. He convinced me that when you have expertise to share that you must write a book so others can learn from you and improve their lives.

Finally, let me say thank-you to my hundreds of clients over the years. They deserve a "congratulations" for their successful deals. Every deal is different and as I am not the type of person who can spend all day doing the same thing, the variety of the thousand's of companies at which I've looked, the nuances, intricacies and personalities make my job fun, which should be a requirement for any and every job.

— 1 —

WHY BUY A BUSINESS?

Pause and think about this. Here are the top nine reasons given by hundreds of people to whom I've asked this question.

- Control
- Reap the benefits of my smart and hard work
- Independence
- Decision authority
- Flexibility
- Income potential
- Equity or net worth
- Creativity
- So I can be the boss

Maybe only one percent of the time do I get the answer I think is the most important; that is, to have FUN! To wake up in the morning with a smile on your face because "It's my business." Yes, there are alligators nipping at you and at your business (just like every business has), but they are your alligators. You get to make the decisions, control the process, and benefit from your actions.

SHOULD YOU OWN A BUSINESS?

That's the first question you need to ask yourself. Ask this before you even consider whether buying a business is the right way to get your own company. You can take tests that will tell you if you are entrepreneurial, and those tests are usually a waste of time and money. It really has to come from your gut. Either you want to do it or you don't. Believe me, there are a lot of "supposedly interested" business owners and buyers out there. There always have been and always will be. They talk a good game but never get on the playing field.

Since 1993 I have trained thousands of business buyers and helped scores of clients get their buy-sell deals done. In 2010 I was given the name, "The Escape Artist™." The person who helped me coin this moniker was thinking of the work I do on the other end of the buy-sell spectrum, helping owners plan how to best escape their business (exiting their business with style, grace and more money).

I, however, saw much more in this moniker because for so many years I have helped executives "escape" the confines of their job, to control their lives through business ownership. I've also helped business owners "escape" the plateau they were on, through growth by acquisition.

During my first year as a Business Buyer Advocate® I met a supposed business buyer. I didn't know at the time that he was simply a tire-kicker. It took a couple years of seeing him chase advertised businesses, only to end up saying that none of them were what he really wanted. It's a little harder to find the tire-kickers these days, because of the prevalence of the Internet. They can remain anonymous as they hide behind their computer screen, but they're still out there. It's one reason some brokers are hesitant to initially put a great listing on the websites that advertise businesses for sale. They know they'll get bombarded with calls from the unqualified and not serious buyers.

REAL LIFE STORY: IT COMES FROM THE GUT

As I said, the desire to buy and own a business has to come from your gut, and the feelings in your gut may change as you gain experience and build up your capital. Many clients have done what Craig did. After being "let go" from Honeywell (also known as being terminated, downsized or fired), he said that he was frustrated and a little angry. It was then he realized that for seven years he'd been thinking of owning his own company, and he became thankful that his employer had given him management and leadership skills, a salary that allowed him to accumulate capital and, finally, the kick-in-the-pants he needed. Now he wouldn't just be dreaming about it, he'd own a business (which he did nine months later).

Self-employment can be great, if you are the right kind of person. My experience has shown me that, when it comes to business ownership, there are four types of people. At one end of the spectrum are the serial entrepreneurs. They are always starting something, growing it to a level where it strains their tolerance for managing, and then wanting to start another one.

At the other end of the spectrum are people like my mother, a college level math teacher who couldn't imagine anything riskier than a monthly paycheck from a government school. Right next to people like my mother are those who get a job with a big corporation, build seniority, and hope to stay there for 40 plus years, whether or not they advance.

The rest of us are in the middle of the spectrum. Here we find people who stumble into business ownership (for example, they will get an idea, and their company doesn't want to move on the idea, so they leave to develop it themselves) or are forced into it (when their company is downsized). The closer someone is to the entrepreneurial end of the spectrum, the faster they will end up with their own business.

Others take longer, and often they make the leap just because they can't imagine going through the job search process again.

I've worked with people who have spent their first 10 years of employment doing nothing but building capital and raising their skill level, because their goal was to own a business. As they weren't the creative type who could come up with a new idea, they knew it was best to buy an established company and grow it. (My good friend, business broker Bill Pearsall of William Pearsall and Associates, coined the term *re-entrepreneur* for people who don't have new ideas and are best suited to manage and grow an existing business.) When a person quits their job to focus 100% on buying a business, you know they're serious.

REAL LIFE STORY: THE MOTIVATION TO BUSINESS OWNERSHIP

A client, age 45, stated that his outplacement firm told him he would have four to five more job searches before age 65. He had never searched for job before because after taking a position out of college he was then recruited by another firm 10 years later. The thought of playing the corporate game of a job search every three to five years did not appeal to him.

It was the motivation he needed to get his own business. He told the outplacement he wouldn't need their services and started the, successful, journey own a business.

Buying a business is like climbing a mountain. There are ups, downs, dangerous crevices and slippery slopes. If you're climbing by yourself, you may make it to the summit. If you are part of a team, you have a better chance of success. If you have a team and an experienced guide, who knows all the danger zones on the trek and how to avoid them, you have an excellent chance of reaching the summit safely, which in this case is a successful transaction.

THREE WAYS TO GET INTO BUSINESS

There are only three ways to get into business. You can start a business (consulting is a type of startup) or buy a new franchise opportunity or buy an established business (let me clarify one thing; when I write, "buy a business" always make sure you mentally put the adjectives "mature," "profitable" and "fairly priced" in front of the word business).

All of these models have advantages and disadvantages depending on you and your situation. At the end of this chapter is a chart comparing some of the key factors involved in starting a business or buying a franchise or an existing business. Some of the primary characteristics of people choosing each option are described in the following paragraphs.

STARTING A BUSINESS

- You're a creative type, you already have ideas for a business, you like the thrill of getting things off the ground and you're willing to risk the odds, as it is a commonly known fact that 65-80% of startups fail.

- You have the time and energy level to devote to a startup. Those rumored 80-100 hour weeks are very true when you start a business.

- Your financial situation is that you have limited capital to invest in a business but you have other income, so you don't need an immediate salary. Working without a paycheck is what is often referred to as "sweat-equity." (This section refers to a business startup in which you are working, using your own money, etc., not one where you have or are seeking angel investors and venture capital that can fund a salary for you as you start the business.)

BUYING A FRANCHISE

- Management experience is not your strength and the idea of a "business in a box" is appealing.

- The brand, franchisor marketing and proven concept make it attractive.

- You need the controls the franchisor places on the franchisees. The controls may cover the product and service you can offer, marketing, advertising, pricing, etc. (Not all bad; while it can stifle a creative and experienced business person, it also keeps less experienced people from drifting off target.)

Another option is to buy an existing franchise, known as a "franchise resale." My good friend Jeff Levy is with The Entrepreneur Source (jeffltheesource@comcast.net) and one of the best franchise brokers/consultants in the country. Here is some input from Jeff on: Considerations when Buying a Franchise Resale.

All franchise owners are subject to the term of their license agreement. It is usually five, ten, fifteen or, on rare occasions, twenty years. It is not unusual that a franchisee will consider selling their business as well as considering their renewal options. When selling is an option, it creates some interesting opportunities and certainly additional checklist items for the potential acquirer.

When one considers acquiring a franchise they must remember there are three parties in the transaction: the buyer, the seller AND the franchisor. In a typical franchise agreement, subject to the Franchise Disclosure Document (FDD), there is a provision for selling the business. This is also commonly referred to as a transfer. Although the franchisor cannot unreasonably withhold their approval, they do have the right to reject the buyer. Normally, a rejection could be based on financial ability, prior bankruptcy or some other anomaly like failing a criminal background check. In all cases the new buyer will have to sign a new franchise agreement or accept the transfer and be subject to its terms. It is important for the buyer to understand if they are getting a transfer or a new franchise agreement. A transfer might mean they will have to renew at the end of the term of the original agreement. A new franchise agreement coincident with a purchase is recommended. This allows you to get the full term and keeps you from being subject to any changes in the franchise agreement for the longest possible time.

There are other considerations when working on acquiring a franchise resale. It is often easier to determine the value of the target company as compared to buying an independent entity. If the buyer has developed a positive communication with the franchisor, they can direct them to other recent acquisitions so the candidate person can see comparable resale data, as one might do in valuing real estate. It is more difficult for a franchisee to hide financial information, as what they have accomplished to date usually has to be supplied to the franchisor. The buyer can verify revenues and margins as well as typical ratios in that business.

When one buys into a franchise resale, they are joining the franchisor's organization and its culture. Experience tells this writer that if the seller has a positive relationship with their franchisor, it is a good sign and may be a predictor of a future good relationship. Remember, all parties have a vested interest in seeing a successful transition to a new, motivated franchisee.

BUYING AN ESTABLISHED COMPANY

- You have experience managing people, processes, money and systems to some varying degree. The company you buy will have an established product or service, skilled employees, a customer base and a competitive advantage, meaning the customers pay enough for the product or service so that the firm earns a profit.

- Buying a business is trading (your) capital for immediate cash flow. You have to come up with 15-40% of the purchase price to close the deal. However, you walk into immediate cash flow. If the deal closes on the 31st, when the 15th of the month rolls around you get a paycheck just like your employees.

- Financing an acquisition is easier than financing a startup. The seller will hold a note and banks (at the time of this writing) like to make acquisition loans, usually through the Small Business Administration's (SBA) guarantee program.

REAL LIFE SITUATION: WHY SELL ONE BUSINESS AND BUY ANOTHER?

It gets in your blood! I have had numerous clients who previously had bought or started a business, grew it, sold it and want to get another one. You may ask, why sell and buy another one? Why not just keep the one you have?

There are three reasons for exiting one business and buying another, based on client experiences:

1. *You get an offer that is too good to pass up.*

2. *Business owners are like everybody else. They often want a new challenge. On average, management level employees change jobs every three to five years. Owners last longer but often want variety.*

3. *Market conditions dictate a sale. It could be consolidation is occurring and will make you uncompetitive if you don't sell, or perhaps you have investors whom want to cash out.*

KEEP YOUR BUSINESS IN SYNC

Many years ago I read about the "three-legged stool of business" and it made a lot of sense to me. This theory states that there are three elements in every business; operations, sales and marketing and finance and administration, and they are dependent on each other. One thing that stuck with me was the comment that operations has to be in sync with sales and marketing, and the finance and administration department gives you the information to know if they are in sync.

When speaking, one of my questions that stumps most audiences, is, "What's worse than having the capacity to make 1,000,000 units a year and only selling 250,000 units?"

It's having the capacity to make 250,000 units and selling 1,000,000. It may be your pricing is too low, your sales staff is too good or your operations under-perform. In any event, if you take orders and can't deliver, your customers will be very unhappy because you've disrupted their business, created problems for them and lowered their profits. In the future, they will most likely order from a competitor and you'll never get that business back (plus, your reputation in the industry now stinks and word travels fast).

What does this have to do with business buying? Everything. A qualified buyer is someone who understands that running a business is managing a number of complicated parts. He or she knows that the example described above is important. You can't concentrate on only sales or on only production or especially on only administration.

Michael Gerber, in his book, *The E-Myth Revisited* (HarperCollins, 1994), expands on the classic line "You want to work on your business not in your business" when he states that technicians work in the business and entrepreneurs work on their business. It's important to know the difference. Our auto mechanic works in his business, fixing cars, as much or more than he works on his business. My business buyer clients often don't know how to do the work their employees do (and don't want to know).

WHAT DO YOU WANT TO DO?

One of my standard questions for business buyers is, "What do you want to do on a daily, weekly, monthly basis?" At least 90% of my clients' answers include the words strategy, vision or planning. The other 10% want to work on strategy but they disguise their answers by saying they want to improve customer relations or take the company to the next level. I never hear, "I want to run the shop floor" or "I want to be chief salesperson, on the road four days a week."

So ask yourself, if you buy a business, the above question? Then realize that you will be asking business sellers this same question to see if what is required in the company matches your goals. The owner who says that they spend their time watching the numbers like a hawk to make sure margins are where they need to be and production is efficient doesn't have a good business for a sales type person. Correspondingly, a business that requires constant customer contact and managing a professional sales force is not a good fit for the operations engineer.

REAL LIFE STORY: BUYER FEVER CAN BE FATAL

When you don't determine exactly what you want to do and what you want out of a business you run the risk of getting buyer fever because a business sounds sexy, cool or its product fascinates you.

An early exposure I had with this is still the most memorable. I have heard many stories about people who got buyer-fever and fell in love with a business that wasn't a good fit for them. As with this story, it's usually a numbers person who is fascinated with a company that makes something.

I was introduced to Tom (a CPA) with corporate finance experience. He had bought a cabinet manufacturing shop, was having problems and was considering selling. His top goal was to get out while being able to recoup his investment in the business. This would prove to be tough because sales and profits were down from when he bought it even though at the time it was a strong economy. Who would pay him this much? He was counting on the "greater fool" theory that states someone will be a greater fool than the seller and will overpay or buy a loser.

When we spoke he had received only one offer. It was for two-thirds of what he paid for the business. However, the buyer would have to use all his capital for the down payment and there would be no money for working capital. Because of this, the deal collapsed. Other buyers told him that, for the money needed as a down payment (so he could pay off his remaining debt), they could buy a larger and better business.

He stated he bought the business because it was "cool" to make something. He loved the idea of making a product and ignored the fact that someone has to sell those cabinets before they could be made. While he lamented that it's tough getting contractors to pay in a timely manner, his biggest problem was his employees.

He couldn't relate to his people, almost all blue-collar workers. He commented that they lived for three things: a cigarette on each break, a beer after work and going fishing on weekends. He was living and breathing his business and couldn't understand why they didn't do the same. It doesn't take a clinical psychiatrist to analyze this situation and realize there was employer-employee conflict.

Let me finish by telling you that he felt the previous owner "cooked the books." He suspected that the owner fudged the figures on inventory to make the cash flow the year prior to the sale 50% greater than the four previous years.

For some reason—buyer fever comes to mind—he bought into the explanation that the prior year was the only year to use for valuation purposes. Oh, did I mention he was a CPA? It seems that it is always the thing closest to our expertise that trips us up, because we get overconfident. How could a CPA miss inventory adjustments? How could a CPA fall for the sales pitch of only using the last, and best, year to value the company? Two words explain this, "buyer fever."

It's easy to get enamored with a business, even one where your skills aren't a match. The above example is not atypical. Know what you want to do and what you want to get out of a business.

WHAT EXPERIENCE DO YOU HAVE IN MANAGING PEOPLE?

As I said, to buy an independent, profitable business a buyer should have experience and skills, to varying degrees, in managing people, processes, money and systems. If your passion for business ownership exceeds your management and leadership abilities, then consider a franchise. With an independent business you walk into an ongoing operation, and to grow it you have to be able to manage and lead.

If you pick up the *Wall Street Journal* or any other major business publication, you will constantly read about people problems in all types and sizes of businesses. It's the number one issue in almost every company. It's one of the largest expense items and one of the most misunderstood areas. A lot of people make a lot of money by solving people problems, in businesses of all sizes.

The ability to manage and lead people is critical to success as a business owner. That doesn't mean order them around, it means being able to motivate them, help them improve and get them to be as productive as possible. It's easily overlooked and when not handled correctly it can cause severe consequences.

REAL LIFE STORY: MANAGING, LEADING AND NOT BEING OVERWHELMED

One of the comments I often hear after a corporate person buys a business is, "I'm overwhelmed." This is normal and it gets better. For example, one client wrote, "My wife and I are into it up to our necks, and loving it."

In the corporate world there are layers of staff and things just get done. One client summarized it by saying he was overwhelmed because he didn't realize he had to know how absolutely everything in the business worked. He went on to say he didn't have to do everything but he had to know who was to do it, when it needed to be done and what it looked like when done right.

The happy ending to the above is that the buyer whom discussed what being overwhelmed meant to him got up to speed quickly, has done extremely well with his company and is looking for another acquisition at the time I'm writing this.

CORPORATE EXECUTIVE—WHY DO YOU WANT A BUSINESS?

A 2011 study by the Bureau of Labor Statistics stated that middle class jobs in America are on the decline. While high-end jobs are predicted to increase, it's not what happens to the population in general but what happens to you. Do you have room for advancement? Will your company keep you on as your salary rises to the top of the range? Will you be happy doing more for the same money as the company cuts staff to please Wall Street analysts?

REAL LIFE STORIES: YOUR EMPLOYER PROVIDES THE MOTIVATION

One of the first business buyers I ever talked to told me what was happening in his life and I will never forget what he said. He told me that he would turn age 50 in three months and he knew what his company did to people when they turned 50. He said, "They will replace me with somebody half my age and one-third my salary." He elaborated that his replacement would also have about ten percent of his productivity.

Before I became a Business Buyer Advocate a banker in my Rotary Club lamented the latest round of staff cuts his bank had just made (to please Wall Street). He told me he was already working long hours, not seeing his kids enough and this just meant there would be more to do for the remaining staff.

Let's go back to the beginning of the chapter and look at the reasons people commonly given for wanting business ownership so that you can judge how important each is to you. First, rate all of the reasons in the following chart on a one to 10 scale, with 10 being the highest, for how important each criteria is to you (they could all be the same number). Then rank them from one to nine, with one being your top reason for wanting a business and nine being your least important.

	1-10 scale	Rank
Be the boss		
Benefit myself from my smart and hard work		
Control		
Creativity		

	1-10 scale	Rank
Decision maker		
Equity or net worth		
Income potential		
Independence		
FUN		

There is no right or wrong, although, in my opinion, if money is the main reason for wanting to own a business, you will not enjoy it as much as if independence, fun and putting your own twist on things (being creative) are your top reasons (not that money isn't important).

REAL LIFE STORIES: BE FOCUSED ON GETTING A DEAL

The above are reasons why your gut should be telling you business ownership is for you. Greg, Ed and Kyle (separate buyers; not partners) stand out as buyers whose gut feelings were so strong they couldn't stand working for someone else anymore and left their well-paying positions to focus on business searches fulltime.

While money was a motivator, other reasons were the more important factors tugging on them. Each of these clients had children in school, mortgages and the other expenses we all have. Yet they budgeted their time and money to pursue their dreams.

But for every Greg, Ed and Kyle, there are numerous buyers like Michael who, in the midst of a drawn out buying process, told me he would get to his next task "after my next game of golf." I came to realize that there would always be a next game of golf. We had a get serious talk, he got the message and asked if we could close in three weeks. We couldn't, but we did close in six weeks.

Small and midsize companies—why do you want another business?

Later in this book I cover in detail why a small business owner would want another company (this might be you in the future if you're a first time business buyer—after you've closed your first deal). For now, let's just look at some of the numerous reasons it can make sense for small and midsize companies to make an acquisition.

Geographic expansion: Why risk opening a new office and taking all the risk? It's almost the same as starting a business. A client bought a distressed Seattle based business that had become distressed because of an unsuccessful expansion into Portland (starting a new business in a new market). When you buy, you assume the customers, market share, and cash flow, and you eliminate the one to five year ramp-up that many start-ups face.

Obtain Employees: Two clients bought competitors. For both, the number one reason was to find competent employees (in a tight labor market for those specialty employees).

Diversification: While it might not make sense to diversify too far from your core business, it may make sense to expand your horizons a little. Perhaps you can buy a company with a product line you can't get on your own (products you can also sell to your existing customers). Or perhaps the company you acquire will give you the service department you don't have now.

Customers: Acquire a direct competitor that allows you to sell the same product to more customers, or acquire a complementary business so you can sell your product or service to their customers, and vice versa.

Synergism: Profits can increase through overhead reduction, more sales to existing customers, increased marketing efficiency, greater purchasing power and more. The owner of a magazine publishing company told me the following Real Life Story.

REAL LIFE STORY: CREATE ECONOMIES OF SCALE

The owner of a magazine publishing company told me, "I found that when I had one magazine it required me to have one switchboard operator. Now that I have 23 magazines, I still need [only] one switchboard operator. I probably get one call a week from somebody that publishes a singular magazine and wants me to purchase his or her company. I know how expensive it is to have just one publication. I do not want a loser, but show me a business already making money and I will make a lot more."

Unprofitable companies scare off most business buyers. The corporate buyer does not need to be as concerned with this. An individual buyer must have immediate cash flow. A company can purchase a profitable, breakeven or maybe an unprofitable firm (if you know the reasons why and feel you can fix them). Often, the best deal is a company not earning up to potential, where you can eliminate overhead and quickly make it profitable. The best deals for growth by acquisition occur when the owner is forced to sell, which could be due to divorce, death, disability, owner disputes, or lack of working capital.

ACTION ITEMS

* Rank the reasons for considering business ownership.

* Evaluate your desires and skills, to determine if buying a business is the best option for you compared to starting one or buying a franchise opportunity.

* Ask yourself if you have the experience and skills to run a mature, profitable business. This means your experience with managing people, processes, systems and money.

* Know what you want to do on a daily, weekly and monthly basis. Is it sales, finance, marketing, operations, strategy or something else?

* Corporate executives: Ask yourself if you can make enough money and be happy working for someone else.

* Business owners: What are the value drivers for growing by acquisition? Is it more customers, skilled employees, geographic expansion, increased sales or eliminating a competitor?

Factor	Start	New Franchise	Buy Independent or Established Franchise
Bank financing availability	Low	Medium	High
Branding	No	Yes	Yes – in niche
Cash needed upfront	Low (can be)	Low-Medium	Medium-High
Cash (yours) needed ongoing	Medium-High (possibly)	Medium	Low
Customer base	Must build	Must build	Exists

Factor	Start	New Franchise	Buy Independent or Established Franchise
Exiting – company marketability	Unknown	Medium – depending on franchise agreement	High
Financing alternatives – acquisition	Low – your money	Medium	High
Financing alternatives – post acquisition	Low	Medium	High
Have sweat equity not cash	Ideal	Medium	No
High energy and time commitment needed	High	Medium-High	Medium
Immediate profit	No	No	Yes
Immediate salary	No	No	Yes
Management skills needed	Medium	Low	Medium-High
Marketing in place	No	Plan available	Usually
New idea imperative	Yes	No	No
Quality employees	Must find	Must find	In place
ROI – Financial	Unknown	Unknown	Known

Factor	Start	New Franchise	Buy Independent or Established Franchise
ROI – Non-financial benefits	Unknown	Some understanding	Good understanding
Success - chances of	Low	Medium	High
Systems (to follow)	No	Yes, in writing	Yes, not always in writing
Transition assistance upon selling (your involvement to help buyer's entry into management of business)	High	Low	High
Want/Need support	No	Yes	Some (in transition)
Written operations manual	No	Yes	Maybe
Rocket ship growth potential	Medium	Low	Low-Medium
Investigative research available	Do it yourself	High (FDD)	Must know questions to ask
Site selection help	No	Yes	Site exists

This list is not intended to be all inclusive of all comparison factors.

For discussion purposes only. There are exceptions to all general rules, please apply the above to your situation with common sense.

How to Know What You Want for Christmas

Finding a Business that Floats not Sinks

Buying a business is like operating a business in that if you have a proven plan and implement it correctly you will be more successful. I used to teach a class on business plans and one of the things I told the students was, "Don't go to the office supply store, buy the latest whiz-bang business plan software, load it on our computer and answer all the questions. Because if you do, you'll most likely print it out, put it in a binder, and it will go on a shelf and become a 'shelf plan,' not a working plan."

Business plans need to be working documents. They need to be not only a plan but also a record of what's worked, what hasn't worked and why. They also need to be flexible, adapting as your market, your team and your product line change.

TIP: HAVE A PLAN AND FOLLOW IT

There are numerous studies on the benefits of a business plan. I've always remembered a study published in USA Today. The telling statistic was that small businesses with a business plan had twice the sales and profit growth as companies without a business plan. This study also gave statistics on how companies with a plan had less debt, better access to capital and offered better benefit plans.

At "Partner" On-Call Network (POCN) we use our proprietary Business Locating and Screening System® as the basis for acquisition searches. There is more in Chapter Three about the actual search process. However, there are some important considerations to cover before you actually start searching, which are discussed here.

The first of these is to determine your passion, which is a consideration that trips up many entrepreneurs and re-entrepreneurs. I constantly read or hear people state that to be happy in business you need to define your passion. However, those entrepreneurs usually take it too deep. At a basic level, as Michael Gerber mentioned in his book, the mechanic, with business skills, should not own a garage because he or she will end up fixing cars, not working on the business.

REAL LIFE STORY: THE BIG-PICTURE PASSION IS WHERE TO FOCUS

Keith Jackson owns Industrial Revolution, Inc. in Tukwila, WA. If you go to my website, www.martinkaconsulting.com, you will see a short video of Keith and me that was on Seattle's KING 5 TV. It's what happens off the video, though, that is more important.

For background, Industrial Revolution manufactures and distributes products for camping and backpacking. Their products include Candle Lanterns, the Ice Cream Ball, mini-tripods and camping utensils.

The cameraman asked Keith if he enjoyed camping. Keith stopped in the middle of the shop and started laughing. He said, "We go to trade shows and people come to our booth and gush over our products. They tell us that we must really love camping and backpacking because of the great products we have." He paused and stated, firmly, "I hate camping." Then with a big smile on his face he said, "I like making things."

Keith's passion was at the 30,000-foot level. It wasn't important that he make outdoor products or indoor products, consumer products or industrial products. He wanted to use his skills on something where he could add value. When buyers get so granular that they that have to own a company that "manufacturers scientific measuring devices" (true example) versus "making something," it is a formula for disaster.

Keep your passion big-picture and, like Keith, you'll have a greater chance of success when it comes to finding a business.

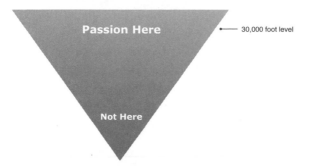

While we'll discuss buying criteria more in the next chapter, there are some basic criteria that all buyers should have on their list. Upon meeting a prospective business buyer, I often get a list of what they are looking for. That list should look like this:

- Profitable company
- Defensible position
- Sustainable product advantage
- High margins
- Scalable
- Proprietary product or service
- Not trendy

In other words, they want a competitive advantage (with protectable barriers to entry), which is what all buyers should want. Also, nobody should think about buying a business if they don't want to grow it. It's that energy that buyers bring to the company that gets the management and employees fired up. It's the fact that a new owner usually asks the employees for their input and pays attention to what they say that adds immediate value.

Your basic criteria can be broken down to three top components and should therefore always include:

- Profitable business

- Competitive advantage

- Growth potential

The more detailed criteria of what makes a good acquisition for *you* will be covered later.

QUALIFICATIONS

SCENARIO ONE: BUSINESS OWNER

(Individuals can skip to scenario two.)

It goes without saying that if you currently own a successful business you are qualified to buy another, assuming your skill set matches up with your target industries, you have the personal bandwidth and the management team to handle an acquisition, transition and increased operations.

Preparing to grow by acquisition is similar to preparing your exit strategy and your business for a sale for the following three primary reasons (assuming you have the financial wherewithal for an acquisition).

Time: During exit planning, business owners are advised to distance themselves from the day-to-day operations of the business. This three-step process involves:

- Fade away from getting involved in operations.

- Plan and take longer and longer vacations.

- Concentrate on strategy and big-picture issues for at least six months. Refuse to get involved in anything else other than for an emergency.

Buyers prefer to see a business not dependent on the owner, so this is integral to exit planning. Buying another company will absorb the owner's time. If you're deeply involved in your current day-to-day how will you manage the acquisition process, transition and added work?

Management: A business with a management team has more value than a company whose largest dependency is the owner. An acquisition will require more than just the owner, so in both cases it's imperative that you build, trust and assign responsibility to a management team.

Marketing: One of my top requirements for a company embarking on preparation for an eventual sale is to have a well-documented marketing and sales plan. When a seller brags about all of the company's potential, the buyer hears, "They're growing slowly, have probably tried every marketing technique known to man, nothing really works so I'm buying a stagnant business."

Thinking of buying another business? Prepare so you have the time for it, your team can cover current operations and the transition and your marketing machine is going strong so your existing business doesn't slow down.

Consider buying another company if you don't want to rely on just organic growth.

Don't get me wrong, these are important subjects but they are what everybody is preaching and doing (or at least trying to do).

There are a lot of strategies to grow a business. Let's cover some of the more traditional ones. Then we'll discuss how you can break away from the pack.

- You can take on more products or services (or start making more products). It may take a while to get the process down, your salespeople and customers educated and general acceptance. If it works, everybody's happy. But there is risk. Inevitably it's more expensive than planned to roll out a new product.

- Expand geographically by sending salespeople on the road more often or perhaps open an office in another city. There are some upfront and ongoing costs to opening a remote location and if you don't sell enough you're going to hurt.

REAL LIFE STORY: SOMETIMES EVEN A BAD BUSINESS IS WORTH BUYING

Many years ago a client and I came across a business that was in a world of hurt. Your first though may be, "Why buy a business that is hurting?" Well, it's because of why it was hurting. The seller expanded into a new geographic area by opening a new office and hiring people. He was not capable of managing those people from a distance and the new office was failing. Then his ego got involved. He insisted he could "sell" his way out of the problems and also bought a building in that market at a market peak.

The buyer bought the original location, not the remote location, with the entire down payment going to the state for back taxes, the key vendor and the telephone company. One of the key motivators was the State of Washington and its Department of Revenue. They were ready to close down the business and sell off the assets for back taxes. They insisted on a letter of intent and closing by certain dates to postpone this. Their actions were added motivation for the seller.

Hire more salespeople and hope they can sell. Keep in mind that one of the most common complaints among business owners, managers and executives is about finding good salespeople who can earn their keep. One of the members of a mastermind group I'm in recently made a New Year's decision to fire their salesperson because he wasn't bringing in enough good business to cover his base salary. Too many salespeople are happy with their base and that's not motivating.

Stealing customers by getting into price wars with the competition doesn't help you or your customers. You can only shrink margins so much. It's like the old Jack in the Box commercial where the finance guy tells Jack that they are losing money on every sandwich. Jack's response is, "That's okay, we'll make it up on volume." You also don't want customers who care about nothing but price because they'll leave as quickly as they came onboard. It's also a disservice to them if they don't get the quality or service they deserve because you can't afford to provide it.

Buying more equipment so you produce more widgets cheaper still means you have to sell those widgets and equipment is a fixed cost that is there whether you sell one more or one million more widgets.

Why not double your sales in months, not years? Don't slug it out in the trenches, soar above the fray. Merger and Acquisition (M&A) people use buzzwords like rollups and consolidations. Often they work, unless the buyer gets greedy and does too many deals without regard for what they are paying (it's big, public company mergers and acquisitions that don't work according to many studies).

Real Life Story: Leverage profits by making acquisitions

As I write this, a client is in the middle of two acquisitions. One recently closed and other is set to close soon. Both are firms in remote locations in relation to his main office. Both provide some of the services his firm offers, but not all. In fact, one of these firms has also been a customer of his for some of his services. He plans to offer all of his services to the target firms' customers, consolidate some overhead and move some jobs to his existing staff (there is capacity), and he projects substantially increased margins on the added revenue.

Let's look at 12 reasons why growth by acquisition makes sense and look at the business buying process, including search, analysis, financing and due diligence. The objective of this is to eventually have you on the other side of the transaction with not only an understanding of what the buyer is looking for but of the emotions they are experiencing.

Acquire great talent

Good employees are hard to find, and they are often not in the job market. Yes, you can use a recruiter, although often a recruiter is quite pricey for a small business. The more skilled your employees need to be, the more this option makes sense. While all buyers want capable employees, most strategic buyers (that may be you) want a solid management team in place.

Great employees, with industry knowledge and experience, are seldom in the job market. When you are looking for great salespeople, there are even fewer. They won't change jobs if they've got a good thing going.

If you acquire their company and create an atmosphere of growth, those employees will want to stay. While I can't comment on the culture in all companies, I do know that many small, family-owned businesses have owners who are coasting. They are doing very well, they aren't working too hard and they don't want to disrupt their moneymaking system. The employees may be younger, have more energy and ideas on how to grow (and challenge themselves and the firm). To the owner, this could mean a bigger payday with the corresponding risk of slightly lower profits if the ideas don't work or a temporary profit reduction if there's an investment needed for the new idea.

As one sales manager said to me a few months after an acquisition, "Thank you. The new owner is like a breath of fresh air." He wanted to grow, the seller wanted to maximize cash flow and the employees liked the growth culture.

REAL LIFE STORY: FINDING EMPLOYEES VIA ACQUISITIONS

At one point I had two clients (coincidentally, both in LA and both distributors) who hired me to find companies in their specific industries. The prime motivator for both was to acquire great salespeople. They needed people with industry knowledge and experience and they were having trouble finding people willing to change jobs. Buying another company, with a good sales staff, made more sense than trying to steal employees.

DIVERSIFY YOUR PRODUCT OFFERINGS

Almost every salesperson has experienced exiting a meeting with a customer (a customer with whom they have a fantastic relationship) thinking, "If only we had the X and Y product line, I could sell it to them, save them money and make more myself." Of course it's tough to get those product lines, especially if you're starting from zero with the supplier.

So why not buy a firm with those product lines and diversify what your people can sell? One of the nice things about this is that you don't have to purchase a huge company. It can be a small company whose purchase will have the full support of their vendor because you can plug the products into your customer base for almost instantaneous growth (of the new product lines).

The products don't have to be similar. I remember one owner who sold packaging materials (boxes). He believed he could acquire any company that sold any kind of supplies to warehouses. What else do warehouses use: paper, tape, janitorial supplies, racks, material handing equipment and more. Don't limit yourself. Think creatively.

VENDOR RELATIONSHIP STRATEGIES

Above, we discussed diversifying your product lines. What goes along with this is access to vendors you can't get on your own. Many have territories and protect their distributors and/or retailers. Acquiring one of their customers gets you in the door. Once in the door you can make the most of the opportunity.

All of this assumes you're buying a company with different products than yours. This also works for buying a competitor (or similar business in another market) with the same product line. For retailers, it means buying a store that carries the same lines that you carry. The end result in either case is that you will do higher volumes with your suppliers and qualify for greater volume discounts.

LOCATION, LOCATION, LOCATION

This is the old mantra for retail and it applies to other industries also. There may be a location you want and can't get. It could be a retail location and it could be, for manufacturers and distributors, a building near a distribution center, on a rail line or close to suppliers. While this may not be common, when combined with some of the other reasons for making an acquisition, it may be your tipping point.

More apropos for most companies is to expand geographically by buying a similar business (competitor) in another market. I'm in the Seattle area. For Seattle companies this may mean buying something as nearby as a competitor in Tacoma. It could be across the state in Spokane or down I-5 in Portland. Or, it could mean expansion into Denver or Salt Lake City, to have a Rocky Mountain presence.

REAL LIFE STORY: EASE INTO ANOTHER LOCATION VIA AN ACQUISITION

One of my clients purchased a California business similar to his Seattle company. It gives him added volume and the opportunity for faster growth, and he was able to hire an industry friend to be the chief California salesperson (the acquired firm had no sales team as the owners, in their 70's, weren't active, they were "coasting").

MAKE A COMPETITOR GO AWAY

Some businesses have more than general industry competition; they have a specific competitor that stands in their way. It may be a fierce rival (along the lines of bitter sports rivals like the Packers and Bears or Yankees and Red Sox) or it may just be that there isn't a big enough market for either firm to break away from the other.

Acquire your competitor (or merge if you're friendly). Getting rid of them may make fast growth easier, cheaper and achievable. It may allow for faster moves into other markets or segments, using traditional growth strategies. This strategy ties in very well with the previous strategy of expanding geographically by acquisition.

SAME OVERHEAD, HIGHER VOLUME

Look at all the reasons to buy another company. Realize that 90% or more of the time you will add volume without adding the corresponding overhead. This is often one of the prime motivators for making an acquisition. If you have 40 employees and two staff accountants and the other firm has 25 employees and two staff accountants, there is a good chance you'll only need three staff accountants after the acquisition. Boom—one salary, tax and benefit package goes to the bottom line. The same can happen with rent, other staff people, phone and Internet, advertising and more.

REAL LIFE STORY: INCREASE MARGINS VIA AN ACQUISITION

A client bought one of his suppliers. It was a small business with a lot of inefficiencies. He was able to move the business into his space, replace at least one production worker (my client had capacity) and coordinate marketing efforts with no increase in his marketing costs. In addition, just think of all the other overhead he could eliminate, including telephone lines, accounting services, utilities, etc. He took a sleepy little company and turned almost all of its gross profit into net profit.

ASSETS ARE CHEAPER AS A PACKAGE

Tangible assets are a sunk cost. Once you have them, whether it's vehicles, machines, forklifts or space, you have the cost and/or payments. You need to make them efficient. All businesses struggle with this (for tangible and human assets).

At some point you have to buy a new machine (or hire a new person) because you're over capacity on current equipment, people are working too much overtime, etc. However, once you buy that piece of equipment your capacity increases and your utilization drops. You have to generate more sales to get the equipment running at a profitable rate.

Wouldn't it be nice if the equipment, just like people, came with utilization? Of course it would, and that's why buying another company can be a good way to get needed equipment with corresponding customers. These assets can be cheaper when obtained as a package (versus buying new or used assets that don't come with customers).

SYNERGY

In an oversimplified example, you sell paper and the company down the street sells envelopes. You sell to the same customer base. Wouldn't it make sense for one salesperson, not two, to call on each customer and sell paper and envelopes? The same holds true for delivery people, warehouse people and accounting (one monthly invoice, not two).

These situations don't come up every day. Savvy owners are always on the lookout for them, though. It doesn't have to be as obvious an example as paper and envelopes. My story above about a packaging company seeking a firm that sells completely different products (like janitorial supplies) to the same customers can illustrate the point just as well.

DIAMONDS IN THE ROUGH

A synergistic acquisition may mean buying a loser, it may mean buying a struggling business (nice personal income to the owner but no real profit) or it could mean buying a business where you can see things that can be done to make it more than it is now.

Often these businesses have no options other than to struggle along, close the doors or sell to another business. Rarely will individuals, equity groups or other financial buyers (those needing an income from the business) buy a loser. That means their options are very limited, as only a small percentage of companies ever consider growth by acquisition (which makes it an even stronger strategy for those who do).

This can be a good find at a low cost, perhaps even on an earnout basis (payments to the seller based on sales or profits and/or the increase of sales and profits and the payments are not guaranteed). And these can still be win-win deals. You get volume, people and other benefits and the seller gets something for his or her company (that they wouldn't otherwise get).

Real Life Story: Let technology increase your acquisition's effectiveness

Technology can often produce large profit growth, even for non-tech businesses. A service business, with burned out owners (actually they were well beyond burned out, they were fried), had a website that acted like a brochure.

To order services the customers had to call in, and we all know how that works. First, there is phone tag. Even if an order is left on voice mail it has to be confirmed. In any event, it takes an employee to process the order and the customer has to take time to make the calls, return calls and talk about the order.

The buyer noticed this during analysis and within months had an online ordering system. It saved the customers' time and hassle and it increased his staff's productivity (a lot). It's not rocket science, it's observing and looking at things through the customers' eyes.

THE TOP THREE REASONS TO GROW BY ACQUISITION

Customers

"This would be a great business if it wasn't for those darn customers" is a semi-serious comment someone made to me years ago. Of course it's the annoying (bad) customers he was referring to. It's good customers we all want more of—customers who are loyal, steady, in good financial shape, growing, pay their bills on time, appreciate the value you offer and consider you part of their team, versus simply want a low price.

I mentioned above that acquiring a new product or service line that you can sell to your customers is a good reason for an acquisition. The same holds true for selling your current offerings to a new group of customers. Often this can be done without any increase in your sales force.

An ideal situation is where there are some overlapping products, so there is some continuity and synergy to be achieved, as shown in the figure below. Your salespeople now have an easy transition to discussing, and selling, their products, and their salespeople have an easy transition to discussing, and selling, your products.

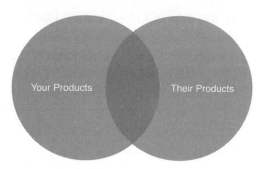

In simple terms, if your primary motivation is acquiring a customer base, you are acquiring market share. It may offer many of the other benefits (geographic expansion, talent acquisition, etc.) but the bottom line is, you are buying customers, and that means top line growth.

REAL LIFE STORY: SELL YOUR PRODUCT TO THEIR CUSTOMERS

During an acquisition of a quasi-competitor, I quizzed my client on the projections we were reviewing. They all made sense, and then he added that an intangible benefit was the fact that the company he was acquiring only offered one of the three services his company offered. While not in his projections, he saw the opportunity of offering at least one of his other services to these customers.

YES YOU CAN!

This is not about ego; it is about building an exit strategy and getting a higher multiple (of profit) as a selling price when you sell. Buying another company, assimilating it into your operation and showing that the combined profits are greater than the two individual companies' profits demonstrates that this can be done, which is attractive to companies that may want to buy your business in the future. You are proving that you have the team that can integrate one operation into another.

This integration could involve integrating your firm into theirs or it could be a signal that growing your business (or now a division of theirs) is possible by further acquisitions. A management team that can successfully integrate other firms without major disruption and create immediate efficiencies is a valued team. Too many big mergers and acquisitions fail (up to 95% of public mergers do not live up to expectations). A savvy buyer, who is your exit strategy, will appreciate this talent and experience.

The bigger they are...

The bigger they are the more they sell for, all other things being equal. A $50 million (revenue) company with 10% EBITDA (earnings before interest, taxes, depreciation and amortization) will sell for a higher multiple of profit than a $25 million company with 10% EBITDA, which will sell for a higher multiple than a $15 million company, and so on.

There are generally accepted ranges for multiples of EBITDA based on revenue. However, too many owners see in the Wall Street Journal that a $250 million company in their industry sold for 10 times EBITDA and assume their small business will also sell for 10 times EBITDA. That won't happen; there's more risk in smaller businesses than larger, so the desired return on investment is higher.

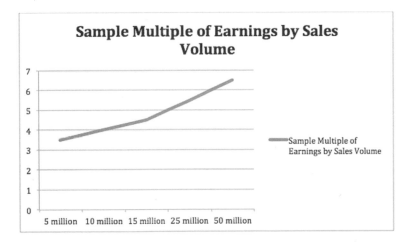

For illustration purposes only; companies sell within generally accepted multiple of EBITDA ranges depending on a variety of factors. Don't assume that a particular company will sell at multiple of EBITDA shown above for that size company.

STATISTICS: LARGER FIRMS SELL FOR MORE

Companies with sales of $5-50 million tend to sell for four to seven times EBITDA. A company on the lower end of the range will usually sell close to the four times EBITDA. Those on the higher end will sell close to the seven times EBITDA. Grow your $5 million company to $15 million and your multiple may increase by one times EBITDA (from four to five for example). Assuming 10% profit (and four times EBITDA) you can see the price go from $2 million to $7.5 million (10% profit at five times EBITDA).

The faster and safest way to grow from $5 million to $15 million is by acquisition. Buy another firm in your industry, a supplier, a customer or an unrelated company that provides diversification to have an immediate revenue increase and a larger platform from which to grow organically. In addition you get the benefits of higher profits along the way and a higher multiple when you exit.

IT'S NOT BRAGGING IF YOU CAN DO IT (DIZZY DEAN, 1934)

A lot of business owners talk about their company's potential or the growth that will occur if the buyer just, "does some marketing." Of course, most of this is just talk. Business buyers, of all types and sizes, are a skeptical lot. When they hear too much about potential they think the seller has tried every conceivable way to grow and can't.

So prove you can do it. Go out and buy another company. Show that you can integrate the people, processes, financial systems, customer service and everything else into your operation. Private Equity Groups and large corporations make multiple acquisitions. If you can buy another firm, and successfully assimilate it, you become more attractive to these buyers.

They will assume you can do it again and that your management team is capable of this. As strategic buyers and equity group type buyers value management teams highly, it can even increase the multiple (compared to having the same size company that has not made acquisitions).

CREATE A BREATH OF FRESH AIR

The sales manager at a recently acquired firm thanked me for getting the deal done and said that the new buyer was a breath of fresh air. The new owner, unlike the seller, listened to the employees' ideas, let them act on them and was willing to take risks. Too often employees get in a rut. They like the company and their job but it gets to be routine. When the boss ignores them, they lose enthusiasm and leave.

You can create a breath of fresh air by buying another business. Enthusiasm is hard to teach but it's contagious. The excitement of an acquisition can fire up your team. It's a new and rewarding challenge. It can also fire up the team of the acquired business. Often their company is being sold because the owner is retiring or burned out. In either event, that owner has probably been coasting while the employees are constantly having new ideas. Putting two fired up teams together and letting them use their abilities is when you have 2+2=32, meaning your results must be exponentially better than just the sum of the numbers.

		Skill	
		+	-
Energy	+	2+2=32	2+2=4
	-	2+2=4	2+2=0

IS IT FOR YOU?

Buying another business is not for everybody. There are risks involved, higher risks than with many other things we do, and that is why the rate of return is much higher than on other investments. However, if your desire is faster growth, a much larger company or to position yourself for an eventual sale, buying another business is probably faster, cheaper, safer and easier to finance than starting a new division, opening a branch in another city and increasing your sales and marketing efforts to grow organically.

If you desire any of the goals associated with growth by acquisition, you owe it to yourself to investigate it. Follow a proven plan and pay attention to the details. By all means put together a team including your attorney, accountant, acquisition advisor and banker (more on this in Chapter Three). Make sure all have experience in transactions of the type you are targeting. Keep in mind that preparation and planning make the process go faster and smoother. As the late Lionel Haines (a noted author of many books on the buying and selling of businesses) said, "You must act like a hunter, not a trapper." You have to get out there and actively search for businesses, as you would prospect for new customers. This is not a passive "sport."

Once you find a good candidate, don't create your own speed bumps or roadblocks. There are enough already out there! There is risk involved, and if you feel your skills balance the risks of the business you are considering, then delve in and find out what makes that company tick. In other words, why are they profitable or unprofitable? Some of the best deals are when a money losing company is "saved" by someone in their industry who can make money on the same sales volume (or, as a better manager, can do little things that make a big difference).

CASE STUDY—GROW BY ACQUISITION

SITUATION

The subject company is a manufacturing and distribution company that has been and is very successful and growing fast. Their growth was organic and centered around two proprietary products. Their only personnel weakness was the lack of a product engineer.

One of the products they distributed was from a small manufacturer whose owner was in his mid-60s and was not a good businessperson, but was a great product designer and engineer. The potential buyer was attracted to acquiring this small manufacturer for three reasons:

- To have 100% of the products distribution, therefore getting higher margins (by eliminating the middleman, which is what his firm was).

- He could bring the manufacturing in-house and eliminate most of the overhead (by getting rid of rent, phone, bookkeeping, etc.).

- As part of an eventual exit plan he wanted to prove he could buy another business and assimilate it into his operation.

INTERVENTION

While there had been some casual conversation between the two owners, once I was brought in we picked up the pace. We met with the seller and seriously talked about a buy-sell transaction. We discussed the company's operations and the seller's role post-closing. One thing we didn't initially discuss in detail was price or terms.

When a business is being sold it is customary that the seller or his or her intermediary prepares a "book" or memorandum about the business. We flipped the usual roles on this and prepared a presentation book for the seller and his wife. As the seller was an engineer, our book gave him the logic to analyze and support his decision.

Our presentation included:

- Valuation methodologies

- Comparable deal statistics

- Other justification for the offer

In addition, we included reinforcement on why the seller told us he was interested in selling (his hot buttons), his future role as a product engineer for the buyer and a section on what makes a business an attractive acquisition candidate. This latter section was to show why his business would be tough to sell to an individual buyer (because the business was him; the company was completely dependent on him).

Most importantly, we appealed to his emotion along with his logic and gave full justification on the price. I like to say that the true economic *buyer in a small business buy-sell deal is usually the spouse. In this case it was very true and his wife had the idea that because they had owned the business for 30 years it was worth a lot (more than it really was). She equated value with longevity.*

RESULT

The combination of logic, emotion and complete backup information worked. The deal closed and the integration into the buyer's company was a success. The company's production was brought into the buyer's shop and the seller became a part-time product engineer who worked on all of the company's products.

This was a win-win deal that provided:

- *The seller with an exit strategy.*

- *Higher margins on what now became one of the buyer's proprietary products.*

- *The successful implementation of a growth by acquisition strategy.*

SCENARIO TWO: THE CORPORATE EXECUTIVE AS A BUSINESS BUYER

I've mentioned that buyers have experience and success managing people, processes, systems and money. When assessing the strengths and attributes a client brings to the table, I ask them to rate themselves on six categories. Rate yourself on the list below, using a one to five scale, with five being excellent and one meaning you are a novice (in regards to small business).

Rating on a 1-5 scale	Category
	Sales— defined as being able to prospect for new customers, keep current customers happy, present your firms value proposition and manage a sales team.
	Marketing— what it takes to attract prospective customers to your business so you can make a sale. It includes advertising, public relations, social media, events and more.
	Operations— of a factory, warehouse, service department, transportation logistics, administration or any other integral part of the business.
	Management—managing people is the primary objective here. Getting the most out of a team, showing leadership and motivation and handling people problems.
	Finance—not public company finance but understanding financial statements, cash flow, having bottom line responsibility, budgets, margin management, etc.
	Technical—your grasp on technical concepts (not just high technology like software) so that you're comfortable talking about it, doing it and not being intimidated or held hostage by technical employees.

A simple version of what makes you a qualified business buyer is my three-legged stool of a qualified business buyer. The 'skills and experience' leg is based on your abilities on the above areas of skill.

No matter what, you must have a good personality. Buy-sell deals for small businesses are always relationship based.

REAL LIFE STORY: ADVICE FROM AN EXPERIENCED BUYER

Jim Bernard started a business, I assisted him in selling it to a larger firm in his industry and then he bought two businesses. While having lunch after the final transaction, we discussed relationships. After three transactions, I found the following statement he made to be insightful and have used it ever since. Jim told me, "I would never buy a business from or sell a business to someone I didn't like."

If you can't like the other party, or be liked by him or her, you won't even get to first base on a transaction.

These deals are relationship based for three reasons.

1. The buyer must trust and feel comfortable with the seller and what the seller is telling him or her about the business. Why would a buyer base a life-changing decision on information from someone he or she doesn't trust? When business buyers are skeptical about the importance of building a relationship I ask them to understand that the seller has built a profitable business because of their relationships with their customers, employees and vendors. If the buyer and seller don't relate, how can the buyer expect to relate to the critical elements of the business's success?

2. The seller must trust and feel comfortable with the buyer because he or she will be financing part of the deal. It could be all seller financing, in which case the seller has to be very comfortable with the buyer's abilities. It could be a small amount of seller financing, if a bank is involved. However, in 2012 that small amount of seller financing is usually subordinated to the bank, meaning the seller may have payments deferred for two years or longer. It also means that if there are any problems with making payments, the seller will not get paid until the bank is paid and the bank is first in line to take collateral including business and personal assets.

3. Small and mid-sized business transactions are more emotion than just about any other business deal. The seller is letting go of his or her "baby" and the buyer is parting company with a significant portion of their lifesavings, whether the buyer is a corporate executive or the owner of another business.

REAL LIFE STORY: NO RELATIONSHIP MEANS NO DEAL

A client complained because, he said, "All the business sellers I'm meeting really didn't want to sell." I pulled out his file and told him that his stack of prospective sellers was three times as large as any of my other clients, the others were searching in the same geographic market, for similar sized businesses, and nobody else was having this problem.

This client did not buy into the fact that it's important to build a relationship. I suspected this and it was confirmed a day before our conversation when an owner (seller) called me to say he wanted to sell his business but not to this person.

My client had a habit of, within 15 minutes of meeting an owner, wanting to drill down into the financial statements, marketing strategies and other secrets of the business. Would you divulge trade secrets like these to someone you just met? Of course not.

He did get a little better. I accompanied him on an introductory meeting or two with sellers but he never fully bought into the importance of relationships. The good news is that he eventually met a seller just like him—person who wasn't personable and just wanted the facts.

The downside was that it took him one and one-half years to get a deal done in a time period when other buyers were averaging nine months. And, the transition was rough because neither party communicated well. The buyer thought the seller should just tell him everything about the business and its operations, and the seller thought the buyer should ask about those things he wanted to know (of course, the buyer didn't know what to ask).

If the adage, "Cash is King" is true, then relationships are the Queen; and, as in chess, the Queen is the most powerful piece on the board.

TIMING

Up until the Great Recession and its lingering aftermath, my client agreement stated that business buyers should allow at least six to nine months from the start of searching to closing a deal. In 2009 I changed that to allow at least nine to 12 months.

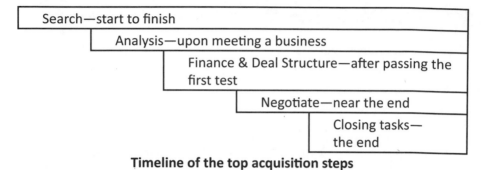

Timeline of the top acquisition steps

It's a sign of the times. Everybody is more cautious. Who can blame them, since there is still a lot of uncertainty? Think back to 2009; would you want to buy a business, putting a large part of your net worth at risk so soon after the stock market collapsed, the banking industry was in peril and the economy was in shambles? Business owners thinking of selling were worried that even if they met a qualified buyer, outside factors, such as the bank not renewing the company's line of credit, could cause the business to derail, ruining what they had spent years building and jeopardizing the note they held (probably a sizable note, as banks were very hesitant to lend then).

As mentioned, buyers had the same concerns as the sellers, most likely magnified many times. At the same time any money in the stock market was down about 50% (in early to mid 2009), home equity was also decreasing, so the ability to make a down payment was tremendously reduced.

The fact that interest rates were down meant nothing. In fact, it might have been a negative factor on deals. Banks weren't lending so it didn't matter to a buyer whether the rate was high or low. Sellers wanting cash because of all the uncertainty looked at the interest rates on money market accounts and usually decided a pile of cash was nice but the return was so low that they would hold off on selling as the profits from their business gave them a higher return on investment, in this case the return on the price they would receive on their business.

Real life stories: When the seller is motivated, you can find a way

2009 was a horrible year for small and mid-sized company transactions. I think back to that year, and while I generated a lot of activity, including new buyer clients, there were very few deals. Two that stand out had unique circumstances and both were deals that didn't require a bank.

One was a business that was overwhelming the owner, who was about 70 years old. The business needed management, plain and simple. As the deal developed—and it started as an almost all cash transaction— the seller asked the buyer if he could finance more of the deal. Why, you ask? Because the buyer was willing to pay 6% interest on a note and the seller didn't know where he could get a safe 6% (he had extreme trust in the buyer's abilities).

Another deal had a very motivated seller, due to a perfect storm of catastrophic personal events. The buyer was a good fit for the business, the business was a bulls-eye on his target of business types and again, no bank was needed. If a bank loan had been needed the deal would not have closed. The business had been performing marginally (a positive to this buyer) and the banking climate had not improved enough to consider an acquisition loan. This buyer was truly the knight in shining armor to the seller. Without him the business would probably have closed within a year, given all the personal issues the seller faced.

Think about it this way, when it comes to timing. Even if you found a business tomorrow, by the time you build a relationship with the seller, analyze information, structure financing, structure a deal and make an offer, negotiate a final deal and get the legalities done, it will take three to four months. For most buyers, even if the first business they find is the one they buy, they want to compare and contrast industries and companies.

Buyers are always cautious and skeptical, but in 2012 the level of caution and skepticism is still much higher than normal, which has buyers acting more like tortoises than hares. There is no mad rush to the finish line. A lot of effort is put into determining if the business was and is truly recession proof. Sellers who state they have a good business that has gone down with the economy are not doing themselves any favors (as they are showing they can't control economic swings).

Banks are also more cautious and in reality today's business buyers are like yesterday's banks. They adhere to President Reagan's statement, "Trust but verify." Banks today are like yesterday's bank examiners and auditors. They rarely trust and they double verify. Because of more sophisticated advisors and the Internet, buyers have access too much more information than ever before and use that information to confirm that a business is all it's claimed to be.

Banks have become sticklers for detailed backup materials on all aspects of the business. Some banks are now asking due diligence questions. Some of those questions are ones that even many buyers skipped over 15 years ago. All of this adds time to the process.

MONEY NEEDED

When I started working as a Business Buyer Advocate in the early 1990's, my mentor and POCN President, Ted Leverette, told business buyers (and me) that the cash a buyer needed from the buyer's pocket for a down payment was the buyer's annual salary (fair market salary for the job of business owner or company president). That was very true then, but it's changed over time.

In the late 1990's I saw changes in the market and by the year 2000 I was telling buyers they would need one to three times their salary in cash for a down payment. By 2010 I was emphasizing that they should figure on two to three times their salary. It's a sign of the times, and buyers hoping to get into a deal with less than two to three times their salary must be very experienced in business buying and ownership to make that happen.

The vertical axis is total investment cash needed.

The horizontal axis is fair market salary for the job of running the company.

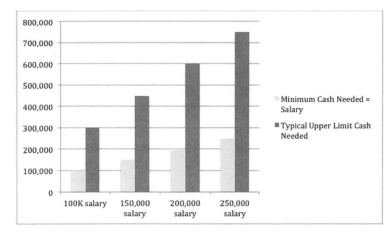

How does this translate into cash as a percentage of the purchase price? My clients over the last few years make down payments of an average of 18-20% of the total price). The range is 12% on the low end to 40% on the high end (with one all-cash deal because it got the buyer a much better price and he didn't want this particular seller looking over his shoulder because of the seller note on a non-bankable deal).

However, the buyer's cash outlay is more than just money for a down payment. There are also closing costs and, most importantly, money for working capital. When asked, audiences usually respond that the number one problem with small businesses is that they are undercapitalized. This translates to not enough working capital to implement the owner's strategies.

One of the changes I've seen since 2009 is more of an acceptance to include working capital in the assets transferred to the buyer. Most valuations and many deals assume a clean slate when it comes to quick assets and liabilities (cash, accounts receivable and liabilities). In other words, the seller takes the cash, collects the receivables and pays off all debt and all bills. With valuations down, it offers sellers a way to say they got the price they wanted. At the same time, it gives buyers a cushion and banks a better feeling about the loan.

REAL LIFE STORIES: BUYERS AND BANKS LIKE CASH KEPT IN THE COMPANY

Two post-Great Recession transactions come to mind regarding work-ing capital left in the business. One was purely psychological, as the seller wanted "his" price. The business wasn't worth his price but it was worth his price with 20% of that price left in the company in net working capital. One way the buyer looked at it was that he got his down payment back at closing.

The other deal had close to 25% of the price included in net working capital ($1 million). This was truly a high working capital need business. There were long lead times on jobs, long lag times from ordering to billing and the typical collection cycles. This deal was not doable with-out the working capital, and the seller knew this. The business was too small for an equity group and too large for 90% of individual buy-ers. Any individual with enough for a down payment and the working capital would buy a larger business. The win-win solution was to keep money in the company.

Finally, have advisors who understand the banking environment, SBA guaranteed acquisition loans and conventional acquisition loans. Your advisors should be able to direct you to the bankers and banks that not only know how to do these loans but also want to do them. In 2011, a lot of banks that previously didn't participate in the SBA pro-gram jumped onboard.

We'll cover bank loans more in the chapter on finance, so for now realize that while you may want the seller to hold the only note (no bank financing), their advisors know enough about this subject to tell them that many banks will use the SBA guarantee program so they (the seller) can get a high percentage of the price in cash at closing. It is a rare deal indeed that has the seller financing the whole deal other than the buyer's down payment.

FLEXIBILITY IN SEARCHING

I described above the level where a buyer's passion should be, not drilled down to the exact product type but rather at the big-picture level. This is truer than ever since the Great Recession. The buyer whom thinks they can wait for the perfect business is going to wait so long they will give up the search.

The buyer who realizes they are not getting married to the business, so it doesn't have to be a perfect match, will be much more successful. Look at the business purely as a business endeavor. If you end up loving it and want to keep it for 37 years, that's great. But don't make that your objective. A business that allows you to leverage your skills should be the goal.

REAL LIFE STORIES: KEEP AN OPEN MIND WHEN SEARCHING

Rich was a few months into a search when I got a call from an owner whom we had contacted on behalf of another client. The original client already had a deal, so I shared this possibility with my other clients.

Rich was fascinated by the industry. He had never realized this industry even existed, and the skills needed to manage the business matched up well with his skills. We changed focus, started targeting this and related industries and after analyzing a number of companies in this niche he ended up buying the company I first presented to him (with the benefit of seeing others and having some industry comparisons).

James had a similar experience, although it was his research that brought him to the point of change. After looking at a variety of companies, nothing was exciting him. As he gave it thought and did some research, he decided on a particular industry (actually a variety of niches under one umbrella). We shifted our focus 180 degrees and within months he had bought two firms.

PULLING THE TRIGGER

A book on business buying would be incomplete and inadequate if there wasn't any mention of whether or not you have what it takes to do a deal. In other words, pull the trigger and sign a purchase and sale agreement, a note to the seller and bank, personal guarantees and more.

My clients pay an upfront commitment fee. It tends to separate the serious buyers from the tire-kickers (also known as lookiloos). I tell my clients there are three reasons for a commitment fee (besides the fact that I'd go broke if I worked for all the people who said they'd pay me a lot larger fee when they did a deal instead of some money upfront and some at closing).

It binds us together. Once they've paid me we have accountabilities to each other, so we can have the best chance of success.

There is risk on each side. They have the risk that if they pay me and then decide, for whatever reason, not to buy a business, they are out the money for the commitment fee. I have the same risk because we could do a lot of work for the (small) commitment fee and I'll lose out on the (larger) closing fee if they change their mind.

Most importantly, it lets me tell sellers that my client has paid me upfront and that means they are serious buyers. Owners are skeptical of buyers (just like buyers are inherently skeptical of any claims that owners make about a business's potential) and have seen too many tire-kickers. This statement to sellers holds a lot of weight and increases their comfort level and interest in pursuing a deal.

However, some buyers pay the commitment fee and then decide that maybe business ownership and all of its responsibilities are too much. Rarely will they say this. They usually take a devious route to escape the business-buying maze. Here are three examples.

Bob had a good background for and the desire to own a manufacturing business. He was so passionate about ownership he convinced his very conservative, cautious and skeptical wife to let him hire me and pursue this dream. Whether it was because of her influence or he just realized the leap-of-faith it takes, he kept changing his criteria so that it became impossible to find a business that met his criteria.

He did this by restricting his acceptable geographic territory. He lived in the heart of Seattle. First he told me that while he didn't want to, he would cross the lake to the eastern suburbs but only go so far. Of course that "so far" kept him in residential areas so he eliminated all of greater Seattle's Eastside area. A bit later he said that the south county suburbs were too far of a commute. Now, the south county is one of the manufacturing hubs of the greater Seattle area. At this point I realized he was losing his guts. It was when he told me he wouldn't cross Seattle to one of the few areas in the city itself with manufacturing and industry zoning that I knew he was done.

Sam took a different tact. He asked question after question after question. One seller, with whom I thought we would do a deal, nicknamed him Columbo because there was always, "one more question." More questions, more demands for information and always wanting something more. I cautioned him that he would blow the deal. His attorney also cautioned him, and the seller's attorney called me to discuss his style, to no avail, and the deal died. To show he wasn't discriminating against this owner and company, he did the same thing on the next potential deal. This was after we had a heart-to-heart talk about exactly what to do. To him, the hunt was truly more exciting than the kill.

Mitch was similar to Brad, although he refined his criteria around business types (eventually, his geographic restrictions and willingness to put up personal collateral became issues also). He wanted a business that produced not only a proprietary product but also one that needed his specific engineering skills. The noose got tighter and tighter until it became impossible to escape the tight criteria confines.

Losing one's guts and not pulling the trigger is rare with my clients. My client's success rate before the Great Recession was about 80%, compared to 10% among all buyers (in *How to Buy a Good Business at a Great Price*, Richard Parker states that 90% of people who say they want to buy a business never purchase one). Since the recession that percentage has declined a bit although many of those buyers who dropped out really wanted a job, and jobs were hard to find in 2009.

REAL LIFE STORIES: MOST EMPLOYEES DON'T WANT TO BE OWNERS

Yes, supposed business buyers lose their guts. We all think big on some things but never follow through. I would wager that among management teams given the opportunity to buy their employer, the dropout rate is very high.

A client asked me to try and structure, coordinate and get a deal done between the senior management team and the owner. About halfway through the process it became apparent the management team was not going to do the deal so I wrote the owner, said I was stopping the project and he didn't have to pay me the rest of my fee (it was a flat fee, no contingencies with two payments).

Four months later I asked a new client what would be a bulls-eye on this target (of business types). He said a $10 million sales firm in a particular industry. The company the management team declined to buy was doing $10 million in sales, in the exact industry he wanted and, to make it even better, two miles or less from his home.

They closed in 90 days including breaks for Thanksgiving, Christmas and New Years.

Harold bought his company after the management team wouldn't personally guarantee loans or pledge collateral (to the bank). The thought of owning the business excited this three-person team. The thought of signing a note with the bank, putting up their homes as collateral and signing a note with the seller scared them out of the deal. The bank had approved the loan with a very small down payment because they were the ideal buyers, being the management team for the firm.

They wanted a risk-free deal, or maybe they thought it would be a guaranteed a job (without any financial responsibility). Harold walked into a great situation, and a very loyal and dedicated team. A side benefit of a management team passing on a deal is that you know they will not be going to out to start or buy a business and become your competitor.

Action items

* Formulate your plan, with an emphasis on search.

* Determine what will fuel your passion (from the 30,000 foot level).

* Rank yourself on the necessary skills (this helps tremendously when screening companies).

* Put together your financial statement and determine now how much of your assets you will allocate for a down payment, closing costs and working capital.

* Owners, analyze the factors that determine if it makes sense to grow by acquisition.

* Do a final gut check. Is being in business for yourself, buying a business or buying another one for you?

— 3 —

TREASURE HUNT

Ninety percent of people who say they want to buy a business never do. Many, perhaps two-thirds of them, aren't really serious, they're dreamers. However, the majority of the rest get disillusioned, and never get a chance to pursue their dream. Why? Because they approach business buying the same way they would approach buying a home. Almost 100% of homes for sale are on a Multiple Listing Service (even those for sale by owner often are also listed). All one has to do is turn on the computer and browse.

Not so with businesses. Statistics from numerous sources, including the International Business Brokers Association, say that only 20% of profitable small to mid-sized businesses are ever advertised or listed by a business broker. That means if you approach business buying like you would home buying you are missing out on 80% of the market.

BusinessWeek coined the term "hidden market" for small businesses back in the 1980's and it's as true today as it ever was. Hidden market is a common term in the job search market and, as we'll see, there are many similarities between a business search and a job search.

Your goal should be to pursue 100% of the market. If you don't, you are shortchanging yourself.

REAL LIFE STORY: A POOR SEARCH MEANS YOU WON'T BUY A BUSINESS

At a bank's Christmas party one of the other guests asked me what I did. After I explained, he told me that he wished he had met me a dozen years earlier when he was searching for a business to buy and wasn't able to find a good one or a good one fairly priced.

When asked, he shared that his search methods consisted entirely of looking at newspaper ads, searching the Internet and calling a few business brokers. When a good prospect crossed his desk he found that numerous other buyers also were pursuing it, some irrationally bidding up the price.

He was now in his mid 60s and would stay at his current job until he retired. He said he still thinks about what might have been.

People in the outplacement industry have told me that 90% of jobs (management and executive level) are found on the hidden job market. The Department of Labor states that it is 80%. No matter, it's an impressive number in both markets and something that can't be ignored.

Another outplacement statistic is that job seekers who have a plan, implement it and follow it find a new job one-third faster than those without a plan or those who don't follow their plan. While I don't have statistics pertaining to business buying and following a search plan, my client observations tell me the results are similar.

It's why we at "Partner" On-Call Network created and provide our clients with our proprietary, "Business For Sale Locating and Screening System®." We know that if they follow the plan their chances of success skyrocket and their velocity to that success is greatly increased.

SEARCH COMPONENTS

As the following chart shows, there are only three search strategies to find a business to buy. You must implement all three to maximize your chances of success.

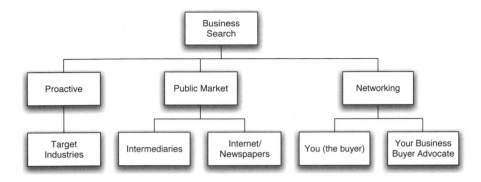

Career coaches and outplacement agencies can train their clients to be the best possible negotiators of job offers. However, if the job seeker doesn't find a company to interview with and get an offer from, those negotiating skills are wasted. In business it all starts with making a sale, also known as getting a customer (or an order). In business search it all starts with finding companies, and the best way to assure you will find one is to know what you want (and implement the plan to find it).

One (supposed) business buyer told me, "I don't buy into all that stuff about defining what you want. I'll know it when I see it." Did he ever see it? I don't know, but I do know that five years later he hadn't bought a company. Buyers with focus are successful and get there faster than those who "wing it."

When you haven't defined what makes an attractive candidate (other than having very general criteria like it must be profitable or have a competitive advantage) you risk having emotion take the lead. Emotional decisions often lead to trouble. Regularly, I get calls from clients asking me to "bring them down to earth." They love a business or at least the business model but the company isn't making money, doesn't match their skill set and experience, or the proposed deal is just crazy.

SEVEN STEPS TO A SUCCESSFUL SEARCH

1. Define your criteria

2. Your presentation materials

3. Assemble your "A" team

4. Build relationships
5. Know why the seller is selling
6. Understand your search is your job
7. Implement your search plan

STEP ONE: KNOW WHAT YOUR WANT—DEFINE CRITERIA

Fill in the following chart of the top 10 acquisition criteria after reading the descriptions of each category.

Criteria	Your resources or feelings
Capital to invest	
Salary	
Cash flow	
Location	
Full or partial ownership	
Daily activities	
Management team	
Employee types	
Sales, marketing	
Travel	

Capital to invest: As mentioned above, buying a business is trading your capital for immediate cash flow. The company you can afford to buy, the salary you will receive and the growth of the company are all tied to the amount of money you have and how much of it you are willing to invest. You should rarely if ever invest "everything." You always want to have adequate personal reserves.

How much you need is a tricky question and is always based on the potential deal. Realize that you are not going to buy a business that can pay you a $150,000 annual salary and have substantial profits if you only have $75,000 for a down payment. As written above, you will, in today's market, need two to three times your salary in your cash.

Real life story: The owner of a profitable business is in the driver's seat

In my early days as a Business Buyer Advocate, before I had a 100% referral based business, I would regularly get calls from business buyers who would say something like the following.

I have $100,000 for a down payment, I need a salary of at least $150,000, and I want to buy a business that can pay me that salary and have at least double my salary in profits. I figure there's an owner who wants to retire, doesn't have any family members to take over the business and, therefore, doesn't have any options.

Au contraire, novice business buyer, it is that owner who has all the options, and selling to someone with inadequate capital is an option low on their list. This seller is not encumbered by having to sell to family; they have a mature, profitable business and buyers with a lot more money than you would beat down the business's door if they knew it was for sale.

Let's look at where your capital will come from. Your top sources of capital usually include the following:

Cash in the bank, certificates of deposit or money market funds: This is your best source because it's liquid and it doesn't fluctuate with the market.

Mutual funds, stocks, bonds: Easily convertible to cash, but at what value? One of the mistakes buyers make too often is keeping their funds in volatile investments (the stock market) hoping and praying the market will go up during their search. When it goes up they are ecstatic and when the market goes down they are filled with angst. This category does not include investments like limited partnerships, notes or anything else that can't be turned to cash quickly and easily.

Investment real estate equity: If you have real estate investments (not a partnership, REIT or other managed and illiquid investment) and you want to use that equity for part of your down payment, then get a line of credit on it ASAP. Don't wait until you're working with a bank on an acquisition loan because they may want the equity as collateral and restrict the cash you can take from it. Long before you go to a bank for an acquisition loan, take a draw against your line of credit and put the money in a bank account.

Notice I didn't include equity in your residence. As I write this, the SBA guidelines state that home equity is not an acceptable source of cash for a buyer's down payment. If you want to use your home equity, get a line of credit well in advance, draw on it, put it in a bank account or CD and let it sit there (losing a few percent of interest a year). If it's done long enough in advance you have a chance of being able to use that money for a down payment. Realize that your business acquisition bank may look at it differently and tell you to repay the line of credit so they can have the equity as collateral. That's why I don't recommend you use this in your calculation of capital available.

Qualified plan funds: Withdrawing your funds and paying penalty and income tax on those funds is not advisable under almost any circumstances. However, there are a handful of third party administrators around the country who will help you set up a new C corporation, install a 401(k) plan and then roll your qualified money over to that 401(k) plan and use it to help buy a business (without tax and penalty). Most banks are familiar with this and comfortable with it. Some of my clients have used Guidant Financial in Bellevue, WA (www.guidantfinancial.com). Please do adequate due diligence to determine if this is right for you.

Let's cover the pros and cons of these programs. The biggest pro is that the vast majority of buyers (and this program is for start-ups and franchise purchases also) would not be able to buy a business without using this money. That is reason enough, if you don't have adequate funds otherwise.

However, let's discuss four possible pitfalls to these programs. First, I'll mention that a small drawback is you must make investment in your new company available to your employees who have money in the 401(k) plan. However, I haven't ever seen any employee invest in their employer's firm, and an attorney who works in this field told me it "never" happens.

1. The qualified plan controls the business: Let's assume the price of your business is $3 million, you put in $500,000 of qualified money and $100,000 of non-qualified money for your 20% down payment and finance the rest. One might assume your 401(k) plan money owns one-sixth of the business. However, ownership is based on the ratio of qualified money to your down payment, so the plan owns five-sixths of the company.

2. Distributions: When you sell the business the proceeds will go into your 401(k) plan, so when you personally take money out of the plan it is taxed at ordinary income rates, not capital gains rates (which currently amounts to a 20% difference).

3. The entity's structure must be as a C corporation: You lose the pass through feature offered by an S corporation or an LLC, and when you sell the business there are more possible tax traps than with a pass through entity.

4. Reporting: An attorney told me that a 401(k) plan, unlike a SEP IRA plan, puts you in the big leagues when it comes to government reporting. This is overwhelming to many small businesses and can be expensive.

All of the above taken into account, if you can't get a business without this money then, by all means, go full speed ahead investigating this program to see if it's right for you. If you can finance your deal without this money, do it. This is why I refer to this method as your "money of last resort." It's fantastic if you must use it, but it does add to the overhead and administration.

Other sources: This includes lines of credit, life insurance cash values and credit cards. My recommendation is to exhaust all other funds, including your qualified money, before considering sources like this. Borrowing personally to make a down payment, in addition to your acquisition debt, is very risky and threatens the viability of your new business. Cash is king, and if you add to your personal overhead it directly affects the business.

SALARY

You hope not to take a drop in salary but it depends on the capital you have to invest, the business you buy and your decision on whether to take a larger than necessary salary or use the money to grow the company. No matter what your earnings history, if you are willing to take a salary of $200,000 or less you will have a quicker search and a greater chance of buying a company. There are far fewer companies that can pay a $250,000 salary (or more) than can pay a buyer $150,000-200,000. Be realistic, think small and get the benefit of growth.

CASH FLOW

There are many definitions of cash flow. I like to use this one:

Profit + owner salary + depreciation + non-business expenses − capital expenditures

This cash flow should be at least two times your salary and preferably three or more. In any event, your starting point for acquisition debt payments should be 50% of profit (the above cash flow less fair market owner salary). The larger the deal, the greater the flexibility you have with the 50% rule. Don't over-leverage, even if the bank will allow you to have a 1.25:1 debt coverage ratio (the 50% rule gives you a 2:1 ratio).

On smaller deals you will often see the term "Seller Discretionary Earnings" (SDE), Owner Discretionary Income or some other variation. This includes salary, profit, perks, benefit, depreciation and just about anything else that can be thrown into the formula. It's a way for brokers and others to get out of the discussion of what is the fair market owner salary for the business (the seller thinks a $50,000 a year manager can run the firm making $500,000, and the buyer believes it takes a $150,000 person). If this number is being used, remember that, for valuation purposes, you can't use the same rules and techniques that you would for a profit figure. And nowhere in the SBA valuation guidelines do they use terms like SDE when defining acceptable valuation methods.

LOCATION

Above I gave an example of a client who let me know he was scared by tightening his geographic area. It goes both ways. Don't be unrealistic and think you'll commute two hours each way for the right business. It will get old fast. If your market has geographical pockets where there is a high concentration of businesses of the type you want, you can't exclude those areas. You may have to move.

REAL LIFE STORY: DON'T OVERLOOK "SIMPLE" CRITERIA

In my first year as a Business Buyer Advocate, I asked a client where he wanted the business to be. He answered, "I wish somebody had asked me that six months ago. I spent three months working on a deal in a city two hours from here. I assumed we would move. My wife assumed I would commute. I should have thought of this before getting involved with a potential deal."

OWNERSHIP

Every business buyer wants sole ownership. Every business buyer should at least consider and definitely tell the market he or she will consider being a working partner, preferably in a majority position. It doesn't happen very often but it can get you a deal you wouldn't have got any other way. It also gets sellers who wouldn't talk to you about selling 100% of their company to talk to you and give you the chance to impress them so they will sell the whole company. Also, key employees with a small percentage, or the seller in a minority position, can add stability.

The third option is a minority position. My feelings are that it has to be a very special situation for a buyer to consider this, or there has to be a contract in place that gets the buyer to a majority position at a fair price (the buyer shouldn't have to pay for the increased value he or she creates).

DAILY ACTIVITIES

What do you want to do on a daily, weekly and monthly basis? Every client I work with tells me they want to be involved with strategy, vision, management and/or leadership. They may go on to say they also want customer contact (sales and marketing people), product development (engineers) or managing the finances (finance people). Never do I hear that they want to run the machines, be the lead salesperson or the in-house accountant.

One of the early questions to a seller is, "What do you do on a daily basis?" This is our first insight into whether or not the business is a good fit for the buyer. An owner whose business is dependent on him or her to program the CNC machine or do product development and enhancements will never be a good fit for a sales professional or generalist manager position.

It's important that you define what you want to do and, early on in the process, find out what the seller does. A quick no is worth as much as a yes.

MANAGEMENT TEAM

The bottom line is, you are buying people and their skills. What skills do you want your team to have? Formulate a general description of where you think you'll need help from your team, realizing that every business is different and there is no one size that fits all. A buyer who is a financial whiz will probably want a strong sales manager and sales department. A buyer who is a sales manager will place less emphasis on this (because he or she knows they can build a sales plan and team) and may want strong product or financial people on their team.

Employee types

I have worked with buyers who have told me they didn't want to have low skilled or (highly skilled) blue-collar workers. I've worked with buyers who didn't want anything to do with white-collar or highly educated employees. There is no right or wrong; it's based on your experience. You need to think about this before going too deep with any acquisition.

In chapter one there is a Real Life Story about the CPA whom bought a cabinet shop only to find out he couldn't relate to the employees. It made his day-to-day life miserable. Take some time and think about the employee types you prefer *not* to have. You may realize that any and all types are acceptable and that's okay.

Sales and Marketing

Do you want to have relationships with your customers or attract them via marketing? Almost all business-to-business sales are based on relationships; you are solving a problem in conjunction with your customer. Many consumer product businesses will use marketing to attract customers. We're decades past the door-to-door Fuller Brush type salespeople who built customer relationships to sell consumer products. Where are your skills in this area?

Travel

It's rare that the owner of a small or mid-sized business will be a road-warrior like corporate sales people or implementers. It is common for owners to attend trade shows, make customer visits in a regional area or travel across the country or across the world to visit factories or top customers.

Decide now if you have any travel restrictions and, especially if you have any limitations, ask the seller, early in the process, what travel is involved. A simple question on travel could save you a lot of time.

REAL LIFE STORY: KNOW YOUR PERSONAL LIMITS

Paul was close to making an offer on a business. He then found out the owner traveled 10 days per month. Paul had two elderly parents who needed care and Paul's siblings had moved away. He couldn't be gone one-third of the time, given his family's needs. He had to pass on a company that fascinated him and that was a business model to which he felt he could add tremendous value.

STEP TWO: YOUR MATERIALS

You don't need a four-page resume best suited for a corporate position and a business card that has your contact information. The long resume is a waste of time. Rarely will a small business owner take the time to read it, and if they do they won't care that the buyer has Six Sigma or some other corporate training program certificate. (As an aside, the best business card a client had included his name, contact info and the tag line, "Looking for my next great adventure in life.")

So, what should a buyer have? Here are your minimum requirements:

- A business card with all or your contact information
- A one-sheet description of what you are looking for
- A one-page resume filled with accomplishments, not platitudes. This means you need to state results like, "Reduced costs by 22% over two years," or "Increased sales by 29% over the five-year historical growth rate."
- Your personal LinkedIn URL

In addition:

- Build a database of everybody you know, send them a notice that you are looking for a business to buy and regularly send them updates of your search, including what you are analyzing, what your criteria are, etc.

- Also consider having your own website that describes who you are, what you are looking for and gives a running update of your search (a blog of your search)

- Post updates and requests on whatever social media vehicles you use (Facebook, Twitter and others)

Once you meet owners, have a sanitized personal net worth statement or (and this is preferred initially) a copy of an investment account statement showing how much capital you've allocated for this deal. Sellers are skeptical of any buyer who won't show their financial capabilities but want detailed information about the business. Realize that once a deal is agreed to, you will have to share your full financial statement with the seller (who is going to finance part of the transaction), who may have a credit check done on you.

Step three: Assemble your "A" team

Sellers don't want a buyer who won't use a team. Well, maybe they do thinking they'll get a better deal but their advisors know that the inexperienced buyer, acting on his or her own, is a sure sign of disaster.

Tip: Use your team to increase your safety

Buying a business is like climbing a mountain. There are ups, downs, dangerous crevices and slippery slopes. If you're climbing by yourself, you may make it to the summit. If you are part of a team, you have a better chance of success. If you have a team and an experienced guide, who knows all the danger zones on the trek and how to avoid them, you have an excellent chance of reaching the summit safely.

As a Business Buyer Advocate I often coordinate the team with the buyer. The usual suspects include:

- A transaction savvy attorney, who has done deals in the same size range as your deal

- A CPA who knows transaction tax and deal structure and can set up the financial systems and structure

- A banker who knows and likes acquisition loans and understands ongoing business banking needs. Often banks will have the buyer work only with the SBA expert. I encourage buyers to meet the person who will be their business banker. It doesn't do any good to get an acquisition loan and then find out your banker can't or won't help you with ongoing working and growth capital needs

The following also needs to be considered, as the deal requires (this list is not meant to be all inclusive):

- A CFO to assist with financial modeling, cash flow projections, budgets and management reporting systems

- A human resources specialist to make sure the company's hiring and other employee policies are current and legal

- A commercial real estate professional (there are now many who don't lease or list property and only work for the tenant, similar to what I do as a Business Buyer Advocate)

- An engineer for specific mechanical or structural issues

REAL LIFE STORY: HAVE ADVISORS WITH THE <u>RIGHT</u> EXPERIENCE

One of my clients told me that he just loved and very much respected his attorney. I questioned if the attorney was the right one, given that his firm was associated with middle market deals, not small to midsized company deals. My client assured me all was okay.

His attorney drafted the purchase and sale agreement and sent it to the seller's attorney. The response was that they would not even read this (57 page) agreement and would take it upon themselves to write one more appropriate (kudos to them). Their agreement came back at under 20 pages (typical size).

When I asked my client about this he told me that his attorney had done such a great job for him in the past. When I probed he confided that the other transaction was when he (my client) was the CEO of a firm that was involved with a completed merger with a European company.

His attorney took his skills for large international deals and applied them to a small business deal. It just didn't work, and we were lucky the seller's attorney had the common sense not to work off of and negotiate off of the middle market template.

STEP FOUR: RELATIONSHIPS

Sometimes I think my clients get tired of me talking about how business buy-sell is a relationship game. In the previous chapter I discussed relationship and quoted Jim Bernard: "I would never buy a business from or sell a business to someone I didn't like."

This subject is too important to just mention once. It is the key to getting any deal done. When clients tell me they met an owner for two hours and spent 20 minutes discussing the business, I reply that it's a good start. We don't know if it will be the right business at the right price but there's hope.

What does this mean on a practical level? It means you have to be prepared for every meeting because you never know if it will be "the one." You must:

- Have an opening statement.

- Be prepared with your questions for the seller.

- Have formulated answers for questions the seller may ask you.

- Be ready to end the meeting with a definitive next step (telephone call, sending of information, next in-person meeting, etc.).

Professional speaking coaches say that you need a strong opening and a strong closing. Audiences whose attention is not captured in the first 90 seconds are lost. Audiences not motivated by a strong ending will drift away, having received nothing of value. Open strong, close strong and, even if your middle (the majority of a presentation) is weak, you will be remembered positively. The same holds true here, although you don't have the latitude to have a weak middle.

STEP FIVE: WHY ARE THEY SELLING?

This is age-old question that raises every bit of skepticism in a buyer, and you will have to get good at (nicely) asking the tough questions to uncover the real reason. Unless there's a definitive event in the seller's life, buyers wonder why the seller would sell a profitable business. A seller stating that they want to "pursue other interests" doesn't hold it with buyers.

As one client (who had previously bought, grown and sold a company) said to me, "The best time to sell a business is one year before you're burned out." Many investment managers don't hesitate to sell a stock when it's at its perceived peak or when they feel they can capture the return on investment they want.

However, there often isn't a catastrophic event that forces a sale. Business owners are like everybody else. In corporate America people change jobs every three to five years. Owners last longer but they do have other ideas and interests. The smart owner will sell before getting completely burned out, when the business is doing well and when they can demonstrate future growth is possible.

As we'll see later, buyers are attracted to companies when they see areas where they can add (immediate) value. All of this said, a healthy degree of skepticism is not only expected, it's encouraged. One can never be too careful (and the same should go for a seller's skepticism of the buyer and his or her abilities).

The reasons for selling that you should look for include the following:

- Death
- Disability
- Divorce
- Owner dispute
- Burnout
- Retirement

- Health (owner or spouse)
- Personal life issues
- Owner is an entrepreneur (and wants to start another business rather than manage the current one)

Real Life Story: Life happens and it can create urgency to sell

Life happens and people don't always make the best decisions. Dale closed on a deal and the seller received no money. In 2007 this owner of half-a-dozen small businesses took all his capital and leveraged it in commercial real estate. By 2010 he was owned by the banks.

The banks forced him to sell his businesses to pay his real estate debt. When Dale moved into his business he looked across the street and saw a building owned by his seller. The building had been vacant for eight months at the time.

Step six: Understand your search is now your job

A successful search starts with having a plan and implementing the plan. This is no different than finding a job, prospecting for a new customer or even dating. If you have a plan and implement it you will be more successful than if you don't. However, even the smartest business buyers often neglect this step. For some reason all of the business acumen disappears when it comes to doing a search for a business.

This could be because buying a business is not like buying a house, but buying a house is what most of us have done more than once. The following provides detail on the major differences.

Comparison: Business Buying, as Easy as Buying a House?

"It's amazing how, regardless of the level of sophistication, experience and business acumen of a prospective business buyer, the acquisition process always seems "easy" to those who have never experienced it."

This is a quote from Richard Parker, owner of Diomo, Inc., www. diomo.com, one of America's foremost experts on business buying, who writes a blog on business buying for BizQuest.com (www.bizquest.com).

Richard wrote the above to me during an email exchange we had about business buyers (in general). Too many of the buyers Richard describes think buying a business is like buying a house. While there are similarities, there are crucial differences in many important areas, three of which are described below.

Search: Finding a house to buy is easy. Ninety-nine percent of those for sale are available via the Internet, whether or not you have a real estate agent. You can filter, compare and contrast all from the comfort of your home.

Buying a business is more like finding a job. First, most of the good businesses, like good jobs, are never advertised. In fact, the International Business Brokers Association and other industry groups state that business brokers sell only 20% of the businesses that sell (follow some of the discussions on LinkedIn and other sites and you'll soon realize this is a frustrating issue for many brokers).

Confidentiality is a primary reason for this. House sellers want the world to know their house is for sale. Business owners fear that employees, customers and vendors will find out the company is for sale and leave or demand a change in terms. This and other reasons mean that a wise business buyer can't just peruse the Internet like they would do if buying a house. They must access the hidden market.

Deal and Finance: Buying a house means the buyer gets pre-qualified by a lender and can pretty much be assured that if the price of the house meets their down payment and borrowing capacity restraints they can do the deal. There are usually many comparable sales to keep prices in-line with reality.

While businesses and buyers may say they are pre-qualified for financing, it has a completely different meaning for each. Yes, a business may get a lender to say they will finance up to a certain amount, but the big question is the quality and capacity of the buyer. Similarly, a buyer may be told by a bank they will qualify for a certain loan amount based on their down payment, but the big question is the collateral and cash flow of the business. Finally, comparable business sale information has never been as comprehensive as for homebuyers, although it was still important. However, there is little to no comparable sales information for deals since the Great Recession, so using historical sales as a benchmark has lost almost all of its validity.

Inspection and Negotiation: Negotiation with the sale of a house is almost exclusively on price, with maybe a little on things that need fixing per the inspection. It's a given that the seller will be cashed out, which is not so when buying a business. The chances are high there will be seller financing, even if a bank is involved. In fact, there's a good chance the bank will insist the seller have some "skin in the game."

So negotiations are about price and terms, with conditions thrown in for good measure. Conditions may include the seller's transition time, his or her health benefits, what happens if a key customer leaves, employment agreements for management and more. Once price is agreed to the real fun starts (whereas in home-buying, price is everything).

Home inspections have become a commodity. Due diligence for an acquisition is part science and part art. A buyer is always making a leap of faith and wants to be sure of what they are getting. They have to ask the right questions and get the right answers without getting bogged down in minutia (for example, as pointed out to one client, you don't need to know what every employee does every quarter hour of the day; they have tasks to do and the firm's profitability tells you whether those tasks are getting done).

Every business has warts, and it's what happens when the warts are discovered that makes or breaks a deal. If the warts are disclosed early, the buyer is a lot more confident about the deal than if those blemishes are kept under cover and are found during due diligence (buyers don't like to be surprised in due diligence; they want to prove what they've been told).

Conclusion: Richard Parker is right. It is not easy to find and buy a business. However, one of the more complicating factors is not mentioned above, and that is emotion. A seller may be selling their "baby." A buyer is committing to millions of dollars that includes draining investment accounts, signing over their home and personally guaranteeing loans, leases and vendor accounts. Even if the process was easy, the emotion would still be a complicating factor.

BE ORGANIZED WHETHER WORKING OR UNEMPLOYED

It is my belief that a business buyer who is unemployed is much less productive than a buyer whom is working, doing consulting or doing contract work. As Michael once told, "I'll get to it after my next game of golf." I soon realized there would always be another game of golf.

If you're not working, realize this is your full-time job until you buy a company. Work it every day and don't take too many days off. If you are working, fit in what you can. Many owners will want to meet at the end of the day or on a Saturday anyway. All of your breakfast, lunch and coffee meetings should have a purpose (to get leads on companies that may be for sale). Whether you've been in sales before or not, you are now. You are selling yourself to your friends, business associates and motivated business owners who wish to sell. Approach it like a salesperson approaches their territory and prospects.

REAL LIFE STORY: GET THE DEAL DONE

It was the middle of June. My client had just come to agreement with the seller on price, terms and conditions. He called to ask what I thought of delaying the deal until September so he could have the summer off. I didn't laugh. I did tell him that he knew me well enough to know that it is my firm belief that the longer a deal stretches out the less chance there was of it closing. He immediately shifted modes, asked if June 30 was feasible. It wasn't, but we did close in July.

Above all, don't get caught up in the "thrill of the hunt." The goal is to make a kill, that is, buy a company. The search is fun. Meeting many owners, seeing businesses and analyzing information is fun. Don't let it get too enjoyable. Keep focused to move forward one step at a time.

Also realize there are *no* perfect businesses and there are no perfect deals. All businesses have issues you'll have to deal with. You will have to give to get. The object is to find businesses where the company's weaknesses are a match for your strengths (while at the same time, your weaknesses will not be exploited). Your goal should not be to get a steal. It is to get you into business ownership as soon as feasibly possible with a win-win deal for a company you will have fun (and make money) with.

When you find something you like, start researching. Never before has it been easier to research. Buyers are more likely to get a deal done when they understand the industry and its future.

Finally, a search is never over until you close on a deal (although most buyers dramatically reduce or stop their efforts once they think they have a deal). Don't stop your search efforts until you are sure it's going to close.

REAL LIFE STORY: KEEP PROSPECTING FOR COMPANIES

Craig worked the plan. He followed it and kept his pipeline of prospective sellers full. When a deal on his top choice didn't materialize he went to his second choice. When that deal collapsed we talked about next steps. It collapsed because the seller's plan was to sell and work, at a low salary, for his church; during our due diligence he realized his non-salary ownership benefits were substantially more than he thought, and he knew he could never support his family with investment earnings and the low salary.

I told Craig to call prospect number three, which we had put on the back burner. He replied that he already had a meeting with them in two days. He met, they came to an agreement and it closed in six weeks. If he hadn't kept his search active when he found his top choice, it could have taken months.

STEP SEVEN: IMPLEMENTING YOUR SEARCH PLAN

As mentioned previously, there are only three strategies you can use to find a business for sale, and all are important. Buyers whom consistently and regularly implement all three strategies have a greater chance of finding a target company and doing so quicker.

PUBLIC MARKET

Some owners try to sell their business by themselves, and these days the Internet has taken over as the advertising vehicle of choice. The two prominent websites for advertising companies are www.bizbuysell.com and www.bizquest.com. Take a look at them and what you'll find is that most of the businesses advertised, especially the good businesses, are represented by business brokers.

While listed businesses may dominate these websites, business brokers handle about 20% of all small and mid-sized business transactions. Often I have prospects and clients who are frustrated with the available broker listings. The complaints I get are that the businesses aren't a fit for the buyer's skills, the companies are losers or they are over-priced. If a company is not a fit it is not a fit, no matter how you find it. Losers are everywhere; it's when someone tries to peddle a loser as a great business (lots of potential) that buyers get upset, at least the buyers I meet, who are sophisticated executive level people.

The overpricing is common and the phenomenon is not unique to listed businesses. Eighty percent of owners believe their business is worth more than it is. A broker's job is to get the best price and terms for their client, the seller, and they must get the listing before they can get a deal.

Sometimes the owner truly wants to sell and is also unrealistic. If the broker can get the listing, they then have the opportunity to educate the seller as a team member, not as a "salesperson." At the same time, the market will educate the seller (when all of the offers come in lower than he or she wants).

TIP: AN UNREALISTIC OWNER WILL LOSE GOOD BUYERS

I get many newsletters, and one caught my attention because it had a section on the pricing of businesses for sale. The following is a quote from that newsletter:

"Should a business be listed at a higher price anticipating a lower offer?

Usually the answer is yes. But if the price is too high, there may be very few looks and possibly no offers."

Business buy-sell is a lot like selling a used car. If you want $10,000 for your car, you don't ask $10,000, you ask $15,000 and give yourself room to negotiate. This is not like going to Nordstrom or Target and seeing fixed prices.

The biggest mistake buyers make is not staying in touch with brokers. They call a few times and if there are no listings that match, they give up (on that broker). It's important that you keep in touch with all the brokers who handle deals in the size range you are targeting.

I have a great relationship with my local (Seattle) business brokers. I can chalk up many deals to these relationships, as brokers like working with my clients because they know my clients are qualified and realistic (I don't work with bottom feeders trying to steal a company). Here are three examples:

1. A broker reached out to my client with a company that was a perfect fit for him. He didn't remember the broker and asked how she came to contact him. She replied that she met him through me (in the last year) and had kept his contact information in her database.

2. My client and the broker attended the same church and saw each other almost every week. Yet the broker didn't know my client was looking for a business and my client didn't know he was a broker. During one of our regular "keep in touch" calls I mentioned my client's name and the broker said he had a business that was perfect for him (it was, given my client's industry experience).

3. A lawyer referred a client to me whom wanted to sell. I referred her to a broker friend and six months later a client of mine, whom didn't like to network with brokers or anybody, met the owner because the broker and I felt he was a good fit. He was cautious because it was an industry not on his target list. We were right; it was a good fit. His monthly sales were at least 10% higher than the same month the previous year for his first year of ownership.

REAL LIFE STORY: STAY IN TOUCH; THERE ARE MANY WAYS BUSINESSES ARE MARKETED

A business broker told me that after securing a listing, the client asked if he'd be marketing it, "everywhere." His reply was that no, he wouldn't do that. Instead, he would make five telephone calls. If he didn't find a good buyer he would make five more calls and keep making calls until he was successful. He did this because he didn't want the business's name out in public to all the unqualified buyers who answer ads. I was one of his first five calls and one of my clients (whom the broker casually knew) was a good fit and bought the business.

NETWORK, NETWORK, NETWORK

Networking is something the majority of business buyers do:

- Right after they start attacking the public market of companies for sale
- An incomplete job of and do poorly
- So inadequately they wonder why they aren't getting a lot of referrals

Most business buyers have not been involved in business development during their careers. They have been managers and leaders and therefore don't understand the process of networking (and marketing in general). Once again I will share what I hear from the outplacement industry, and that is that their clients rarely have a network while they are working and don't know how to meet people and make the right impression.

In step two I listed the materials you should have to conduct a viable search. Materials are great and social media is a fairly new tool, but neither are substitutes for face-to-face meetings. You have to meet with people to make your best impression

Real Life Story: Finding a business is a contact game

Many years ago, at a professional group meeting, a crusty old salesman pulled me, a young marketing neophyte, aside and drew the following picture on a piece of paper.

$$.) (.$$

He asked me if I knew what the drawing was, I didn't know and he told me that no matter what the circumstances, the best way to make a sale was to get belly-to-belly (the drawing represents two people standing belly-to-belly).

Fast forward many years, and meeting people one-on-one still is the best way to communicate and get the results you want, especially for business buyers.

So, whom do you connect with? The answer is everybody you know.

Start by putting together a list of family, friends, business associates, alumni and others, such as your dentist, doctor, CPA and other service providers. Your second step is to rank them using a simple A, B, and C system. All can receive emails at the same time, but prioritize your in-person meetings. Realize you can't meet with too many people. This is a numbers game and the more people you contact the better your chances of success.

From now on, every breakfast, coffee and lunch meeting should be related to your search. Seek out trade groups, Chambers of Commerce, networking events and professional associations, as they are all viable situations. Don't be afraid to get to the point. This is not a time to be wishy-washy. Tell people your objective point blank, which is to buy a mature, profitable business.

Then stay in touch. A weak link in networking (all networking, not just as part of a business search) is the lack of staying in touch. I suggest an email every four to six weeks that gives a summary of your activities, mentions companies you have looked at and reminds people that your objective is to buy a business, so ask them to please refer to you any situations where the owner may be even thinking of selling. Here is what one client sent as part of his update (and notice it's in the P.S. because that is the second most read part of any letter or message, after the headline or opening sentence.

> P.S. As a reminder, I'm searching for a small company with a defensible niche position in the Greater Seattle area. My ideal acquisition target is a manufacturing or distribution company in a mature industry with $5M - $12M in annual revenues and an owner who wants to exit. Here is a link to my acquisition website.

As a Business Buyer Advocate I also network on behalf of all my clients, and every time I track results the deals that are found via networking are at about a 50-50 split between my clients' and mine. Mine come from my established network and theirs come from getting out and meeting people. About half of businesses referred to clients are from people they didn't know when they started searching.

REAL LIFE STORY: EVEN INTROVERTS CAN NETWORK SUCCESSFULLY

One of my clients, Robert, an engineer and typical in that he was not comfortable networking, realized he had to meet people to be successful. We created a package of materials for his search and he used them as his "crutch" (his term) to give him an entrée in networking. By being aggressive and using his crutch, he estimated he had a 50% greater chance of getting a lead compared to before he had his crutch.

I summarized Robert's activity and strategies to my other clients in a memo. Here is how I closed the memo, to emphasize that you should never stop prospecting.

Robert is scheduled to close on April 1. As of last week (March 10) he was still "prospecting."

Finally Robert found the company he is buying by networking, * and said having a number of opportunities always on his plate made him more confident when dealing with the seller.

> * To show how a search is a moving target, I introduced Robert to somebody I knew. Robert talked to and gave his materials to this person, who later told me he had a lead for Robert. I called the referral, introduced him to Robert and the start of a deal was in the works.

I volunteer and teach a class at the Seattle SBA offices on starting and growing a consulting business. In the section on networking I tell the students that I've read and thrown away more books on networking than most people have even seen (much less read). Too many of these books are centered on "working a room." You don't need to work the room, you need to make a good contact or two at meetings, impress the people you know and stay in touch with everybody.

If you're not a mingler, like Robert and me, find your personal "crutch." Never forget that a business search is the same as being in sales, it's a numbers game. The more people you meet the greater your chances of success and faster success. It's a relationship game between buyer and seller and between buyer and his or her network.

People like to help other people; especially people they know and like. That's why you shouldn't be hesitant to directly ask for their help or to stay in touch. There is also a give-to-get karma on this planet, so anytime you can help someone else, do so. In fact, when you meet with someone, and are asking for their assistance to help you find a company to buy, ask if there is anything you can do for them, someone you can introduce them to, etc. I built a network of over 100 referral sources, from a base of three, within one year by asking for names of other professionals, and as I started meeting those people I then offered to introduce them to others.

BE PROACTIVE

The third way to find a business to buy is to target industries and reach out to companies to see if they are interested in selling. There are many owners who are thinking of selling, and if your timing is right you just may find a prospective seller.

Many owners I talk with just don't know what to do and are scared to death regarding confidentiality, or the lack of it. One of your biggest obstacles when prospecting directly to companies is confidentiality. If an owner tells you they are interested in discussing selling their company, for all they know you are with a competitor that will use that information in the market place. As a shameless plug for using a Business Buyer Advocate, when your Business Buyer Advocate contacts an owner, they can impress upon them their ability to hold secrets. If word gets out that an intermediary violated confidentiality they are out of business.

So, owners who don't know how to sell keep operating the business, even if the drive and passion is slipping away. You probably want to ask, why wouldn't they call some business brokers and put the business on the market? Here are three reasons.

1. Confidentiality is again on the top of the list. Owners fear that, even with confidentiality agreements, word will get out because a broker's job is to market the business. This may be unfounded (as good brokers are very careful) but it is a fear.

2. They don't know whom to call. There's a wide range of deal sizes and the IBBA says that the average price of broker sold businesses is about $300,000. If an owner looks on the Internet they see the majority of businesses for sale are small and that bothers them. If they expect to get seven or eight figures for their business, they fear working with someone who is out of their league with their size company. It's the same reason they use a CPA for taxes and not the tax preparer in the kiosk at the mall.

3. A few people who use manipulative techniques to get a listing have tainted the brokerage industry. Here's how it goes, and every owner has experienced this or heard about it from a friend. A broker cold calls an owner and tells them they have a buyer for their business. The owner goes to the broker's office, finds out they have to sign a listing agreement to meet the buyer and when they do they are told the buyer was looking for something in their industry (say manufacturing in

general) not their particular business. Usually the buyer is not interested or qualified. It's called fishing for a listing and I regularly get asked if I am fishing for a listing even after I tell someone I don't list businesses. Good brokers don't do this, but they all get lumped together.

Using the criteria we previously discussed, you need to come up with a list of target companies and reach out to them. You will do this by letter and/or telephone. Based on your criteria, your skills and interest, pick industries that seem to be a match. There are numerous list brokers and the two largest databases (that I know of) are Salesgenie (part of InfoUSA) and Hoovers (a division of D&B).

Inc. magazine once published an article that stated that the average profit for small businesses is 7-10% of sales. Widen this to 5-15%, figure that profits will be two to four times the fair market salary for running the business and determine the size range of companies you will target. For example, if you want a business that can pay you a $200,000 salary, you can figure the profit for that company will usually be $400,000 to $800,000. Knowing that most firms will have profit of 5-15% of their sales, you know that the 80-20 rule says that the sales range for your target companies will be $2.5 million to $16 million.

This is a wide range, so use some common sense. Distribution businesses tend to have lower margins and therefore will be at the higher end of this range. Very few distribution businesses will have $600,000 or more of cash flow (salary and profit) on $3 million of sales. Service businesses can have incredible margins and will tend to be in the lower half of the range.

Here is a sample prospecting letter (taken from a combination of sample letters in *How to Buy a Good Business with Little or None of Your Own Money* by Lionel Haines (Crown, 2000), *and a number of the many books written by Arnold Goldstein.*

I want to acquire a manufacturing business located in the greater (city) are with annual cash flow (owner salary plus profit) in the $600,000 to $1,000,000 range. The firm I am looking for should have annual sales in the $2.5 to $16 million range and be well managed. I prefer a firm with clear, well-defined market niches and a strong reputation for quality and customer service.

I am a principal, not a broker, with adequate capital and financing.

If you have an interest in selling, please call me at your earliest convenience. You have my assurance that I will hold all matters in the strictest confidence.

If you are not interested in selling at this time please keep my enclosed business card for future reference. If you know of any other good companies that meet my criteria would you please contact me?

Thank you for your assistance in this matter.

Sincerely,

After sending letters you may want to send them again to the same companies if you don't hear from enough owners with good, profitable businesses. However, you will have to pick up the telephone and call everybody you sent the letter to in order to maximize your results.

Here is a script for telephoning owners. Adapt this if you have to leave a voice mail message. Under no circumstances should you tell anybody else in the firm why you are calling. Your saying nothing more than that you are looking to buy a business will start rumors flying that the company is for sale.

Ms. or Mr. owner, this is (your name) and I'm looking for a business to buy in your industry. I recently sent you a letter but didn't hear from you so I decided to call to see if you are interested in discussing selling your business or, if not, if you know of someone who may be interested in selling.

Real Life Story: Outside factors can influence your results

You don't want to put all your eggs in one basket. In this case, don't send all your letters at the same time. Spread them out over 3-5 weeks. This prevents outside events like weather, disasters, politics, etc., from distracting the recipients and decreasing your odds of success. Also, if you send all your letters at once, the chances of you making the follow-up calls in a timely manner are slim.

We once mailed letters for a new client. There was absolutely no response. Not one call and most interestingly, no letters returned as undeliverable (around 5% always come back). Two weeks later we mailed the letters again, staggering the mailing over three weeks. The first week my phone started ringing and our search was off and running.

These letters were sent from Seattle to Kitsap County, WA, which is across Puget Sound from Seattle. To this day I believe there is a good chance the first mailing ended up on the bottom of Puget Sound.

Remember, it's a numbers and a timing game. The owner not interested in selling now may be in interested in four months. If you make a good impression they will remember you and call you when the time is right.

Your search is the most critical component of business buying. There is nothing else you can do if you haven't found any businesses interested in discussing selling. You dramatically increase your chances of success if you are active with all three or the search strategies. Stay in touch with the appropriate brokers, network efficiently and effectively and proactively contact owners.

ACTION ITEMS

* Define your criteria.

* Segregate your down payment funds (don't have it at risk).

* Determine your personal cash flow needs so you're prepared for all viable deals.

* Create and assemble your marketing materials.

* Build your advisory team (including numerous bankers).

* Work on relationships of all kinds.

* Make search your priority; you can't buy a good business until you find a good business.

* Attack the market.

— 4 —

First Date

Overview

Understand that once a company (or companies) is found, all the rest of the steps on the road to closing are intertwined. It is not linear. In fact, financing has jumped to the initial analysis stage, because of the Great Recession.

Above all, don't get caught up in the "thrill of the hunt." The goal is to make a kill, that is, buy a company. The search is fun. Meeting many owners, seeing businesses and analyzing information is fun. Don't let it get too enjoyable. Keep focused to move forward one step at a time. The next step we're going to discuss is the initial analysis.

As you start analyzing a company, realize there are *no* perfect businesses and there are *no* perfect deals. All businesses have issues (red flags, blemishes, detriments, etc.) you'll have to deal with. The object is to find businesses where the company's weaknesses are a match for your strengths (and your weaknesses will not be exploited). You will balance your skills and risk quotient with the red flags you are encountering. What might be a deal killer for one person is an opportunity for another.

Your goal is not to get a steal. It is to get you into business ownership as soon as feasibly possible with a win-win deal for a company you will have fun (and make money) with.

When you find something you like, start researching. Never before has it been easier to research. Buyers are more likely to get a deal done when they understand the industry and its future. If things "check out" it's one risk factor that's been mitigated.

Clichés: Don't judge a book by its cover, or, the glass is half full, not half empty. We hear these all the time. When it comes to analyzing a business, don't fall into the cliché trap. For example, you may say that a business is "bursting at the seams." That is not a bad thing; it means they're busy. A bustling place and pace is good. A facility that is not pristine may be a result of success.

A buyer complained that the shop floor was crowded. The answer was because having a smaller space kept money in the business's bank account, not in the landlord's bank account. One buyer complained was that it's a messy facility (not dangerous or unhealthy, just messy). The complainer came from an office and sales background. Another buyer, a manufacturing engineer, didn't give it a second thought and said it meant sales and production was up.

Remember Pareto's Principle ("A minority of input produces the majority of results"). This is also known as the 80-20 rule, and in this case it means don't spend too much time on the last bits of information because they won't change the end result too much. Look for the big signs of success. It's more fun that way. (This does not mean you should ignore red flags, just don't get hung up on the superficial.)

As I've been taught, keep in mind that it's not about perfection, it's about success. Every business has warts. But if the company has profits, concentrate on whether it's reasonable to assume the profits will continue.

Buyers often worry prematurely about things they don't have information about. In other words it's needless worry. There are enough risks in buying a business without stressing yourself over things you don't have information on.

Here's a typical comment and question: "I think the company is doing 'X.' What do I do about it?" My answer is always, ask them if they are doing 'X,' why they are and how has it worked. Just because the strategy is different from what you did at your previous company or in your previous business doesn't make it wrong. Just because it doesn't "make sense" to you, doesn't make it a bad decision. In fact, what you should be looking for is something you feel could be done better—expenses that are excessive or efficiencies you can improve.

Real life story: Take a breath and think it through

Business buyers often get irrational, especially individual buyers. This is simply because they are making the largest financial decision of their lives (in most cases). As an FYI, sellers get like this also, and it shows itself in what is known as "seller remorse," or the hesitancy to part with their "baby." Customers are one of the biggest concerns, so this irrationality often manifests itself around customers.

Buyer irrationality tends to manifest itself late on Fridays, so that it can expand exponentially over the weekend. I received a call from a buyer first thing on a Monday morning, two to three weeks before closing. He had had an uncomfortable weekend because late on Friday he posed this question to himself, "What if the seller is doing everything possible to irritate the customers and when I take over they will be mad at the firm and stop doing business with us?"

By the time Monday rolled around this was reality, in his mind. I asked if he had any evidence this was happening; the answer was, "No." I asked if it made sense for the seller to do this, given that he was taking a note and any deal can collapse, leaving him to have to work with those customers; the answer was, again, "No."

TIMELINE

Timelines are important to the whole process, especially once a deal is struck and you're heading to the closing. For now, create a mini-timeline, even if it's just for you. Analysis is one of the shorter time blocks in the process. Your goal here is to get an initial understanding of the business, not delve deeply into it. This is not the time when a seller will divulge his or her secret sauce or trade secrets. That comes after you've signed a letter of intent.

It's my practice and belief that this part of the process should be as follows:

- Buyer and seller meet, build relationship
- Buyer analyzes initial information and seller reviews buyer's overview (money and experience)
- Buyer reviews company financials with one or two banks
- An offer is made based on big picture information
- A letter of intent is signed
- Due diligence starts and the buyer proves what he or she has been told (as does the seller)

It starts with building a relationship, and relationships are the key to sales, not just to buying a business. An example of this is given in an old article on selling, from *BusinessWeek online*.

The author writes, "I promised to share a better way to sell in today's tough economic environment. Selling is not a competition, it's a connection. Rather than putting the competitive instinct in overdrive, devote your energies to making connections with customers, their co-workers, the people in your own organization, and beyond. This strategy will not only increase sales and profits, it will speed up the sales cycle.

Many years back, I lost a big sale because I didn't have a good connection with my prospective customer. I learned the hard way the truth of this piece of selling wisdom: "When two people want to do business together, the details won't hold them apart. When two people don't want to do business together, the details won't hold the deal together." Learn from my mistake. Look for connections, develop them, expand and leverage them."

Like it or not, buying a business is a selling game. You have to sell yourself, as does the seller. Do the things you're supposed to do, create a relationship and follow through, and you'll be successful. A broker shared with me that a deal fell apart because, while the money was there, the seller just didn't like the buyer.

Part of doing what you're supposed to do is to manage your time and the seller's time. I tell sellers and brokers that we can quickly analyze a company without disrupting it. Remember, whether a deal happens or not, the owner has to manage the business every day. Respect their time.

Part of this management involves creating a timeline. Look at what needs to be done, create a chart with deadlines and share it with the seller so you're on the same page when it comes to working towards you making an offer. Work together to make it happen so the seller isn't surprised by the information you request.

REAL LIFE STORIES: ADDING VALUE

Buyers get attracted to a company when they see something (or some things) to which they feel they can add significant value. Here are three quick examples.

Buyer one noticed that the elderly owner took numerous two, three and even four week vacations. He said he knew he could grow the business, "Just by being there." The business quadrupled in three years and has grown since.

In buyer two's case, it was the website that needed improvement. This was a service business and the website was nothing more than a brochure. Employees and customers wasted time making telephone calls, leaving messages, playing phone tag and having the usual chit-chat that goes on when in-person contact is made. Within three months the buyer had his website expanded to be an online ordering system and this saved money and his customers' and employees' time. His employees used that freed up time to do more marketing, and the company doubled in size within two years.

Buyer three realized that the two owners, both about 65, were coasting. They had another business that was a cash cow and just "showed up" at the company he bought because they liked it. This was confirmed when the primary vendor told him that they really liked the sellers and wished they would take advantage of more opportunities in the market. The business tripled in less than five years.

FINANCIAL INFORMATION

To start, you should get three to five years of financial statements (income statements and balance sheets), year-to-date statements and any big picture explanations of items like accelerated depreciation (which, with the current and ever-changing laws, can make a real difference on a company's bottom line). At this point, and all the way through the process, give yourself a gut check. If ever your gut tells you something is amiss, either investigate thoroughly or back off.

At this time I have my clients give the seller "Partner" On-Call Networks Initial Disclosure Form (for a copy of this form email me at john@johnmartinka.com. It is the only form I ever want a seller to fill out on his or her own. Every other questionnaire at this stage or during due diligence should be gone through in-person. Note that this form asks a lot of big-picture questions; it doesn't go into detail. At this point in time big-picture information is all you need. You should tell the seller, "I'm going to ask some questions that will let me know if there are any red flags. If there are, we will discuss them. I'll use the answers to these big-picture questions and your financial information to formulate an offer. My due diligence will prove what you've already told me. Like all buyers, I look at due diligence as a time for confirmation not surprise."

Once you are comfortable with the initial information about the business, it's time to go a bit deeper on the financial statements. You'll want to know, if it hasn't already been shared, if there are any non-essential expenses on the income statement. This could be adjusting the owner's salary to market, the annual corporate meeting in Hawaii in January, the owner's or spouse's car payments, personal expenses run through the business or, and this is bad if even mentioned, income (usually cash) not reported.

This is a serious subject and is known as recasting or adjusting the profit and cash flow. We'll go into detail on this in Chapter Six. It is too bad that many owners turn their business into an extension of their personal checkbook and the company becomes a lifestyle business. Owners thinking of selling should be positioning their business and it's profit and loss statement as if they are trying to win the contest of, "Who has the most profit?" When speaking, I tell audiences to "ignore your CPA." After the stunned silence I say, "Ignore their advice to reduce your profit and taxes. Show a lot of profit because banks and buyers love profit on the tax returns."

EXAMPLE AND APPLICATION:

If the seller is a C corporation, the owner may be taking an extremely high salary to minimize corporate profit and corporate taxes. Smart buyers understand this and will add the salary to the profit and deduct a fair market salary for the job as company president to get a true profit figure.

S corporation owners face the opposite situation. They often take a low salary to create a high profit that flows through. The profit is taken as a distribution without paying FICA and Medicare tax on it.

My advice to owners is: If you want to sell your business for the highest possible price and get the most cash at closing (and assure the business's continuation post-sale), then treat the business as a business. Don't funnel personal expenses through the company, don't hire family members who really don't work for you or do anything else that reduces profit. Show as much profit as possible for at least a few years. It will come back to you in multiples. Too few owners take this advice.

REAL LIFE STORY: PLAYING TAX GAMES CAN COST YOU

Pat got a great deal because the seller was forced to sell due to her spouse's terminal illness. The goal was to move from Las Vegas "back home" on the east coast so he could spend his final days with family.

The seller admitted she had the ultimate lifestyle business. Her personal overhead was minimal as everything, and I mean everything, was run through the business. Because this was a forced sale, due to a catastrophic event, she didn't have time to remedy this. She admitted that the amount of tax she had saved would have come back to her three to four times if she had the time to change from a lifestyle business to a business maximizing profit. The lost proceeds from a lower selling price was in the mid-six figures, a substantial amount.

Here's one final note on this subject. Owners, and that includes you, post-transaction, should realize that hiding revenues or padding expenses is fraud. An IRS auditor told me that in either case it's fraud to the IRS. Now the penalties may vary greatly. It could be a warning or slap on the wrist, a penalty or criminal prosecution (the agent alluded to criminal prosecution, primarily for not reporting revenues).

The more blatant an owner's actions in this area, the more distrust he or she creates with buyers. And this happens at all levels of business. One owner told us he sold his titanium scrap on the side and pocketed an unreported six figures every year. We walked away from him based on this and other statements that put his level of integrity in question.

EXAMPLE AND APPLICATION

I rarely work with buyers of retail type businesses that do cash business, and with the advent of credit and debit cards the use of cash has significantly declined. However, I remember saying the following when faced with a situation where an owner stated their profits were higher than reported because of the cash they took.

"What's worse, the owner who states their profits are really 20% higher because they skim cash or the owner who states their profits are 20% higher because they skim cash, but really don't (skim any cash)?"

Be careful in this area. Don't fall for it and don't do it. As an owner, make your bottom line look as healthy as possible.

Again, what does your gut say? Is everything appearing aboveboard or are you like the buyer who walked away from a seller perceived to have low integrity?

GETTING A BANK INVOLVED

It's during this initial analysis that you'll want to talk to two or three bankers who are with banks you believe are favorable to making business acquisition loans. The last part of the previous sentence is the most important. Some banks, and bankers, love acquisition loans. Others are fearful. I can send my clients to numerous banks that I know will do all they can to make an acquisition loan (on a good deal to a good buyer, which is what we always try to have). Others will loan against the liquidation value of the assets and tell you they don't loan against an "air-ball" (also known as blue-sky or goodwill).

DEFINITIONS

I've used the term "goodwill" numerous times, so let's define it. In simple terms, goodwill is the difference between the value of the assets of the company and the company's value based on other valuation methods (the value created by profit). Every buyer, seller and even banker should want a lot of goodwill. It means the company is getting a great ROI on its assets.

Some bankers, and unsophisticated buyers, will often call it blue-sky. Some bankers refer to it as an "air-ball," meaning it might not have any value because it isn't collateral they can attach to. My feeling is that goodwill is valid, it's a number based on profits. Blue-sky is on top of goodwill and a number based on unrealized potential.

In the post-Great Recession economic climate it is more important than ever to get banks involved early. There is no point in even dreaming of a deal structure without knowing what banks think about the company and about you (as an owner in the industry), and what they might finance (unless you are not using a bank, which is rare).

There will be more on this in the next chapter but for now let me say that the chances are the bank will use the SBA loan guarantee program. That gives the bank protection and offers you a longer amortization period. It also can throw in some complicating factors, so ask upfront about all the conditions.

EARLY PRICING

The seller may throw out a price or may not. Realize that this is somewhat like selling a used car. If you want $10,000 for your car you don't advertise it for $10,000. You probably advertise it for $13,000 (or more).

If the seller doesn't give you a price, you have to educate them. There will be more on valuation and pricing in Chapter Seven but for now, here's a short script I use and encourage my clients to use (adapt it if necessary for larger or smaller deals).

Script:

"I'm like most buyers in that I'm a financial buyer. That means I need a salary to live on and profits to pay for the business and build equity. Most buyers are looking for a rate of return of 20-30% on their investment. Appraisers and historical data agree with this range. This means a buyer will want to pay 3-5 times profits, usually 3-4 times, after a fair market owner salary, for a small business. The profits must cover the payments, whether they go to you, the bank or back into my savings account to provide me with a return on my investment.

Where the price will be within that range, or if it even makes it into that range, is determined by the non-financial factors like customer relations, employee abilities and loyalty, the lease and more. Does that make sense?"

Caveat: If you are considering a restaurant or retail business, the range is lower. Usually it is 2-4 times profits (a 25-50% ROI). If you are buying a business with sales greater than $10 million, adapt this based on the information in Chapter Seven.

Don't be like one of my clients. We met to review his list of prospective companies. He said there weren't any on the list and that surprised me because I thought there should be at least 10 on it. When I asked him why he told me that none of them were worth pursuing, he said it was because what the owners told him on the phone that they wanted for the business was too much (in his opinion). I immediately told him to call every owner back, get in front of them, see the business and use the above script.

Real Life Story: Sellers rarely know the value

Here is a perfect example of the process and why my advice that you work on the relationship, be patient, and "go slow to go fast" is important.

In a first conversation the owner stated profits as $200-500,000. It was a pretty wide range, but that's what he said (they were consistently about $400,000). His stated salary of $150,000 was actually $184,000 plus numerous perks. Annual sales of $4 million were actually $3.5 million. The seller said he thought his business was worth about "$2 million or so."

The buyer met with the seller and said he spent most of the first meeting getting to know a lot about the owner and a little about the business. They built a terrific relationship.

About 10 days after the first contact and a few days after the buyer and seller met, the seller sent the buyer a long e-mail covering many issues about the business and stating he thought the business was worth $2-3.5 million and that he would like $1.5-2 million as a cash down payment.

The deal closed four months later. The sale price was $1,525,000, with half down plus a small earnout.

If you like the company and the owner, put some time in to investigate the business and educate the owner as to how deals get done. It can be well worth the time.

DON'T GET ANAL RETENTIVE

This is a time for discovery, not for overwhelming yourself or others with minutia. We're talking small business here, and the fact that there are no perfect businesses or perfect deals. One of my favorite sayings is:

"The bigger the spreadsheet the less chance of a deal."

At this point you want to move things along, as described above. You don't want to be like my client mentioned in Chapter Two, who was nicknamed "Columbo."

REAL LIFE STORY: THE CURSE OF HARRY

Harry ended up starting a business and is happy and passionate about it. Why he didn't buy one is what I affectionately call "The Curse of Harry," because Harry wanted three things:

- To be able to know it when he saw it

- The perfect business

- The perfect deal (more risk on the seller than on him)

If you think you'll know it when you'll see it, you'll never see it. If everything is okay but nothing excites you, you'll never find a business worth owning. There has to be some focus. That said, I've had clients who have bought businesses without a crystal clear business-type focus. However, they focused on what the business should do (distribution channels, manufacturing processes, etc.). What the company actually made, sold or serviced was secondary.

Harry's business had to (as we joked about) "save the whales." If it wasn't socially redeeming it went to the bottom of his list. The deal had to be perfect. This meant that if anything went wrong after the sale, Harry was protected. This means the seller had more risk than he did. Harry's "deal from heaven" included a low down payment, a seller note and an earn-out that got the seller to the "full-price" if everything, and I mean everything, went better than planned.

In other words, the seller, not by Harry, felt any hiccup. You see, Harry didn't look at what the business could do, he looked at it from the perspective of "how is my butt covered if the sky falls, I'm not as good as I think I am, the market changes, etc." You buy a business based on a combination of its history, the potential you see and the value you bring to its future. There is risk in business ownership and where there's risk, there's reward. You have to make sure the risk is manageable and the reward is greater than the risk. But you won't find the perfect business or the perfect deal. If that's a buyer's goal, they won't ever be happy (and probably never close a deal).

Harry also built incredible spreadsheets, including one that ranked the tangible and intangible factors of the business. It had relevant things *like working capital needed and growth potential, as well as more eso-teric things like does it save the world (on a 1-10 scale) and is the office environment suitable for my dog. The tipping point was when he pur-sued a business he said he really didn't like but his spreadsheet said he should like it. My comment was, "I'll bet that means there's a dog run behind the office."*

Early warning signs

Five killers

- **The company has been losing money**: In 19 years of working with business buyers I've had less than five buy distressed companies and there was always a known reason why the business was in trouble (and the buyer knew exactly how to fix it). Usually, losing money is a sign to run.

- **The industry is saturated**: Often this means that price is a focal point for customers. Franchising in the industry is often a sign of saturation (because it means the model is easily replicable). Be careful!

- **There is no lease or you can't get a lease long enough to cover the term of your loan**: In the mid-1990's I would tell buyers this and they would laugh. Then the SBA started enforcing the rule that requires a lease, including fixed options, to be at least as long as the term of the loan or the term is reduced (except if the business is an accounting firm, training firm or a similar business that can get office space easily).

- **You can't determine if the business has a competitive advantage**: This is one of the questions every buyer should discuss with every seller (not just ask what the advantage is). It's important and you need to delve into it. This is what allows a business to make sales at a price high enough to produce profit.

- **Growth opportunities are limited**: I have never worked with a business buyer who wanted to buy a business and keep it at the same sales and profit level. Every single one of my buyer clients has wanted to grow the company. If there is no growth potential you are buying a job (and not a job as the company president but as a worker bee).

WARNING SIGNS

The following is from an article I wrote, which was aimed at business owners, titled, "20 Reasons Why Your Business May not be Worth What You Hope It Is." As stated above, the real killers are when a company that is losing money (and this article was for owners of profitable business) and the other four reasons listed. The following factors are for you to consider in your early analysis, realizing that every business has some blemishes. It's how these factors match up with your skills and the level of your risk tolerance that determines pricing and if you'll proceed towards a deal.

1. **Dependency on owner**: Too many businesses suffer from the all-controlling owner who not only knows how to do everything but also insists on being part of everything. Don't let yourself be the bottleneck. A buyer may pass or offer a lower amount when they see how big the shoes they have to fill are.

2. **Customer concentration**: No buyer wants to see that a small number of key customers account for a disproportionate share of your volume. Diversify your customer base and realize if you have a highly concentrated customer (or industry) base you may be asked to include an erosion clause that lowers the price if a top customer leaves.

3. **Financial statements and tax returns differ**: There isn't much to say about this. Have good accounting systems and safeguards and accurate statements. Don't rely on too many adjustments for the tax return or an overwhelming amount of 'add-backs' (to profit).

4. **Dependency on a key employee**: A company recently had severe problems when their top salesperson left and took most of their accounts. This problem could manifest itself with a technical expert, machine operator or office manager (who knows how everything in the firm works; see dependency on the owner above).

5. **Poor lease or no lease available**: You may think a month-to-month arrangement is great as it offers flexibility. Buyers and banks think about how expensive it is to move. In fact, for other than a professional type business (like consulting, accounting, etc.) your buyer won't get a bank loan for longer than the term of the lease, including options. Too short of a lease means too short of a seller and/or bank loan and too high payments to make the deal feasible.

6. **Behind the curve on technology**: While some people will think this is an opportunity for a buyer to do things more efficiently, in reality there is a cost to hardware, software and implementation. Use your business experience to get technology up-to-speed, show increased efficiencies (and profits) and sell for a higher price.

7. **Skimming cash**: There isn't a CPA around who will let a buyer be convinced to pay a price based on unreported cash. First, you are cheating the IRS. Second, is it worse that you're skimming or worse that you say you are but really aren't?

8. **Too small**: A business doing $2,000,000 in sales will not get the same multiple of profits as a similar business doing $20,000,000. There are just more risk factors the smaller the business is. An issue that is a major disruption to a small firm is a minor hiccup to a larger firm.

9. **You are blending too many personal expenses into the business**: Yes, there are advantages to paying for things with pre-tax dollars instead of after-tax dollars like employees have to. Carry it too far and it's almost as bad as skimming. Bottom line, buyers and banks like to see profits. Show a lot

of profit, pay some tax and it will come back to you in multiples when you sell (and make it easier to sell and finance the business).

10. **You have to work too hard in the business**: Buyers look for businesses they can work on not work in. They may not have your passion for your product or service; instead they have business skills to leverage what you've done. Get out of the business of doing things an employee could do. If your industry requires a high level of industry experience, a buyer without that experience won't get an acquisition loan. However, you may get a higher price by financing more of the deal.

11. **Financing is hard to get**: Banks don't like your industry, your business or acquisitions in your industry.

12. **No business or marketing plan**: While the absence of a plan may not directly reduce the value of your firm (other than via the fact that companies with a plan have significantly higher profits), a business and marketing plan may add to the attractiveness of the business and the price a buyer is willing to pay.

13. **Poor or no management team**: Buyers like to manage and lead; they don't like to do. A poor team means a lower value.

14. **Salary is not profit**: An appraiser will want to know the fair market salary for the job of running the company. If you weren't there you'd have to pay someone to be president and that salary is not profit (by a long shot).

15. **Saturation**: This is often a function of franchising and/or low barriers to entry. Eventually this leads to competition based on price, and it's hard to win in that situation.

16. **Special skills or license needed**: About two thirds of all small businesses need an owner with general business skills and business common sense. Those are the types buyers like the most. If you have to be a PhD in an advanced scientific

field to own the business, well good luck finding someone with money who wants to buy the business.

17. **Vendor concentration**: Don't overlook this. The vendor(s) may not pull any tricks, but what happens if your sole source has problems, goes out of business, etc.

18. **Working capital needs**: You pay your people this week. You pay your suppliers in 30 days, the rent and other overhead every month and your customers pay you in 90 days. That's working capital and that's why fast growth can be a problem. It takes cash to grow and if you don't have access to enough cash you've hit a bottleneck (see the first reason on this list).

19. **You have a job and it's not as CEO**: In other words, you work in the business not on the business. If the business can't survive if you're not on the shop floor, you aren't a manager you're a working employee. This probably means growth is stagnant, as you have no plan, leadership or management.

20. **You've bled the business**: Every last cent goes into your take-home pay and the assets are in need of repair or replacement. This leads to lower profits. One owner was so cheap he wouldn't buy a new printer. After the sale the buyer bought a new printer, the accounting department stopped having their systems freeze up when something printed and their efficiency soared.

Action Items

* Stay focused with guarded optimism and a healthy dose of skepticism.

* Create timelines for all segments of the process (as they occur).

* Be on the lookout for where you can add value and make improvement.

* Collect basic financial and non-financial information.

* Meet bankers (plural).

* Understand pricing parameters for the size of company you are analyzing; educate the seller on those parameters.

* Watch for risk factors and warning signs.

* Look for big-picture red flags (save the minutia for later).

— 5 —

LOOKING INTO THE CRYSTAL BALL

The best thing a seller can do for the buyer is to have put his or her company through a "mock" due diligence. As a buyer, you are by nature skeptical, and if you're not a natural skeptic then the chances are you will quickly turn into one as you see all the overpriced and unprofitable businesses that dominate the Internet.

If your seller has put the business through an internal due diligence process, they will be ready for you and not be surprised by the depth of your questions. As Lisa Forrest writes in the guest article in Chapter Six, "Lenders are going to get nosy." So are you (going to be nosy), and a prepared seller makes it much easier. Everything in this chapter should be looked at assuming that a mock due diligence and a buyer's due diligence would be the same, if done correctly.

However, as a buyer, don't hold your breath waiting for a company that has done this. They are few and far between. A 2008 *Wall Street Journal* article stated that 90% of medium sized businesses are not prepared for a sale. This same article said that 70% of owners planned to sell in the next decade (from 2008). In early 2012, I conducted a survey of business owners; 70% admitted not being ready to sell and 50% say they plan to exit in the next decade.

Hopefully, the seller will anticipate what a buyer will ask and have the business ready for investigation. As with many things in life, Pareto's Principle holds true here (stating, for example, that 80% of a company's sales comes from the top 20% of its customers). Buyers of all types and sizes will be concerned with the same 80% of issues in an acquisition target.

The Pareto Principle says that 80% of buyers will not be very interested in doing much legal due diligence because they will not want to buy the company's stock. There are two types of transaction structures for sales: a stock sale or an asset sale. The terminology relates to how the transaction is taxed, not what the buyer gets. If the company's legal structure is an LLC, a Partnership or Sole Proprietorship, there is no stock, so it will have to be an asset sale.

LEGAL DUE DILIGENCE

Disclaimer: In these sections on deal structure, I am not giving tax or legal advice. I am passing along big picture information and strategies. Both buyer and seller should have experienced tax and legal advice on all of these matters.

Legal due diligence is negligible if it's an asset sale (described below) because the history of the corporation is as important as you aren't buying the legal history (you're buying the business history). If it's a stock sale, the history of the corporation is very important and the buyer's legal team will be busy.

I'm not going to describe legal due diligence because I'm not an attorney. I will describe some basic transaction facts and strategies and have a guest article on legal due diligence for a stock sale.

One of the first things you will want to ask about is the business's structure. As mentioned above, if it's an LLC, Partnership or Sole Proprietorship there isn't any stock to sell (and every deal will be structured as an asset sale, described below). If it's a corporation, either a C or an S corporation, there is the option of either a stock or asset sale; if it's a C corporation, be prepared that the seller will want it to be a stock sale (to avoid double taxation).

STOCK SALE

In a stock sale, you are buying the shares of the company just as if you were buying shares in a publicly traded company. If the seller's cost or basis in his or her firm is $1 million and he or she sells the shares for $7 million, there is a capital gain of $6 million and (as of this writing) that gain will be taxed at capital gains tax rates.

When shares are sold it includes everything including cash, accounts receivables, accounts payables and other liabilities in addition to your operating assets like inventory, vehicles and equipment. (Often the amount of net working capital left in the company is negotiated and is part of the contract.) The transaction also includes future warranty claims, future legal claims regarding past events and everything else, known and unknown, which go with the operations of a company. This is one reason buyers prefer not to buy your stock and why lawyers put in overtime making sure the buyer is covered if a skeleton comes out of the closet (in the form of a lawsuit or something similar).

The asset values and depreciation schedules on your current balance sheet are part of what is being sold. If there is $2 million worth of equipment and it is depreciated down to $200,000, then the buyer gets assets valued at $200,000 and the current depreciation schedule—even if those assets have a fair market value of $1 million.

YOUR ATTORNEY'S ROLE

The following is from Mike Larson, Pivotal Law Group in Seattle, Washington, 206-340-2008, www.pivotallawgroup.com.

What is a Stock Sale?

A stock purchase and sale transaction usually involves a shareholder selling his or her share in the company to another in exchange for a purchase price. This transaction may seem simple, generally only requiring the shareholder to endorse the back of his or her stock certificate. However in actuality, the sale of stocks is not a simple transaction at all, and requires much thought and consideration on the part of the purchaser, prior to the actual sale.

This is because when you are purchasing stock from a corporation or shares in an LLC, you are essentially purchasing the underlying business, and will, therefore, be responsible for all of the liabilities of the company being acquired. Examples include federal and state tax obligations and pending claims and lawsuits from the failure to pay employees and vendors to warranty and other claims. Therefore, in order to protect yourself in such a transaction, always remember to: (1) perform due diligence on the business; (2) properly value the business; (3) request adequate representations and warranties from the seller.

Due Diligence

Due diligence is the investigation and review of a business in connection with a stock sale transaction. Due diligence allows the purchaser and/or their lawyer to formulate a better understanding of the business and its operations, which will then assist the purchaser in determining whether to buy the stocks, at what price, and on what terms and conditions. Due diligence is usually done prior to or during the negotiating of definitive documents, and includes the investigation and review of:

- Company's financial information (financial statements and tax returns)
- Operational structure of the business
  - Interviews with management
  - Touring the business facility
  - Review of sales and marketing programs, supplier and customer lists
- Organizational docs
- Debt and equity documentation
- Material contracts
- Employment arrangements, including employee benefit plans
- Real estate and environmental matters
- Intellectual property

- Existing and past lawsuits
- Regulatory compliance

The purchaser or their attorney should consider completing a due diligence checklist prior to entering into a transaction.

Valuation of a Business/Stocks of Business

Another important part of stock sales is valuation of the stocks being purchased. In order to properly value the stocks, one needs to do a proper valuation of the business. Of course it may not be possible at the beginning of negotiations to know the exact value of the business; therefore, coming up with a range of values should be adequate. An investment banker, an accounting firm, or a company that specializes in valuation services can do a valuation of a business. There are also many different ways to value a business, and some of the more common methods are: (1) discounted cash flow approach; (2) historical performance of the company; (3) asset valuation; (4) industry comparable sales data.

Representations and Warranties

Last but not least, if you are a buyer, it is always important to require the seller make certain representations and/or warranties about the company. There are many reasons why a purchaser should have a seller make representations and warranties, such as: to obtain disclosures from the seller about the company, to secure future indemnity rights for any "losses" occurring from a breach of the representations and warranties, and to possibly have walking rights if the sale transaction is one with differed closing. Some of the general representations and warranties made by a seller are regarding:

- Operation of the business
- Financial and physical condition of business
- Assets of business
- Existing lawsuits

- Capitalization of seller

- Affirmation that after due diligence disclosures there is nothing else the buyer has not seen, and the seller has not disclosed

A purchaser should try not to have the seller expressly limit their representation to known things. This is because unless the representation or warranty is expressly limited to the seller's knowledge, the purchaser may recover from the seller for misrepresentations and incorrect representations as well, even if they did not know of the facts and circumstances surrounding the breach. Some of the other considerations for the purchaser to consider when trying to decide what kinds of representations or warranties to request from the seller are: whether to set time limits on the representation and/or warranties, whether to set a minimum/maximum amount of liability for the seller, and whether to set a minimum threshold amount of losses incurred by purchaser before the indemnity clause starts to work. Additionally, you should always remember to have the seller include in the seller's representations that there is nothing else the purchaser has not seen regarding the business or its operations.

These representations and warranty obligations should be secured by a personal guaranty of the seller, remembering the seller's personal guaranty is only as good as their financial situation. That is another reason a buyer should be inclined to pay part of the purchase price in a deferred obligation to be paid later. The deferred obligation, say a promissory note payable over time, provides the buyer some time to discover misrepresentations or nondisclosures of hard to discover liabilities and use the deferred payment as a source of compensation from the resulting damages.

In closing, it is imperative that you, the purchaser, investigate to the best your abilities, and do your due diligence prior to purchasing stock, since the representations and warranties are only as good as a person backing it up.

ASSET SALE

Half of the business buyers I meet erroneously assume that an asset sale means they don't get everything in the company, only the tangible assets like inventory and equipment. The term Asset Sale is strictly for tax purposes. The buyer can buy all assets, tangible and intangible, and can even purchase liabilities. It's similar to going to the grocery store and filling your cart with what you want.

Buyers always want the operational assets and the intangibles like telephone numbers, website URLs and email addresses. Negotiations will determine which non-operational assets are part of the deal; these could include cash, accounts receivable, prepaid expenses and perhaps even some corresponding liabilities.

Why do buyers usually prefer an asset purchase? First, as mentioned, they aren't buying past problems. In an asset sale, if a customer or employee sues the company for something that happened months before the transaction, the buyer is simply part of the conduit between the plaintiff and the company. In a stock sale, the buyer owns everything and is responsible for the lawsuit. That said, good lawyers, on both sides, recognize this and can easily write clauses in the purchase and sale agreement to protect the buyer, but this can dramatically increase the legal hassle factor.

An asset sale gives the buyer some important tax advantages compared to a stock sale. Here are three common advantages:

1. The buyer can create new depreciation schedules. The $200,000 of assets with a fair market value of $1 million mentioned above could be put on the buyer's books at $1 million with a new depreciation schedule and if they are five-year assets the buyer can now write off $200,000 per year for five years. (Note: consult with your CPA or tax attorney on all of this, as there are many exceptions to every IRS rule and varying state regulations.) Also, you, the seller, won't want to have "depreciation recapture," which means that they could pay ordinary income tax rates (not capital gains rates) if the asset values are allocated at an amount above book value.

2. Goodwill can be amortized over 15 years. In the above example there would be $6 million of goodwill and the buyer would have $400,000 of annual amortization for 15 years. Combined with point one, the buyer can get a tax savings of about $200,000 per year for five years (at 2011-12 rates) and two-thirds of that for another 10 years.

3. While the non-compete agreement is considered goodwill, some of the asset allocation can go to transition training and be deductible the first year. Both are ordinary income to the seller, so some of the non-compete agreements allocation can be shifted to training to benefit the buyer.

REAL LIFE STORY: NOT ALL CPAS ARE CREATED EQUAL

The seller's CPA was not experienced in transactions, although he thought he was. When it came time to allocate the assets, he put $500,000 towards the non-compete agreement. We noticed this and I pointed out to him that this would be ordinary income to the seller. His first reaction was that all intangibles were goodwill so there was no difference to either buyer or seller. Upon researching it he realized his mistake. The buyer's CPA suggested reducing the total amount of the non-compete plus training to $75,000 ($50,000 to training) and received no resistance from the CPA. (As in point one, consult your CPA and attorney on these matters.)

C CORPORATION TRAP

The owner of a C corporation may face double taxation with an asset sale. In simple terms, the corporation may pay capital gains tax and the seller will pay tax when the proceeds are distributed to him or her personally. Therefore, sellers and their advisors will resist an asset purchase if it's a C corporation.

Buyers will generally want to discount the sale price if the seller insists on a stock sale. The more experienced and sophisticated the buyer and their team, the more likelihood this will occur.

AN ALTERNATIVE TO THE C CORPORATION TRAP

If the company is small enough (if the purchase price is under $5 million and definitely if it's under $3 million) you may be able to follow the precedent known as the "Martin Ice Cream" case. My clients have been involved in numerous transactions that utilized this strategy and you should keep in mind that while advisors will tell you the risk is low, and it may be, almost all of the risk is on the seller. That said, it has never stopped any seller on deals I've been involved with from not using this strategy.

In simple terms, there are two transactions. There is a stock sale at the value of basis (the seller's investment in the company). There is also an asset sale for the amount of goodwill that is structured as personal goodwill and the agreement is with the seller individually, not with the corporation. The courts have validated the Martin Ice Cream case (it is not part of the IRS code at the time of this writing). In this case, the seller claimed that much of the growth and profitability of the business was attributable to him personally and was therefore personal not corporate goodwill. The seller got a stock sale at a low amount, the sale of goodwill personally and avoided double taxation. (Definitely consult your tax and legal advisors on this.)

The reason I gave a maximum company and deal size above is that as a company gets larger there's less chance the goodwill can be personally attributable to the seller (rather than the corporation).

REAL LIFE STORY: PROPER COUNSEL

On a $3 million transaction utilizing the Martin Ice Cream case precedent, we had a two-hour conference call with buyer, seller, intermediaries and both CPAs. The CPAs, especially the buyer's, grilled the seller on his role with the company. They wanted backup justification for the personal goodwill allocation. The buyer's CPA didn't take this lightly, even though the onus was on the seller. He didn't want to be involved in a structure that couldn't be fully supported.

So why would a buyer agree to a stock sale? It could be because the seller won't consider anything else and the buyer desperately wants the business. Other reasons include that the cost of an asset sale far outweighs the tax advantages or there are contractual relationships with customers or vendors that would be violated with an asset purchase.

REAL LIFE STORIES: WHEN A STOCK SALE MAKES SENSE

Stu and Sherry sold a service business with hundreds of long-term leases on assets the firm rented to their customers on a short-term basis. Because they were an S corporation, there was no tax disadvantage to an asset sale. However, it was a stock sale because the hassle and cost to the buyer of changing hundreds of leases, with separate vendors, far outweighed any tax savings and ran the risk of increased costs (higher rates from the vendors).

Warren bought a company that produced products under a license agreement with a Fortune 100 company. Those licenses were solid if the firm's stock was sold. However, with an asset purchase they were open to reconsideration. The seller was a valuable partner and was also in financial trouble with the licensor (the licensor's team welcomed the buyer and the transaction as long as they didn't have to reconsider the license agreements). Both sides recognized that it made no sense to get the licensors legal department anywhere close to the deal.

There is an old adage applicable to every type of deal (business sale, real estate or even the sale of a piece of equipment) and it is:

It's not what you get that's important; it's what you keep.

As a business buyer, don't let the seller get fixated on only the price. Balance the price with the terms, conditions and taxes. Sometimes the highest price is not the best deal.

Initial financial due diligence

I am not a CPA or a CFO. However, I have worked with hundreds of clients and together we have looked at over 1,000 companies. Let's hope your seller gets their CFO and CPA involved in the process sooner rather than later. You'll want to do the same.

In today's world, accountants typically look backward as they prepare financial statements and tax returns. CFOs and other finance people look forward and help with budgets, systems and management reporting. Both are important, as is telling them your objective so everybody is striving for the same thing.

Here are six areas to concentrate on, based on my experience with what buyers, their advisors and banks will be most concerned. This summary is not meant to be all-inclusive. The larger the firm and the more complicated the business, the more scrutiny you will put it through. A buyer off by 10% on a $1 million deal can survive a lot easier than a buyer off by 10% on a $10 million deal.

Financial statements

In-house financial statements are fine for an initial overview but they won't mean much to a buyer or a bank when they start due diligence.

Many experts advise a business and its owner to start the exit planning process and the preparing of the business for sale three to five years prior to when they want to sell. One of the big reasons for this lead-time is related to the financial statements.

Buyers and banks will ask for three to five years of financial statements and tax returns. Anything less won't allow them to see trends and, often, going back further will not be relevant. The changes made during any planning and preparation will manifest over this time period and be reflected in the financial statements.

Tracking what the business did and when it was done will allow you, the buyer, to peg activities to future financial statements and see the results of the seller's actions.

There are three basic types of accountant prepared financial statements and they are compiled, reviewed and audited. A laypersons definition of each is:

- Compiled statements—the CPA simply takes what the business gives them from the in-house accounting system and puts them together in proper format.

- Reviewed statements—the CPA reviews what is given them to make sure that everything is done properly to accounting standards. The CPA will accept what the owner gives them as true and correct.

- Audited statements—the CPA audits the books to verify revenues, costs and everything else. They may perform or assist in physical inventory and verify tangible asset values.

The larger the deal, the more the need for audited statements.

Realize there are differences between Generally Accepted Accounting Practices (GAAP) statements and tax return statements. For example, if the seller bought the company and is writing off goodwill, that is only done on the tax returns, not on GAAP statements.

There are two ways to track revenue and expenses. It can be done on a cash basis (you record them only when received or paid) or on an accrual basis (you record revenue when billed and expenses when you are billed). Work with your CPA and realize that cash basis accounting causes more consternation and more work for your bank and you. It is too easy to manipulate the recording of expenses or revenues and, therefore, it is easier to disguise what is the company's true financial position.

Cash basis accounting can delay the recording of profit by postponing year-end deposits (to the next year) and accelerating expenses to reduce taxable income. In periods of growth, this can be a good strategy. However, if growth slows or stops it creates an inaccurate tax burden in the year of the slowdown. Cash accounting can also be used for the opposite effect. By accelerating revenues and delaying expenses, a business can show higher profits as the sale of the business gets closer. This is what scares buyers and banks.

FINANCIAL SYSTEMS

A business's financial systems actually produce the financial statements but attention to the systems usually comes about if there are questions about the accuracy of your statements. The accounting system (Quick-Books, Peachtree or similar) is simply the tool used.

Here are some areas to pay attention to:

- Does the business have a meaningful chart of accounts that provides useful information?

- Are the accounts in the right place so you are looking at accurate margins? For example, sales commission is often a variable cost and comes between cost of goods sold and overhead and is used to find the contribution margin (contribution to overhead). If it is lumped into overhead it will give inaccurate budget projections. If it is put in cost of goods sold the gross profit is misstated.

- Are there proper allocations for tax purposes? One deal became hung-up over the proper accounting of the overhead calculation for inventory in a manufacturing business (in simple terms, a manufacturer is to allocate overhead costs to inventory and not expense those costs until the inventory is sold).

- Is there a budget for at least the next 12 months? The closer past budgets are to actual results, the better. Be sure to have the seller explain differences, both positive and negative.

MANAGEMENT REPORTS

Work with your CFO to have meaningful management reports for your target business. This allows you to know where you are, where've been and where you are going. A good management reporting system goes way beyond financial statements and any reports produced by Quick-Books type systems.

When I've brought in a CFO to work with clients, they take the information from the accounting system and put it in reports that allow the management team to know what their margins truly are, what their sales pipeline is, what their sales closing rates truly are, what the true inventory turns are and much more. The purpose of this book is not to go into detail on this subject. The purpose is to make you aware that having these reports adds value to the business you are buying and makes operating it smoother once your own it.

My good friend Dennis Hebert, with CFO Selections in Bellevue, WA, www.cfoselections.com, created a list of Financial Reporting Truths to best convey that these reports are tools; they take time and effort to create and are not a silver bullet solution.

Here are Dennis's 12 Truths.

FINANCIAL REPORTING "TRUTHS"

1. You're **never done**. You can always make improvements to existing reports and develop new ones.

2. Reporting is **never perfect**, but tends to get better with additional time, systems, and people.

3. Collecting and reporting information **requires time**, it's **not free**.

4. You'll **never have all of the information** you want or need.

5. **Information results in dissatisfaction** because it creates the desire for more information, which may not be readily available.

6. Reporting should be like **peeling an onion**; "big picture" summaries followed by supporting detail.

7. **Numbers alone mean very little**. History, goals, and industry and company knowledge are essential to bring context.

8. There is great **danger** in looking at **short periods** of time.

9. Reporting provides information for **analysis and problem-solving**, not answers.

10. Ideally, financial reporting should **reflect what is happening** in your business.

11. Data not useful today may be **useful tomorrow**.

12. Favorite reporting question: **"What are you going to do when you find out?"**

BALANCE SHEET

A client who spent most of his career as an operator managed an equity group I worked with. One thing he shared with me was that, as he evaluated acquisition prospects, he had a newfound appreciation for the balance sheet compared to when he ran divisions of major companies and was more concerned with the bottom line.

Don't ignore the balance sheet! Work with your banker and others to understand all of its nuances. Banks tend not to like businesses where the owner has maximized his or her personal cash flow (at the expense of the business). A buyer will worry that there may be capital expenditures that will be their responsibility. High cash flow is great; almost as high cash flow with a strong balance sheet is better.

REAL LIFE STORY: WATCH OUT FOR NEEDED UPGRADES

Almost every deal I've been involved with recently, and almost every company I've consulted with, has needed computer system upgrades. Sometimes this is very evident and other times the importance is overlooked by the buyer or dismissed as irrelevant by the seller. Keep in mind that buyers don't acquire a company to maintain the status quo. They acquire a company because they feel they can add value and contribute to more growth.

Keeping your technology up-to-date can come back to a seller in multiples when they sell. It can also provide ongoing benefits. One seller was extremely cheap on capital improvements, specifically on technology. The buyer did some upgrades, one of which was nothing more than buying a new printer. The old printer took "forever" to print reports; the accounting staff was frozen waiting for this printing and because the new printer printed reports immediately, it noticeably increased productivity (as per the buyer). This seller was "penny wise and dollar foolish" and it cost him productivity and profits.

PROFITS

The previous section's emphasis on high owner cash flow should come with a caveat, which is that many owners turn their business into an extension of their personal checkbook and the company becomes a lifestyle business.

An owner whom wants to sell the business for the highest possible price and get the most cash at closing (and assure the business's continuation post-sale) will treat the business as a business. They won't funnel personal expenses through the company, won't hire family members who really don't work or do anything else that reduces profit. Showing as much profit as possible, for at least a few years, makes the buyer and bank happy. It also makes the deal progress faster.

One final note on this subject; realize that hiding revenues or padding expenses is fraud. An IRS auditor told me that in either case it's fraud to the IRS. Now the penalties may vary greatly. It could be a warning or slap on the wrist, a penalty or criminal prosecution (the agent alluded criminal prosecution is primarily for not reporting revenues).

The more blatant the actions in this area the more distrust there is toward you, the buyer. And this happens at all levels of business. I was referred to an owner interested in preparing his company for sale. He told us he sold his titanium scrap on the side and pocketed an unreported six figures every year. My associate and I decided not to work with him based on this and other statements that put his level of integrity in question.

INITIAL NON-FINANCIAL DUE DILIGENCE

There will be much more on this subject in the next chapter so, for now, let's cover the basics— those non-financial areas that buyers start with. At "Partner" On-Call Network we use the acronym CELBS to represent the non-financial factors. CELBS stands for:

- Customers
- Employees

- Landlord
- Banker
- Suppliers

The CELBS represent any and all other non-financial factors that affect the business and the level of its future profitability.

Buyers will usually start with questions about customer concentration and loyalty and the competence of the key employees and management. The more sophisticated the buyer, the sooner they will ask about other factors and the deeper they will go.

Appendix XXX is a master due diligence list. For now, let's discuss the CELBS and the top items on the master list.

CUSTOMERS

The first factor buyers and banks will ask about is customer concentration. No matter what rationale a seller has, the higher the concentration of sales the bigger the red flag. A business with 60% of sales spread out over 60 customers has a lot less risk than a business with 60% of sales concentrated with just three customers.

The chances are the seller knows who the top customers are, the relationship the firm has with them and their percentage of annual sales. If the business has customers with whom they are doing more than 10% of its annual sales, it's worth analyzing the relationship in detail.

Don't dismiss this as irrelevant because the customers "love" the business. Love can be fickle. Your goal, as a buyer, should be to have no customer accounting for more than five percent of sales. This does not apply only to end-users. Having thousands of end users being serviced by a handful of distributors or reps is the same as having a handful of customers.

REAL LIFE STORY: ONE YEAR'S NUMBERS CAN BE DECEIVING

George was selling his manufacturers rep firm to his key salesperson. On first look the customer concentration was horrible. The top customer accounted for 25-30% of sales. However, upon further analysis I noticed that it was a different top customer every year. On a three-year average no customer was accounting for more than 10% of sales. If you encounter a situation similar to this, be sure to look at the long-term picture, don't focus only on one year, and understand the dynamics of a firm that always has at least one large project.

EMPLOYEES

Initial questions will center on the quality of the management team, the key employees and their role. As with customers, the more spread out the responsibilities of employees the better for the business (and you).

The big issue is, are there any dependencies and if so, how easily correctable are they? You don't want the largest dependency to be the owner! In Chapter One I gave two examples of how owners taking vacations can be good for buyers and for giving a management team responsibility.

REAL LIFE STORIES: A COASTING OWNER CAN BE GOOD OR BAD

Often I talk to owners (sellers) who tell me they don't work too hard, they are coasting, etc. They speak of this as a positive and it isn't always a positive. I briefly mentioned this story before. Keith bought a company that was truly coasting. The owner was 70, sales had peaked when he was 65, and one thing that attracted Keith to the business was he saw that the owner took numerous vacations of up to four weeks each every year. He knew that just by being there the business would do better; and it did after he bought it. The vacations created a stagnant company and a lower price than the seller might otherwise received.

Scott on the other hand discounted the value of a company he really wanted to buy because it was evident that not only was the owner coasting but also there was a culture of "not working hard" in the firm, of doing just enough to make the living the owner and sales people wanted to make. Scott realized there would be resistance to the energy and drive he would bring to the company (it was an aging employee base; it's a lot easier when the employee base is younger, as was the case with Keith's company).

It can be tough for an entrepreneur, but you have to hope the seller has learned to delegate. Contrary to what many company founders and owners believe, it is not a sign of losing control. In fact, delegating responsibility is the opposite, it's gaining control.

REAL LIFE STORY: STICK TO WHAT YOU KNOW AND DELEGATE THE REST

This is often more a mental attitude than anything else and often it's because the owner feels the employees don't have the same passion for the business as he or she does (they don't and won't when getting paid $15-20 per hour). Therefore, the owner's feelings are that "I can do anything better than anybody else so I'll be involved in every aspect of the business."

Sam had this attitude. It didn't matter that on accounting and finance he was a novice, he gave instructions to his accounting department. He could sell his product like nobody else, so any closing ratio less than his meant an incompetent salesperson. Thinking on the job was a waste of time; employees needed to be constantly "doing." Anyone found not being busy was admonished.

It was no wonder he constantly worried about everything, even when things were going well. It took a while to get him to allow his people to use their skills and to coach him, not admonish them. But it worked and he had a much stronger team.

LANDLORD

Often overlooked until late, this can be a critical area. Unless it is a consulting or accounting type firm, a bank will probably not give you a loan for a term any longer than the term of your lease including fixed options. It's expensive to move and the bank doesn't want the business uprooted in the middle of the loan.

A landlord's willingness to assign the lease or give a buyer a new lease, at a fair rate, is also important. The supply and demand for the type of space your company needs is one of the biggest factors in all of this. If supply is tight, a landlord can play tough. If supply greatly exceeds demand, the landlord will do all they can to keep the business as a tenant.

REAL LIFE STORY: A BAD (OR NO) LEASE CAN LOWER THE VALUE

The shareholder agreement dictated that if one of the equal owners of a food manufacturing business wanted out, the other had to purchase the shares (after a prescribed process). During the valuation process, we discovered that there was no lease, the owner was elderly and quite ill and his daughter and owner wanted to get rid of all the small tenants in the building and find one or two large tenants.

The cost of a forced move with 30-days' notice was equal to one year's profit. The value of the company declined by over 30%. After the buy-out the owner, within six months, made an orderly, planned move at a reasonable cost. Financially he was way ahead. Emotionally, he was even further ahead.

BANKER

What does your banker (and other bankers) think of the industry? Is it one where they will demand you have direct industry experience (as with restaurants) or will general business management skills suffice? What about your target business in particular? Are receivables collected fast enough to make them happy? Is there adequate cash flow to meet your debt coverage ratios? And the most important question is, can the business, in its current state, handle acquisition debt?

REAL LIFE STORY: BANKERS LEND TO THOSE THEY LIKE

In another example of one partner buying out another, the banker made it very clear that they would do whatever they could to support the buyer. They loved the business; they loved the buyer and his attention to financial details. In practical terms, this support meant that the selling partner could be removed from the loan guarantees, which was something the buying partner did not expect and thought would be a sticking point in getting a deal done.

SUPPLIERS

A lot of attention is paid to customer concentration. Equal attention should be paid to supplier concentration, supplier innovation and the health of the suppliers' companies. There's not much more to say on this other than the example that follows.

REAL LIFE STORY: SOME PEOPLE NEVER LEARN

A former client invited me to lunch and shared that his top manufacturer, accounting for 60% of his revenues, had dropped him as their distributor. It was nothing he did wrong, other than being small; it turns out a larger competitor lost their (competing) line when their manufacturer took all sales efforts in-house and his vendor switched to the larger competitor.

MISCELLANEOUS

Here is a list of some areas that every owner should review. We'll go into more detail in the next chapter. For now, make sure you have a handle on all of these topics.

- Licenses or certifications—are there any special requirements for the business or its people?
- Litigation—is there any history, anything ongoing or anticipated?

- Warranties—any ongoing potential obligations should be made clear.

- Environmental—this should come up early if there is any chance of environmental or hazardous material issues arising.

- Off Balance Sheet items—typically this is unused vacations, sick days or contracts such as the yellow pages, equipment leases, etc.

- Technology—make sure all software is legal and subscriptions are up-to-date. Make sure hardware is also current and viable for growth.

- Restrictive agreements—this could be a licensing agreement, distribution agreement or a franchise.

- Marketing—is there a plan? Does it document activities and results?

- Competition—does the seller have a good handle on his or her competition and the suppliers' competition, and can they succinctly state the firm's competitive advantage?

REAL LIFE STORY: OFF BALANCE SHEET ITEMS CAN ADD UP

Ray was selling his business and the subject of vacations and sick leave came up. Ray was 70 years old and truly coasting. He simply wanted to keep everybody happy and thus had an extremely generous vacation policy with 100% rollover. When the buyer investigated this area he was shocked because most of the employees had been using about 50% of their vacation time for years and had stockpiled months of vacation. Of course, this was not on the balance sheet.

It cost Ray about $100,000 to pay for this vacation time. It took the buyer almost no time to consult with an HR professional and implement a new, realistic vacation policy with a use it or lose it feature.

ACTION ITEMS

* What deal structure makes the most sense (stock or asset)?

* Perform legal due diligence (if necessary).

* Review the financial statements and financial systems.

* Ask for management reports (the more there are the more sophisticated the systems and managers).

* Pay attention to the balance sheet.

* Do a quick adjustment to profits to reflect normalcy.

* Do an initial review of the non-financial factors.

— 6 —

Borrow $100,000 and the Bank Owns You
Borrow $10,000,000 and You Own the Bank

Let's first make an assumption that you are a qualified buyer for the business you are buying, it is a good business (profitable) and therefore it should be financeable. The big question, is how will it be financed? Will it be your money, the bank's money, the seller taking a note, creative finance techniques or, most likely, a combination of all these methods.

In today's deal environment the most common structure is:

1. A down payment from the buyer's personal funds (10-40%)

2. A bank loan to increase the down payment received by the seller (40-80%)

3. Seller financing via a note to the buyer (10-50% or more)

When I started as a Business Buyer Advocate it was much more common, in fact it was the norm, to have the buyer make a down payment and the seller finance the rest. With the popularity of SBA guaranteed loans (more on them later) the seller started getting more cash at closing. Now, it's rare that a seller will be the sole source of financing to the buyer. It happens but it's rare.

One big reason for this is that the seller's advisors have been educated. His or her attorney, accountant, consultant or other advisor networks and goes to educational events. They hear from banks that they want to make acquisition loans and they hear how the SBA program expedites the loan process. They then advise their clients on the availability of bank acquisition loans and how a seller should expect to only finance a small part of the deal.

Here are my three rules of deal financing:

1. **Cash talks**: As mentioned, in the book entitled *Transaction Patters*, by Toby Tatum (RDS Associates, 2000), Mr. Tatum states that, "Acquisitions, which were financed by the seller, sold for a 15% (median) higher price than all-cash transactions. The average down payment was 37%. This difference is more pronounced if we compare the all-cash transaction to those selling with seller financing of 70% or more. In these deals, the median sale price was 27% higher price than all-cash transactions."

2. **Creative Finance**: It is not financial hocus pocus or wishful thinking. It is using the assets and the cash flow of the business to help finance the deal.

3. **Banks**: The Golden Rule in business states that, "He who has the gold, makes the rules." In this case the rule means, "The bank has the money and the bank makes the rules." Don't forget this. It's why I urge you to go to banks early to get their feel for the deal. Also, keep reminding your seller of this and keep him or her apprised on possible terms as banks relay them to you. One of the last things you want is a surprised seller when you get to deal specifics (because they didn't realize some of the terms and conditions the bank and SBA put on the loan).

Real Life Story: Cash talks

Does cash really talk? In this case, yes! The asking price on the business started at $700,000 and we soon were at $625,000, and the seller was willing to finance 50% of the price. The buyer had another idea, and that was to lower the price and make it all cash. There were three reasons for this.

1. *The business was in an industry that was difficult to finance, especially without direct industry experience.*

2. *He was able to get the price down by 25%, to $470,000.*

3. *The buyer didn't want the seller, a micro-manager, having any involvement with the business, which the buyer would have had if there was seller financing.*

Now and into the future, I'm sure, financing will be a key to any deal. In this chapter I will:

- Discuss acquisition bank loans (as of the time of writing)

- Present two guest articles from bankers on acquisition loans

- Show a list of creative finance techniques and discuss some of the more common techniques

- Give you a lot of real-life examples

Banks and acquisition financing

As of early 2012, banks, in general, like making *good* business acquisition loans. The emphasis is on the word "good." During a roundtable discussion in 2011, a business broker made the comment that it was tough to get deals done, because of the banks. He said that banks insisted it be a "really good deal" in order to make a loan.

It reminds me of the time a client said to me, "The bank's not being very creative on this deal." My response was, "The bank's not in business to be creative; they're in business to get paid back." Of course it has to be a good deal. With a 4% interest rate spread between what the bank pays on deposits and what they charge on loans, it takes a lot of good loans to cover one bad loan.

One reason banks like acquisition loans is that businesses have not been borrowing since the September 2008 trifecta of bad news:

1.   Severe dropping of the stock market

2.   Collapse of the banking industry

3.   Economy devastated by the previous two factors which were heaped upon an already tenuous situation

Many businesses weren't in a position to qualify for loans. Those that did qualify weren't interested in taking the added risk of debt. So banks have money to lend and (good) acquisitions are one place to do so.

WHAT ARE BANKS LOOKING FOR?

The Five C's of banking

When I started in the consulting business as a Business Buyer Advocate, banks were big on the Five C's. In the rah-rah days of cheap credit (the 2000's), they didn't seem to matter and then, poof, we're back to where we were. The emphasis now is, "How do we get paid back?" Keep in mind that the Five C's go back to before anyone reading this was born.

Whether you are dependent on a bank or not, pay attention to this because the chances are your buyer will need a bank to fund operations and growth, and the more your business is attractive to a bank the more confident a buyer will be (meaning a better price, better terms, easier process and perhaps a quicker payoff to you).

- **Capacity**: How will you repay the money? The business must have the necessary cash flow to support your debt payments or why would anybody lend you the money and you'll be dependent on the next factor (collateral).

- **Collateral**: What does the lender get if you can't make the payments? Believe me, the bank does not want your truck, house, car, equipment or anything else. They want to be repaid, and this is why they severely discount the value of the assets used as collateral.

- **Capital**: This is your skin in the game, also known as your risk. As shown in the story below, your skin in the game (as an owner, buyer or seller) is more important than it was in recent years.

- **Conditions**: What is the loan for? Banks usually want to tie long term needs (a piece of equipment or a business acquisition) to a term loan. Short term needs (working capital) will be tied to a line of credit loan like an accounts receivable line of credit that will be paid back when your customer pays you.

- **Character**: As when you sell your product or sell your business, it's a relationship game with your banker. You must come across as competent, trustworthy, experienced and of having a solid reputation.

REAL LIFE STORY: THERE ARE NEW BANKING POLICIES

The following is from my Weekly Memo and my blog from the fall of 2011. These insights are very timely in this post-Great Recession era. Numerous bankers commented, in agreement, when I sent this.

Mike Flynn, former publisher of the Puget Sound Business Journal and now active in the world of raising capital, spoke at my Rotary Club. When talking about banking he said the following.

"The most important change [in banking] is that the days when a business owner could get new capital without putting up a key chunk or himself or herself are over. The point now being made by those with money to place is this: If you aren't confident enough in your business and its prospects to mortgage your house and put your lifesavings into it, then why should have I confidence in you? Now is the time for maximum skin in the game. As the chairman of a Washington State based bank told me later when I asked about this: "That should always have been the case. It wasn't. But it is now. And it will be in the future.""

This is very well stated. I often hear from business buyers and owners that, "The bank doesn't want to take any risk on this deal or with my company." I have to explain to them that banks aren't in business to take [excessive] risk; they are in business to get paid back. It appears banks are moving back to the Five C's of credit.

My experience is that if it's a good deal (for the borrower and the bank) that banks will make the loan. A good deal means adequate debt coverage, a quality borrower and enough collateral (which can be the cash flow, especially in SBA guaranteed situations).

WHAT ARE THE ODDS (OF GETTING A LOAN)?

If it is a good business, a good (fair) deal, the proposed loan meets bank covenants and you are qualified to run the business—financially and managerially—there should be no reason that you won't get a bank loan. That said, loans are turned down all the time. I get clients referred to me by bankers because they couldn't make a loan on the business the buyer brought to them (these are qualified buyers).

What are the reasons you won't get an acquisition loan? Here are the top reasons, and realize that they may vary from bank to bank. One client got a fantastic loan package from one bank, term sheets from two others and at the same time, one (large) bank wouldn't even talk to us about the deal because they didn't feel he had enough industry experience. It was funny, because the seller worked less than 20 hours per week and did nothing more than the bookkeeping. It had been years since he actively managed the business (there was a general manager).

- **Losing money**: Banks don't like losers and neither should you. They look for sources of repayment, and cash flow is on the top of the list (for all loans, personal and business, this is the prime consideration).

- **Bad industry**: This will vary among banks. Restaurants are on the black list of many banks. I had one client turned down for a loan, at the very last minute, because a manager, based on a previous deal, didn't like the asset mix of the business (even though the business had adequate cash flow).

- **No industry experience**: This creeps in and out, and in 2012 it is back in vogue, as mentioned above. It seems, in my opinion, that the larger the bank the more they will concentrate on this issue. I vividly remember a client not getting approved by a large bank. A small community bank made the loan and the bank president told me they looked at the complete package. The buyer was an entrepreneur, he's started and successfully run and bought other companies and they were loaning on him as much as on the business.

Tip: Some companies are just hard to finance

When discussing an exit strategy and possible management buyout recently, I told the owner the following three things:

1. *You have a unique business and the skills needed to buy and price your product are crucial. Those skills require industry knowledge and years of experience.*

2. *A bank won't lend to a buyer of your business if they are without direct industry experience. Since you will be financing part of the deal, why would you lend to a buyer without the proper experience?*

3. *The only real option you have is to sell to your managers.*

Lending is all about getting paid back. If a banker feels a business buyer's experience is inappropriate they won't make the loan. The good news is, there are a lot of companies that need an owner with solid management and leadership skills, not specific technical skills.

- **Weak personal financial statement**: You must have adequate financial reserves after the deal closes, in addition to making an adequate down payment. No banker wants to force you to put all your money into a deal. Remember that the bank cannot use any qualified money (IRA, 401k, etc.) as collateral (more on how to use this later). Whether you have $250,000 or $2,000,000 of assets, if the deal requires 100% of them you may not get a loan.

- **Too small a down payment**: This gets you over-leveraged and you won't meet the banks debt coverage ratios (which are usually a very low 1.3:1, which means you need $130,000 of profit/cash flow to make $100,000 of annual loan payments.

- **Lack of collateral**: While one bank may look at your acquisition loan from (almost) a purely cash flow perspective, another bank may want a certain level of collateral, whether it's business or personal. If it's a service business with limited assets, the cash flow is tight and you have very little in the way of personal assets (including home equity), you may get a smaller loan or declined.

REAL LIFE STORY: BANKS ARE OFTEN A MOVING TARGET

The bank had a history of making acquisition loans primarily based on cash flow. The relationship managers working with my client were excited about the buyer, the company and the deal—until they went to the credit manager and were shot down.

It seems the bank had taken a couple $250,000 hits in the last six months. They said they would loan only to the amount of tangible collateral. Even with the SBA guaranteeing 75% of the loan, they weren't willing to risk having any uncollateralized loan amount. The bad loans they recently experienced were a large sum to this small bank and they were taking a very cautious position, at least for a while.

- **Too much debt**: This is similar to not having a large enough down payment, although it takes into account other business debt you may inherit, and your personal debt.

REAL LIFE STORY: THE 50% RULE RULES!

At "Partner" On-Call Network we have our "50% rule" that states that your acquisition debt benchmark should be no more than 50% of profit *to acquisition debt payments. Now, the larger the deal, the more you can vary from this guideline. On a $500,000 transaction you'd better stay at or above this level. On a $5 million transaction, you have a lot more leeway, as there is a lot more cash flow to play with.*

When I started in this business in the early 1990's, we said it should be 50% of after-tax profit to principal payments. I soon realized that this translated to being about the same as 50% of pre-tax profit to total payments. In these days of accelerated depreciation, writing off of goodwill and other tax reduction techniques, I like to start with using this rule on pre-tax profits and then calculating the net, after-tax and after debt payments cash flow to make sure the deal has enough cushion.

- **No relationship**: Your relationship with the banker (not the bank, the person) is critical. The banker must like you, respect your abilities and trust you. A client told me he believed he had an in where he personally banked, at a large national bank. I cautioned him that it didn't mean much, it would have to be a good deal and the business banker he would work with was the critical relationship. Sure enough, a week later he reported that they told him he was like everybody else and his personal banking relationship meant very little. (This is not a slam on this bank or any other. It simply points out the importance of the relationship with the right person.)

REAL LIFE STORY: BANKERS NEED RELATIONSHIPS TOO

This is a true story and from a memo sent to my business buyer clients and emphasizes the above point on why you must have a good relationship with your banker (because no relationship equals no loan).

A banker's first comment to me was, "We're getting more comfortable with your client." The bottom line is, just like with a seller, you have to build a relationship with all the parties involved in getting a deal done. You can't walk into a bank, drop off the company's tax returns and expect the loan to get approved.

With all banks, but especially with smaller banks, you need to build a solid relationship with the lender. They have to feel comfortable with you. They have to have warm fuzzy feelings for you and your ability to successfully manage the company.

SUCCESS STATISTICS

Business buyers' experiences with banks and acquisition loans are about as similar as snowflakes; no situations are exactly the same. Here are seven examples (I could provide many more but you'll get the point).

1. The buyer went to 18 banks and got two solid term sheets. It was a little puzzling as he had capital, ownership experience and the business was fairly priced. One of the banks that offered a term sheet declined a few levels up the approval ladder because of an experience that manager had years prior. The only reason we came up with for the lack of offers was it was a business in a very narrow niche.

2. This buyer called four banks, didn't like one banker, one bank was lukewarm and he concentrated on the other two banks. One took the lead and he put all his eggs in that basket and they made the loan. He knew the risk, but he was very relationship based and felt it would work out.

3. A lesson was learned on this deal; go to the banks before making an offer. What was surprising was that my client was a former banker. He went to 15 or more banks and did get a loan, but only after we learned to not assume we knew what a bank might do but to find out in advance. This was the tipping point for me to get clients to banks early in the process.

4. When you have great business, a great buyer and a fair deal you get this buyer's experience. He went to eight banks and got eight term sheets. He cherry-picked the best deal.

5. Again, a good deal for everybody and multiple offers, although one banks declined because it was a tech-service business and

they didn't want anything to do with technology, even if all the company did was use it to help other businesses improve productivity. This was interesting because after meeting with the bank the buyer decided to offer more cash to the seller and drop his capital infusion (because the bank was willing to lend more than everybody thought they would).

6.   A specialized business can mean trouble. In this case it was because the final decision maker (out of five; it was a large bank) had a bad experience with a company in the industry a decade before. No worries, however. Two other banks came to the rescue and the deal closed as scheduled.

7.   There were three banks competing for the deal. Two were offering SBA guaranteed loans and one was conventional. Cash flow the first year was a key issue, so we negotiated. The buyer ended up with a five-year note, a seven-year amortization period and payments the first year at about the rate of a 12-year amortization period (to help compete with the SBA loan that had a 10-year amortization). The deciding factor for this buyer was the cost of the SBA loan. The fees outweighed the longer payback period.

SELLER FINANCING

You will get some seller financing (I say, with almost 100% certainty) and you want it, as does your bank. Banks like it when the seller has "some skin in the game." What are the exceptions?

- Very small deals

- Certain industries, like restaurants and retail, where every seller has been warned that the nature of their industry is such that whatever they don't get at closing, they will never get

- Existing franchises where the franchise has national financing arrangements, and those arrangements include cashing out the seller

- Large enough deals that are quasi middle market

- Situations where you don't want the buyer to be involved at all (see the story above)

- For almost every other deal, from $500,000 to $10 million, expect the seller to carry at least a small part of the deal. A seller should think of it this way:

- The business is worth 100

- To get all cash they have to discount it 70

- Could I take 60-80 in cash on a price of 90 to 100

- The chances of the buyer failing or not paying in the first couple of years are slim and the seller is still ahead

Part of your job as a buyer is to educate the seller on this issue (as you will on pricing of businesses, which is discussed in Chapter Six). It is usually in the seller's best interest to be willing to carry a note.

Expect to sign a personal guarantee to the seller on the note they hold. Don't plan on pledging personal collateral to the seller (you will to the bank). This means the seller doesn't get a lien on your house, investment portfolio, rental or vacation properties or bank accounts.

Real Life Story: Does personal collateral mean anything?

I went 17 years without a buyer client pledging personal collateral to a seller on an acquisition loan. Then a CPA was making every attempt to impress his client and insisted the buyer put the seller in third position on his home equity. After a lengthy discussion, the buyer agreed to do so. His rationale was that if things got so bad that his home equity was taken, the chances are it would be the bank taking it not the seller. He figured he had little to nothing to lose. The good news is he's done extremely well with the business and this is a moot point.

TYPE OF ACQUISITION LOAN

CONVENTIONAL

This is a typical bank term loan. The bank will offer you a loan over a certain number of years with monthly payments at a (usually) fixed interest rate. The term will usually be four to seven years. Sometimes, with a shorter term (four to five years), you may be able to get a longer amortization period, with a balloon payment due at the end of the term.

Conventional loans are often more directly tied to collateral than SBA guaranteed loans. This means the bank will consider cash flow less that the secondary source of repayment (the collateral they attach). The bank has complete discretion on the terms and conditions of the loan. I've seen cases where they've put no restrictions on the seller note other than it couldn't be paid off quicker than the bank loan, but I've also seen them impose restrictions such as not allowing any note or earn out payments to the seller.

SBA GUARANTEED

The first fact to remember is that the SBA does not make loans. They guarantee a portion of the loan to the bank. Typically this is 75% of the loan amount, and it is the bank that is protected, not the borrower. In other words, if you default on your loan, the SBA covers the portion they have guaranteed so the bank only loses their percentage.

The second important fact to remember is that while the SBA has a set of regulations regarding their guarantee program, it is the bank that applies those regulations to their loan policies as they see fit. As long as they don't violate the SBA regulations, they can manipulate them as much as they want. This is why you may hear different things from different banks on the same proposed loan. The bank sets their own terms and conditions and overlays the SBA regulations on them.

As more banks are jumping into the SBA program, make sure you are working with a lender that is comfortable with SBA loans. Some understand only the written rules. Others understand the intent of the rules and will adapt to that intent.

Here are some various facts, features and feelings about SBA loans, as of 2012.

The guaranteed portion of the loan is taken off the bank's books and doesn't count towards their reserve requirements. This is one reason why banks like them; they don't have to hold as much capital to cover bad loans as they do for conventional loans.

An SBA loan portfolio can be packaged and sold on the secondary market.

The term is generally seven to 10 years.

There are no prepayment penalties.

If goodwill is more than $500,000, expect to have to get and pay for a business valuation.

The maximum loan is $5 million, and this means the SBA guarantee to the bank is typically $3.75 million.

The SBA is placing a renewed emphasis on relevant industry experience.

The bank/SBA will take your home equity as collateral (and will possibly also take your rental or vacation home equity).

As with all loans, your qualified money can't be used as collateral.

I have not seen the bank/SBA take investment portfolios as collateral (put a lien on it). I have seen them require the borrower to not liquidate the assets without the bank's permission (they allow borrowers to manage the money but not turn it into cash to put into the business or another business).

The SBA loan program is a cash flow lender. That is, they consider cash flow a form of asset and will include it as a consideration in their decision.

The buyer pays a fee (about 3%) that covers the losses on loans in this program.

As of 2011, the SBA loan program was profitable; it was not dependent on tax dollars (I don't know if this includes staff salaries and other overhead, because the SBA does a lot more than guarantee loans).

Earn outs (variable payments dependent on the future performance of the business) are not allowed.

The seller can't have a written consulting, transition or employment agreement (or combination) longer than one year.

They require the buyer to contribute 25% in equity. If the buyer doesn't contribute 25%, then all or part of the seller note will be put on a standby payment program and will count towards the buyer's contribution. Standby means the buyer can make no principal or interest payments to the seller, usually for one to five years, at the banks discretion.

REAL LIFE STORIES: NEW RULES, NEW STRATEGIES

The buyer contributed 12% of the price in cash. The bank loan was for 47% and the seller notes were for 41%. I say notes because there were two of them. The first was for about 15% and was on full standby for five years, with a balloon payment or regular payments allowed after five years, with the bank's permission. The second note was for the remaining 26% and allowed regular payments to the seller as long as the buyer was in compliance with the bank's loan ratios.

The bank put the seller on a two-year full standby with terms to be determined after two years (from closing). The banker looked at the buyer and me, told us there were to be no principal payments and no (wink wink) interest payments. He said that if interest payments were made there would be no way the bank would find out, as long as they were "disguised" properly and the buyer was in compliance with the bank (the bank doesn't audit books when everything is okay).

With both types of loans, but especially with SBA loans, it is my experience that you will need a lease, including fixed options, for at least as long as the term of the loan (or your loan term may be shortened). The exceptions are if you buy a business, such as a training, consulting or accounting company that can be in any office building.

HOW TO PRESENT TO A BANK

My best clients and those with the most success getting offers from banks have taken the time to put together a book for each bank. They use a 3-ring binder with 10 tab dividers. They include:

1. Business financials (3 years)

2. Business tax returns (3 years)

3. Personal net worth statement

4. Personal tax returns (1-3 years)

5. Short business plan

6. Bio of buyer

7. Letter from seller on why buyer is a good fit, and reference letters from friends and associates

8. Other information on the business, like asset descriptions, accounts receivable and accounts payable aging, customer list and concentration, org chart, management duties and bios

9. Proforma P&L and balance sheet (the balance sheet is very important to banks) with realistic projections, including a projection assuming the first year is the same as the seller's last year and another projection with mild growth

10. Month-by-month historical cash flow and projections

As you can see, it's easy to fill up 10 tabs and keep the copier busy.

GUEST ARTICLE: PUTTING TOGETHER A BUSINESS LOAN PACKAGE

The following article is from Lisa Forrest, Union Bank SBA lending officer, Seattle, WA, 425-999-2042. Lisa wrote this for my book, "Without an Exit Strategy you have no Strategy" so it is aimed at business owners. As a buyer, you'll be able to pick up tips on what banks will want from your seller and you.

PUTTING TOGETHER A BUSINESS LOAN PACKAGE...how *you prepare your business for sale and how your buyer applies for a loan can help increase your odds for a successful sale with more cash to you!*

With all that we've heard about the tight credit market, one important fact seems overlooked: banks are in the business of lending. Would-be sellers can increase the feasibility of a lender wanting to help finance an acquisition loan for a buyer through thoughtful preparation and attention to details. And currently the Small Business Administration (SBA) loan program is an excellent avenue that banks can use for business acquisition financing. The SBA has certain guidelines and parameters that every participating bank must follow when offering this type of loan; however, each lender will have their own requirements and terms, at times causing increased confusion and some amount of trepidation. While the uncertainties of these economic times mixed with inconsistencies in the banking environment can be unsettling for business owners considering a sale, there are definite steps owners can follow to control critical aspects of the sales process when it comes to acquisition financing.

Here are nine points for the seller to consider that can help make their business a stronger candidate for SBA acquisition financing:

1. Business Owner Planning and Preparation. Planning to sell your business can take years. Knowing when it is the right time to sell takes thought and preparation. For most of the successful acquisitions I have been involved with, preparation started months, and in most cases, several years prior to the actual loan/acquisition close. Being a prepared and organized seller is key.

2. Exit Strategy Advisors. Because your business is usually one of your biggest investments, having outside advice is generally going to increase your opportunities for success. As owners, you are experts in your industry and have built a successful business; however, when it comes to selling your gem that you have spent years creating, I have observed that outside expertise and perspective will usually serve the seller well. See #1 above.

3. Buyers and Lenders will have similar perspectives. The buyer and their lender will have the same questions and want to see the same documentation, books and records. The buyer and the banker interests are well aligned, so when you think about questions that the bank will have, they are most often the same exact questions that your buyer will have. This is an important notion to understand because a seller should be preparing for the buyer and the banker in much the same way.

4. Buyer "Due Diligence Team". As a banker specializing in Business Acquisition financing for more than 20 years, I have come to appreciate the buyer whom has his or her own Due Diligence Team. And, as a seller, you should also come to appreciate this as well. When the buyer comes with outside advisors it signals to me that they are serious and prepared to take the process all the way through to a close. This team usually consists of a CPA, Attorney, Banker, and Buyer Representative. And, for sellers that are prepared, having a buyer with a team of trusted, experienced acquisition advisors will actually help move the process along faster.

5. Documentation for a Bank Loan Package. Having your financial documents organized and up-to-date, and ready for the buyer's Lender are critical. Generally, the Lender will *initially* require: Three years of business tax returns, Year-end Financial Statements, Year-to-Date financial statements including Profit and Loss Statement, Balance Sheet, Accounts Receivable and Payables Aging Statements, and Debt Schedule. The Lender will also require Three Year's Personal Tax Returns on the buyer, Personal Financial Statement and complete Resume. The Buyer's background, industry experiences and/or complimentary work history is also critical for consideration. Letter of Intent on the transaction will be required for initial underwriting. If initially available, copies of leases are helpful at the outset. These are the basic documentation requirements to get the package started and additional

information will be required along the way depending on each specific project.

6. Lender Underwriting… Business Considerations. Once your buyer has submitted a complete loan package, their bank's underwriter will generally take about 2 -3 weeks to thoroughly review the loan request. Each Lender will have their own credit policies, but because the Business Acquisition project is usually always lacking full collateralization, Lenders will generally all require acceptable Debt Service. Your business' existing cash flow must show the ability to cover the requested bank debt, appropriate salary for buyer's Personal Living Needs, plus a "cushion" or margin for error on top. The Lender will also analyze performance trends. An organized seller will have prepared, in advance, explanations for any unusual adjustments, seller discretionary add-backs, or negative performance issues. Having written statements at-the-ready for the buyer's Lender always impresses. Having access to the seller's CPA can also be a help to the Lender during underwriting, especially if there are interesting adjustments or complicated add backs to more clearly understand.

7. Lender Underwriting & Buyer Qualifications. The Lender is going to look for the following in your Buyer: Industry and/or complimentary work expertise, resources available for down payment and post closing personal liquidity, collateral support, credit score, and secondary sources of repayment.

8. Mitigations. In a perfect world, the Lender would review a project with 100% positive trends in all areas of debt service, performance trends, buyer industry experience and liquidity. In all my years of SBA lending, it has been a rare occurrence to have a project with perfect scores in all areas. That's what makes my job fun. There is a real art to helping put an SBA acquisition project together. As Lenders, we are always trying to find the right blend of loan amount, buyer down payment and seller carry back

financing to balance the particular strengths and challenges of the each specific acquisition project. The more prepared the seller is for the buyer's underwriting process, the more they can play a positive role in providing critical information and being sensitive to what the buyer will be going through on their end.

9. Be Open to the Financing Process. Take a deep breath and persevere. I don't mean to sound too dramatic, but Lenders are going to get nosy. And, please understand that Lenders ask all these questions and require the documentation simply to educate themselves on the merit of your specific project. I never seek to offend but only to understand. I have the utmost respect for business owners who have spent years building something of value and my goal is to reach a win-win- win for the seller, buyer, and bank. I love my job because I always... always... come away from each project knowing more than I did when I started. And, I find with the right mindset and preparation, the same can be said for all involved.

REAL LIFE STORY: AGAIN, RELATIONSHIPS ARE KEY

The business was going through a transition with one of the three owners buying shares to get to a super-majority position. This might have led to some issues with the bank because the departing shareholder had a large personal net worth and was a co-guarantor on the line of credit. However, it wasn't an issue at all because the bank "loved" the buyer, who was the CEO and COO. They loved his management style, attention to detail and work ethic. A new bank wouldn't have that history and would have stricter requirements.

This is the kind of relationship you need to build with a bank. Not after you buy the company, but in the month or so prior to applying for a loan.

CREATIVE FINANCE TECHNIQUES

I own three books with titles similar to, "Buy a Business with No Money Down." My associate, Ted Leverette, wrote, "*How to Get ALL the Money You Want For Your Business Without Stealing It*" ("Partner" On-Call Network, LLC, 1997) and it has 50 pages on financing buy-sell transactions. Following is a list of the more common techniques we at "Partner" On-Call Network cover with our clients as we help them implement our program, "The Street-Smart Way to Buy a Business®."

The bottom line is that almost all of these creative finance techniques will be no value to you. Creative financing is deal-specific, and if your deal doesn't meet the criteria for a specific technique it doesn't matter how much you like the idea, it won't work. What you need to do is keep the following list handy and review it every time you analyze a company. Pay attention to the stories in the next section; they'll provide insight in real life financing situations.

27 FINANCING TECHNIQUES IN ALPHABETICAL ORDER:

1. Asset versus stock purchase—consult with your attorney and CPA on this; an asset purchase structure should allow you to write off the goodwill and re-depreciate the fixed assets. On the flip side, a stock purchase may allow you to negotiate a lower price and lower down payment (especially if the seller has a "C" corporation and may face double taxation).

2. Assume debt (business or seller's personal)—take over the company's debt as part of the deal. It could even be loans due the seller. Personal debt takeover may be trickier; it is rare and requires a high level of trust.

3. Bank loan—an obvious choice and, as previously mentioned, the seller's advisors most likely know that banks are very willing to make acquisition loans. Starting in 2010, I started telling people that the SBA loan guarantee program was a form of creative finance because without it there wouldn't be nearly as many loans.

4. Broker loan—I've never seen this except in a book written by a business broker. It doesn't hurt to ask the broker to finance his or her commission (get paid when the seller gets paid versus getting commission on the full price at closing).

5. Cash—cash talks, not matter what the size of deal. Use more cash to get the price down. Consider using all cash to get a great deal (you may want to put some in escrow to make sure the seller provides the agreed-to transition help).

6. Credit cards—sure, it's expensive, but if you need a small amount of cash to supplement your other funds and feel you can pay them off quickly, it may cheaper and faster than a traditional bank loan (SBA or conventional).

7. Deferred down payment—if you can see how you can get excess cash out of the business in the first few months try to structure the deal so you can make the down payment via multiple payments (not all at closing). See the example from my associate Ted Leverette in the next section.

8. Delayed payments—put off paying the seller note for months or years. It's not that hard to do if the seller is getting a lot of cash or there is seasonality (and you're buying the business during the slow time of the year).

9. Earnout—an earnout is when part of the price is contingent on future performance. A seller may go for this if you offer an upside to allow for their risk (that they may not get the earnout). For example, if the price is 100 with 70% down, perhaps you can negotiate to pay 80 with 60% down plus an earnout that can get the seller to 120. Yes, you give up upside but your cash outlay (in this example) is 31% lower.

10. Equity partner—get an investor who will own part of the business. In these days of low interest rates and volatile stock markets, this may be easier than ever. Be careful if your investor owns 20% or more, as that usually means they will be guarantors on any bank loans (they could also be if they own under 20%; that's the bank's call).

11. Factor accounts receivable—buy the receivables and turn them to cash ASAP. You can factor them or use your bank line of credit. In any event, you get the cash.

12. Friend or family loan to buyer—friends and family are an old source of funds for many startups so why not for an acquisition? After all, buying a business is faster, safer and cheaper than a startup. Plus, it's much easier to get bank financing for an acquisition.

13. Home equity loan—take out a home equity line of credit and use it to get cash, even if the cash goes in a money market account (and you lose a couple points a year). The worst that can happen is the bank tells you to pay it back so they can use your equity as collateral. Be sure to check the SBA rules on this as they have some restrictions on how and when home equity loans can and can't be used as buyer equity.

14. Investments and savings—this is the most likely source for the bulk of your down payment. Just don't plan to use all of it. After all, you wouldn't put all your money into one stock, would you?

15. Keep the cash and AR—let the business provide your working capital. The price may be higher but you're financing it over 5-10 years and that helps cash flow big time.

16. Qualified money—use the money in your pension, 401k or IRA. It is taxable income, and if you're under 59.5 there may be penalties. However, as described in Chapter Three, there are programs that allow you to use this money without tax or penalty. Your new company and its 401k plan will own shares in the business.

17. Refinance existing debt—assume the business's debt and refinance it. Or, combine it with your acquisition debt package for a better rate and terms. Many owners focus on paying off debt quickly, and it straps their cash flow. Get longer terms and free up cash.

18. Seasonal payments—with seller financing, structure your payments so you pay more in the busy season and less in the slow season. Of course, it must be a business with wide swings to make this work.

19. Sell equipment and then lease—If there is equipment with a high fair market value, you can sell it and lease it back. This is similar to refinancing, usually a bit more expensive and can get you cash fairly quickly.

20. Sell excess assets (equipment, vehicles)—it's amazing how many owners love machines, of all types. During due diligence, if you find that there are too many trucks, machines or anything else, then sell them.

21. Sell excess inventory—managing inventory is critical to cash flow. See the example in the next section on this. Too many owners don't manage inventory correctly.

22. Sell shares to employees—there may be nothing better to the long-term health of the company than to tie the management team to the firm with small ownership shares. It gets you cash now and, in most states, minority owners don't really have many rights. It's not like there's a market for the shares.

23. Seller financing—this is a must for most deals. You, and your bank, want the seller to have skin in the game.

24. Seller keeps AR as part of price—negotiate a price that is all-inclusive and then have the seller collect the AR as part of the payments.

25. Supplier loan—suppliers will loan you money to keep the account or to become your sole supplier (for what they provide). This is more common when you buy another company, especially if the acquisition target uses another supplier and you're going to switch.

26. Tax deductible payments—pay the seller part of the price via a consulting agreement or as an employee. You get to deduct these payments

27. Vacation or investment property equity loan—take a loan against other real estate you own. Get advice on the SBA rules on this first and, as with a home equity loan, get the line of credit and exercise it in advance, stockpiling the cash in a bank account.

REAL LIFE FINANCING

Following are some short examples of financing strategies and techniques. The overall objective is always to get the deal done, so any financing strategy has to work for both buyer and seller.

- **Cash talks**—and the buyer knew it. He wanted the business, knew what he could do with it and didn't want to slow things down. When the seller told him how much he wanted, the buyer agreed and said he'd write a check for half if the seller would finance half—no bank loan. They closed in less than two months, including Thanksgiving, Christmas and New Years.

- **Deductible payments**—The seller wanted a certain price for bragging rights. The buyer got there by making part of the deal an employment agreement and part of it a consulting agreement. Use this strategy of making tax-deductible payments if the seller wants to stay active and is willing to take payments in this way.

- **Manage inventory**—The seller loved assets. He loved seeing full racks of "stuff." The buyer managed the inventory better and in less than one year turned $250,000 of inventory into cash.

- **Analyze the assets**—A lot of business decisions are emotional. In this case the seller had a fascination with big trucks. The problem was, the business didn't need big trucks, it needed small trucks. The buyer sold the big trucks, bought small trucks, pocketed the difference and had lower operating costs.

- **Buy the AR and AP**—Buyers make a leap of faith; the objective is to make that leap off a chair not a roof. Sometimes, though, it pays to take a gamble. Craig made a gamble on accounts receivable and accounts payable. The business's records were a mess and initial due diligence told him that the company was better at paying their bills than in doing their billing and collecting (technicians running a business was the situation).

  After wading through stacks of accounting paperwork, he went to the sellers (multiple owners) and cut a deal. To save time and the hassle of analysis, Craig would take all the AR and AP. They agreed and within a week Craig was doubly rewarded. First, he found unbilled jobs for over $100,000 in the mess of papers and then a couple checks arrived for orders that didn't show up in the AR. His gamble really wasn't that big because of his analysis, it was similar to the gamble professional card counters take at the blackjack table. He knew the odds were in his favor.

- **Buy working capital**—Al and Will were in similar situations. Their deals were at the upper end of their capabilities and the businesses required working capital—over $300,000 in Al's case and at least $1 million for Will. Luckily, both owners understood the importance of working capital. And, at the size of these deals, it is more accepted for buyers to purchase a full package (whether it's structured as a stock or asset purchase).

  Both deals were in the generally accepted range (3-4 times EBITDA and 3.5–4.5 times profit) and provided the buyers with the cash to operate the business—cash they didn't have to take from savings or through another loan. As a plus, their respective banks like the structure and that made it easier to justify large loans.

- **Seller employment**—When Bruce bought a competitor he made a cash down payment, gave the seller a percentage of sales his company made to the seller's customers and hired the seller to be a salesperson. This is a combination of an earnout and an employment agreement.

- **Use the working capital to fund the deal**—I have seen this only one time, and because the buyer was a former banker I told him that if he was comfortable with the structure I was too. He put together a package of his money, a term acquisition loan and an immediate line of credit (collateralize with the AR left in the company). This is not typical; most lines of credit are used for working capital. I've never had a banker suggest this to a buyer, but because my client was a banker and the bank agreed I figured it was okay.

- **Interest only note**—having the seller take an interest only-note has become more popular, given the SBA rules implemented since 2008. Bob got his seller to take an interest-only note for the full term of the five-year loan. This gave him better cash flow, and at the end of five years he will finance it with the seller or with his bank.

- **Seasonally adjusted payments**—Robb bought a very seasonal business, showing the power of seller financing. There was no bank involved in the deal as the sellers liked and trusted Robb immensely. The payments were structured so they were half of the regular payment for the first six months and 50% more than the regular payment over the following six months. This allowed Robb to keep his debt manageable 12 months a year.

- **Earnout**—The seller's advisors will usually scream "run" when they hear the word earnout, but with the right circumstances it can work. Bob had to have an earnout because the business was floundering and the seller knew it. Bob paid for the assets plus an earnout as a percentage of gross profit. In another case there were some inconsistencies with the accounting system and financial statements. The sellers (husband and wife) were honest; they just didn't understand accounting.

Because of this, there was an earnout. It covered the buyer if things weren't as they appeared on the financial statements.

- **Pay the company's debt**—The business had got into trouble and Sean knew how and why it happened. He bought the company by paying off the debt to the primary vendor, the telephone company and the State Department of Revenue. The seller got an earnout. Sean didn't take on any more of the firm's debt, only what he had to take over to keep operating.

Action points

* Look at a variety of financing options.

* Determine what banks want.

* Determine what's best for you, a SBA guaranteed or conventional loan.

* Pay attention to the 50% rule.

* Work the odds; see a lot of bankers.

* Present yourself and the deal well; it's more for those credit people you don't meet than the lending officer with whom you build the relationship.

* Pay attention to the points from SBA lender, Lisa Forrest.

* Remember to tell your seller that the bank will be nosy.

* Look for creative financing opportunities, but don't get hung up on them.

— 7 —

PLAYING POKER

This chapter is adapted from the chapter titled, "What's it Worth?" in my book, *Without an Exit Strategy You Have No Strategy*, which I've written for business owners who are preparing for an eventual sale. Valuation and pricing methodologies and approaches should be the same whether done for a buyer or a seller. It's the interpretation that may differ.

As you plan your exit and the sale of your business one of your first meetings should be with your financial advisor. It's important that you have a sound understanding of where you are financially as you prepare for your next great adventure in life. It doesn't matter if your goal is retirement, another business, acquisition or startup, consulting or just a couple years' hiatus.

It may pay to get multiple opinions or to find an advisor who does fee based planning. This is especially true if you don't have a long and trusted relationship with an advisor.

One of my clients was planning for the sale of his business. His goal was to get enough for the business that when added to his current asset base there would be enough income generated to last 40 years. He was in his mid-60s and his wife was over a dozen years younger. His goal was income to last, under reasonable circumstances, until she was at least 90.

He met with his advisor and got the impression that the numbers were "made to work" because the advisor saw a sizable amount of funds about to come under management. The seller was then referred to someone from a major life insurance company and, again, his impression was that the end goal was to sell product. He ended up with a fee-based planner whom did not manage money or sell financial products.

Too many sellers go into the process blind. It's when they find out that they need 50% more than the business is worth that they panic and try to change or kill the deal. It's mandatory that you know what you need to make the rest of the process work and, if your business's value won't get you there at this time, what that value needs to be.

It's what you keep that's important

One key ingredient to the exercise of determining what you need is to know what you're going to keep (after taxes and transaction fees). There is an old adage of, "It's not what you get, it's what you keep." Not too much more can be said about this so I'll give two examples and remind you again to not forget taxes and fees. Later in this chapter we'll discuss terms and deal structure because there are different tax rates and various applications of those rates.

Real Life Story: Pay more and keep less

Greg showed the seller how he could accept an offer with a price 10% less than he wanted, get more cash (because the bank was willing to have a better loan package at a lower price) and have more money after-tax than he would get at his asking price (with standard deal components). Some of this was because of tax concessions the buyer made. However, those concessions got the buyer a better deal with about the same amount of after-tax acquisition debt payments. Most importantly, it got the buyer the deal on a very profitable and stable company (growth of the top and bottom lines every year during the Great Recession).

Whom do you to trust?

I'll say upfront that I don't have any certifications or designations in business appraisal or valuations, and doing valuations is not the primary focus of my business. However, I have been around hundreds of deals and potential deals and I do know the standard valuation methodologies.

I do some letter report or ballpark valuations if they don't involve a bank, the IRS or any type of dispute. There are plenty of people who can do complicated valuation projects and I regularly send people to those appraisers. There are SBA loan specialists, IRS specialists and appraisers who do business valuations when a government unit condemns a property for road expansion or something similar (eminent domain).

But you have to watch out. I saw a backroom bank employee do a valuation for a buyer (and the bank) that was complete garbage. Why? Because he did not even try to understand the business and its financial statements and relied on very simplistic formulas, most of which were meaningless. It's important for anybody valuing a business to get a feel for the business beyond the numbers, because there are so many ways for a small business to reduce taxable earnings; accelerated depreciation disguises asset values and earnings and the non-financial factors are a huge part of the process.

I talked to a life insurance agent who told me that they did a valuation on a company I knew, for planning purposes. I'm not sure if they wanted to impress the owner (with what his company was worth) in order to sell some product, but I couldn't understand how they came up with the value they did on a low-asset business that was running at breakeven and very dependent on a controlling owner.

On the flip side, a client of mine had a valuation done by a well-known, well-respected and experienced appraiser. His report came back with one-third of the value weighted on (very optimistic) projections. Of course, the business owner fixated on the total value in the report even though it was based on (dynamic) future growth. It had to be pointed out that banks using the SBA guarantee program aren't allowed to use valuations with projections and that looking at the report without the projections gave a value at about 70% of the stated figure (I said they were optimistic projections).

If you get a valuation, my advice is to understand what you are getting and whom you are getting it from. Also realize that the balance sheet can play as important a part in the valuation as the income statement.

REAL LIFE STORY: WATCH OUT FOR AGENDAS

I titled this section, "Whom do you trust?" for good reason. A business buyer client of mine hired an appraiser. We all got together to review the numbers, the methodologies used and the discussion points with the seller. At one point the appraiser said that we would use a factor of "X" in one formula because my client was the buyer and we wanted the value to be low.

This wouldn't pass any industry standards or code of ethics. In fact, it goes against such standards (see the section in this chapter on standards). Sellers should also be careful if anybody suggests they are using factors to increase the value because the report is being done for the seller. This can easily backfire if:

- The bank won't finance the deal at that level

- The buyer's advisors see through the strategy

- The deal goes through but the buyer has trouble making the payments

A PLETHORA OF INFORMATION

There are thousands of books on small business valuation and many more articles that have appeared in business and trade magazines, not to mention everything on the Internet. One of the books I have uses the words "simple" and "easy" to describe its contents. Yet, it is filled with almost as many formulas as college textbook type books.

REAL LIFE STORY: DON'T MAKE IT TOO COMPLICATED; THIS IS SMALL BUSINESS AFTER ALL

On a "Partner" On-Call Network teleconference we had one of our "Partners" do a presentation on business valuations. This person had a financial background and had some middle-market acquisition experience.

We followed along on an Excel spreadsheet and he discussed statistical analysis, standard deviations and many other things I vaguely remembered from college math and statistics courses. When he was done there was a stunned silence (which was unusual for this group of assertive people).

After what must have been 10-12 seconds I said, "Would you please explain what you said after your opening?" Following a bit of laughter we got into a realistic discussion of how small businesses are valued.

One can face information overload and get tangled up in a process that is often exhausting. Realize that no matter what method or what formula or statistical analysis is used, it comes down to the fact that there are some generally accepted ranges where (most) deals happen. One of the best examples of this is a chart created by Rob Slee in conjunction with Pepperdine University and published in *Midas Managers* (Burn the Boats Press, 2007). Here is Mr. Slee's information (copyrighted by Rob T. Slee, 2007, all rights reserved).

Sales Range	Classification	EBITDA Multiple Range
Under $5 million	Small Businesses	2-3x
$5-150 million	Lower Middle-Market	4-7x
$150-500 million	Middle Middle-Market	8-9x
$500-1,000 million	Upper Middle Market	10-12x
Above $1 billion	Large Companies	>12x

Let's apply some common sense to the above chart (and realize that there are occasionally exceptions). As stated previously, the larger the company, the higher the price, all other factors being equal. That means that a company doing $5-10 million in sales will sell for close to four times the EBITDA of a company doing $50-100 million in sales.

This book is for the business buyer of a company in the lower middle-market and small business range on Mr. Slee's chart. If the target firm is on the lower end of the lower middle-market range, don't focus on the small business multiple range, as it most likely won't happen. However, given the Great Recession, you might expect the low end of each range to have dropped a half a point (3.5-7x versus 4-7x).

TIP: UNDERSTAND THE BIG PICTURE

The company was at the $5 million in sales level and growing fast (projected over $7 million in two years and over $12 million within five years). The owner and I were discussing multiple ranges for a possible management buy-in.

He understood that as a $5 million company he should be using a 3-4x multiple of EBITDA range and taking into consideration the non-financial factors and the terms. You can't accept any guideline, range or rule-of-thumb as gospel. My cynical comments about formulas and statistical analysis should be taken with a "grain of salt." There is a lot more that goes into this than simply plucking a multiple for a range (as we'll see in a few pages).

WHAT ARE THE COMPANY'S ASSETS AND LIABILITIES (AND WHAT DOES IT MATTER)?

BALANCE SHEET

There are many components to every business, and when it comes to valuation, using a quick multiple approach ignores the balance sheet, which is a mistake. As a private equity group partner told me years ago, as he put deals together his appreciation for the importance of the balance sheet increased.

For valuation purposes, assets are divided into two classes. Essential assets are those necessary to deliver the product to the customer. They include inventory, furniture, fixtures, equipment and vehicles (FFE&V). Without them you can't do business. They are generally included in the total value of the company.

Non-essential assets are necessary to having a business but not necessary to delivering the product to the customer. Common non-essential assets are cash and accounts receivable. Many businesses have little to no money in their bank accounts and can still deliver product. Many businesses have no accounts receivable and can still deliver their product (retail and restaurants are good examples). On the liability side, accounts payable are often treated the same as accounts receivable (non-essential). The net of these assets and liabilities are often added to the value of the business that is formulated, based on profit or EBITDA multiples and other standard valuation methodologies.

Does it matter what the value of your essential assets is? For inventory, it definitely does. A seller can't expect to get the same price for a company with a lot of dead inventory as it does for a company with inventory that is 100% salable and that turns at or better than the industry average.

However, when it comes to FFE&V, there are two factors to consider.

What are the anticipated capital expenditures? In other words, what will you, the buyer, have to spend to maintain the business at its current growth rate? If the assets are at the end of their lifespan then future cash flow will be less, all other things being equal, than if there are newer assets with a longer projected life before replacement. Allowing for capital expenditures after determining EBITDA (or profit) gives buyers their Free Cash Flow figure, which is what they have available to pay their debt, taxes and fund growth.

With all of the accelerated depreciation techniques available today (and constantly changing), the book value of FFE&V is almost meaningless. What's important to a bank is the fair market value of these assets (actually, the bank may be more interested in the liquidation value). This is collateral, and will affect the amount of the bank loan your buyer can get. But be careful in this area. Consult your CPA about depreciation recapture because the seller won't want any part of it. When this happens part of the sales price will be taxed at ordinary income rates, not capital gains rates (in general terms, this comes into play if you allocate a value of an asset higher than its depreciated value on your balance sheet).

INCOME STATEMENT

This is where the fun begins. Rare is it that we find a small business that has a tax return or income statement that accurately reflects the true profit of the company. Part of the reason for this is that there are tax techniques such as accelerated depreciation and amortization of goodwill (if you purchased the company and are still writing off the goodwill). The other big reason is that owners funnel non-business expenses through the company.

Business owners should approach their bottom line, at least for three to five years prior to selling, as if they are in a contest to have the most profit and pay the most tax. However, that's tough for most owners. They either have a great aversion to paying taxes or their CPA takes it as his or her mission to reduce the client's taxable income by any means possible.

In the section on financial due diligence I mentioned how it is considered fraud to not report income and to deduct personal expenses through the business. I don't recommend it but it happens, and that is one reason it is common to "recast" or adjust the income statement to show the true profit and cash flow the buyer should expect.

The following chart is a simple tool to help you calculate the real profit or cash flow that will be available for acquisition debt payments and growth. Most of the categories are self-explanatory, but let's review some of them. First, realize that in an S Corporation the owner often takes a low salary and high distribution, and in a C Corporation it is the opposite. Therefore, we add back owner compensation to net income and deduct the fair market salary for the job being performed by the owner.

Excessive owner benefits: If the seller has life insurance, deferred compensation or a pension plan weighted in his or her favor, you can add these back to income. Do not add back standard medical benefits, similar to what all employees get and what you will expect.

Non-essential expenses: Does the seller deduct car expenses, yet use the car only to commute? Or perhaps he or she deducts their spouse's car (or the kids' cars)? What about that annual board meeting in Hawaii in January? These are not expenses essential to running the business. While the annual board meeting is legal, I recommend you consult with your CPA about auto expenses, other travel you write off, entertainment you write off, etc. before taking those as business deductions.

Depreciation: Work with your CPA to get a cost of asset usage expense (which is really what depreciation is, other than all the acceleration techniques) and anticipated capital expenditures.

Interest and rent: If the seller has an acquisition loan you should add back the interest on it to income. Realize that if the seller has a line of credit, you will have a line of credit, and should factor that cost into your calculations. Rent is adjusted only if the seller pays under or over market (usually if the seller also owns the property) or if you expect the rent to change.

Category	2 years prior	Last year	This year	Explanation
Net Income				
Owner salary				
Owner salary tax burden				
Excessive owner benefits (life insurance, etc.)				
Travel & Entertainment (not essential)				
Owner auto (not essential)				
Depreciation adjustment				

Category	2 years prior	Last year	This year	Explanation
Amortization (of Goodwill)				
Interest (not continuing post-sale)				
Rent adjustment				
Other				
Other				
Total				
Less: Fair market owner salary				
Less: Fair market owner tax burden				
Less: Anticipated capital expenditures				
Less: Other				
Total adjusted net profit/free cash flow				

There are too many businesses that have become "lifestyle" businesses for the owner. There's a blending of the personal and business checkbooks (talk to your CPA or attorney about any risks of "piercing the corporate veil" involved with this blending). Some CPAs are aggressive and tell their clients to write off any and everything. Others are incredibly conservative and will question why your annual board meeting wasn't at your office.

Sellers should realize, for the sake of exit planning and selling the business, that banks are increasingly more suspicious when there's a long list of "add-backs" (of personal expenses). Many bankers will discount these and thus reduce the cash flow they use to calculate debt coverage ratios. Also remember the story I told earlier about the owner whom saved on taxes by running her household expenses through the business and lost out on four times the amount of taxes saved on the purchase price.

I have seen and heard just about everything when it comes to deducting personal expenses. The list includes the liquor store, Costco, the toy train store, Best Buy, shotgun shells, the cigar store, spouse cars, family cars, family salaries (for people not working at the company), the weekly grocery bill, vacations, home remodels and more. I once wrote a newsletter about an article in the Minneapolis Star-Tribune about a Twin Cities business owner whom was put in jail for not reporting income and writing off things that make the above list seem tame.

I've had owners brag about the cash they skim and one owner even asked me, being dead serious, if I wanted to see the real books or the books he shows the IRS.

Many years ago a CPA told me he fired a client because of above type of manipulation (a CPA can lose their license if they knowingly sign a fraudulent tax return). He said he told his client that because the client owned a well-known and successful restaurant, lived in one of the nicest neighborhoods in town and drove an exotic car that he, the CPA, couldn't sign his tax return showing he made a minuscule amount of money.

Seller's should play it straight, maximize profits, pay taxes and adjust his or her income for legitimate reasons. You and your bank will be glad you did.

CASH FLOW TERMINOLOGY

Profit, EBITDA, SDE, ODI, recast income, free cash flow and other terms bounce around the buy-sell industry like a racquetball in a fast-paced game. What's worse is that these terms are often defined differently.

Let's take a look at them, what they really mean and how to apply them. Because, no matter how a valuation methodology is applied, it comes down to a return on investment (ROI), and using one term versus another can create drastically different results.

- **Profit**: As mentioned above, this would be easier if businesses operated to maximize income instead of paying less in taxes. We'd get a truer picture of the income viability of a company. Small business reporting is not like public company reporting where the public company wants to show maximum income to encourage their stock price to increase. For this reason the profit figure on the income statement or the tax return is rarely valid.

- **Adjusted or recast profit**: As per the worksheet previously explained, this is a much better indication of a company's status. It allows a buyer and a lender to know what the buyer's available cash will be. This is a very valid figure.

- **EBITDA**: The acronym stands for Earnings before Interest, Taxes, Depreciation and Amortization. This is supposed to give an indication of true cash flow because, in theory, depreciation and amortization are non-cash expenses, and interest is included because a buyer may have different financing than the current owner. However, EBITDA doesn't make allowances for needed assets or the cost of working capital, which for many businesses is a critical and needed expense. As with adjusted profit you must allow for a fair market salary for the job of the owner. This is a corporate term and you don't see public companies adjust and add-back management salaries to profits.

TIP: WATCH OUT FOR EBITDA

For fun, Google "EBITDA and Warren Buffet." Here are a couple choice quotes from Mr. Buffet on the use of this term.

"You get depreciation by laying out money first -- the worst kind of expense. It's the opposite of float, where you get money at the beginning and pay out at the end."

"References to EBITDA make us shudder. Too many investors focus on earnings before interest, taxes, depreciation and amortization. That makes sense only if you think capital expenditures are funded by the tooth fairy."

- **Seller's Discretionary Earnings**: Also called Owner's Discretionary Income (ODI), this is often EBITDA plus owner's salary. The theory is that all money to an owner is discretionary and it's the owner's decision if he or she takes a salary, uses the money to grow the business or pay acquisition debt. I know how it came about; brokers got sick of arguing about what the fair market salary for a business's owner should be. In reality, for most owners and buyers, a salary to support their personal life is not discretionary. An appraiser (and banker) would always allow for a fair market salary. In my opinion, this is a term that loses all effectiveness once a business's adjusted profit plus salary gets to $500,000.

- **Free cash flow**: In simple terms, take EBITDA (including the adjusted profit figure that allows for a fair market owner salary) and deduct anticipated capital expenditures and operating interest (not acquisition interest). This is a figure equity groups and similar type buyers often zero in on, especially in these days of complicated and changing accelerated depreciation schedules. It also gives a seller credit for recent capital expenditures that will reduce the buyer's need for capital expenditures.

TIP: UNDERSTAND THE DIFFERENCE BETWEEN S AND C CORPORATIONS

A buyer reviewed a company's tax returns and said, "I like the business but it's not making any money." The company was structured as a C corporation and the owner took a salary of about $750,000, which left only $50-100,000 on the net income line. Adjusting for a fair market salary gave a true adjusted profit figure in the $650-700,000 range.

Of course, I've seen buyers get excited when they first look at an S corporation's tax return and see an inflated net income line because the owner was taking a salary of only $40-50,000.

MULTIPLES

The above definitions are important to understand because, as previously stated, it all comes down to Return On Investment (ROI). Your buyer, banker, appraiser and you will all be concerned with the factor used as a multiple of earnings. The following example shows the differences, which are explained after the chart.

For this example, let's assume the company does about $5 million in sales, reports 10% profit before adjustments and has a solid asset base (that needs regular upgrading). For this example, we are assuming there are no serious red flags like high customer concentration, a tenuous lease that may require huge moving costs or market factors that will negatively affect the industry. For simplicities sake I am assuming the non-essential assets are not included in this sample calculation.

Also, I'm assuming this is a manufacturing, distribution or service business because retail and restaurant business have some additional factors, and their multiple of earnings is often lower because of the higher (perceived) risk associated with those business types.

	Profit	EBITDA	SDE	Free cash flow
Reported profit	$500,000	$500,000	$500,000	$500,000
Adjustments	$100,000	$100,000	$100,000	$100,000
Depreciation		$100,000		$100,000
Operating interest		$50,000		$50,000
Owner salary			$150,000	
Capital expenditures				$-50,000
Operating interest				$-50,000
NET	$600,000	$750,000	$900,000	$650,000

Profit: Buyers for businesses in this size range typically want a 20-25% ROI, which means a multiple of four to five. This gives us a price range of $2.4-3.0 million with a $2.7 million mid-point.

EBITDA: As we saw with Robb Slee's chart of EBITDA multiples, they increase as the business gets bigger. The same is true for the other factors. In Slee's chart we see that a $5 million business is on the border of a three and four multiple. This gives us a price range of $2.2-3.0 million with a $2.6 million mid-point.

SDE: Your first inclination might be to want to use SDE, because it's a much higher number than the others. Of course, the generally accepted range of multiples is lower. Around the year 2000 I was being recruited to join a prominent Seattle business brokerage firm. Their typical deals were from $1-10 million in price, and they had a great reputation. One thing that stuck out to me was that in their weekly meetings, when discussing possible listings (of only profitable companies) they always used a range of two to three times SDE. The potential listing agent usually argued for the high end of the range and the other agents gave reasons why that wasn't realistic. Using this range we get a price range of $1.8-$2.7 million and a mid-point of $2.25 million.

FCF: You'll find free cash flow multiples to be similar to profit multiples, and they grow as companies get to $10 million in sales and above. In this example, we get a price range of $2.6-3.2 million and a mid-point of $2.9 million.

	Profit	EBITDA	SDE	Free cash flow
Mid-point value	$2,700,000	$2,600,000	2,250,000	$2,900,000

You can see why I feel SDE loses importance as a business grows. The owner's salary becomes less relevant compared to the lower multiple range. The other prices are in a pretty tight range and then the influences become, as always, the non-financial factors, terms, relationship and buyer and seller motivations.

I can tell you that some business brokers would read this and immediately argue that the range of multiples, the calculations or other factors all give too low value. At the same time, buyer representatives, accountants and others would tell me that the above is too optimistic.

As with any guidelines, use them only as such—a guideline. The above is simplistic and is presented to make a point. That point is that there are different ways to calculate earnings and different multiples for those methods. Buyers of $5 million businesses want a 20-25% ROI, buyers of $15-50 million dollar businesses will lower that to about 15% ROI. There's enough evidence and history to show these are viable ranges, and these are the ranges necessary to allow for the risk of a small business (versus the risks a large, public company faces and can handle).

REAL LIFE STORY: IF THEY LOVE YOU THE PRICE IS GREAT

The seller gave us the asking price and after the meeting the buyer and I looked at each other and simultaneously said, "What should we negotiate?" You see, the price was more than fair, so we didn't want to disrupt the deal. We negotiated part of the seller financing and a few conditions and that was it. It's too bad they're not all that easy.

COMPARABLE SALES

Historical sales information, i.e., comparable sales, is a little bit like the Bible. There is one Bible and many different interpretations. The same can be said for the interpretation of done deal benchmarks, and that was before the Great Recession. If a business is below average, the owner or selling team will point to average multiples as a way to increase the price.

We can learn a lot from history. Of course, we have to pay attention and allow for other factors. One area that especially requires special attention is the pricing of a business and the relationship between current pricing and comparable sales information from pre-Great Recession.

My opinion is that if the business being evaluated has done well during the recession, the comparable statistics are an acceptable benchmark. However, if the business has suffered, it's tough to make a valid comparison with deals from less turbulent times. This means that businesses that have had a rough three to four years are hit with a double whammy. Their earnings are down and their multiple of earnings factor will also be lower.

As mentioned above, consider your use of average selling prices. I've had discussions with many people about the validity of (historical) average selling prices. Rarely will a business be average. Don't get caught in the trap of using averages as gospel.

Toby Tatum, Certified Business Appraiser and the author of *Transaction Patterns* wrote my "Partner" On-Call Network associate Ted Leverette (in late 2011) and said, "Using a 3X multiple of Seller's Discretionary Earnings for the vast majority of businesses represented in the Bizcomps database will tend to yield a value conclusion that is approximately double the correct amount." Or, a small percentage of good businesses are raising the average price of all the others. So be careful.

REAL LIFE STORY: USE COMMON SENSE WITH COMPARABLE INFORMATION

There weren't enough historical sales for the distribution company's SIC (Standard Industrial Classification) code, so we looked at distribution companies in general, at a size range that straddled this firm's size and eliminated all firms losing money. We noted the ratio of price to earnings (the multiple) and, just as important, the ratio of earnings to revenues.

The firm had earnings 20% greater than the average (for example, if the average was 15% then this firm had 18% earnings). Our assumption became that this firm was an above average firm and the justified price should be above average. This is just one way to use comparable sales information.

My advice to buyers and sellers is to not get hung up on comparable sales information. This is not like real estate, where it's a regulated market. Submissions to the databases are voluntary (unlike tax records) and there are no double checks on the information submitted. This information is really a guideline or rule-of-thumb and should be used accordingly.

We also don't know exactly what was included in the reported information. If two owners sell for five times profit and one keeps all the working capital and the other includes it in the deal, we have vastly different sales that are reported with the same price to earnings ratio.

Valuation methods

According to IRS revenue ruling 59-60:

> The fair market value is the price at which the property would change hands between a willing buyer and a willing seller when the former is not under any compulsion to buy and the latter is not under any compulsion to sell, both parties having reasonable knowledge of relevant facts.

Well, the IRS should have said "hypothetical" buyer, or hypothetical situation. Because never will the buyer and seller know the same things, perceive them the same way or have the same motivations to do a deal now versus *maybe next year*.

This ruling covers some valuation methodologies, some of which are usually appropriate and some of which aren't. In the early 2000's the SBA came out with their list of approved methodologies (I'm not sure if they still adhere to that list, but they do now require appraisers to have a certification if they are to be approved to do valuations on SBA program transactions).

For example, the book value of a company is rarely reflective of the true worth, yet it is an approved method. Similarly, calculating the investment needed in a startup to get to the place where the company being valued currently is not often valid. Both of these may be useful for unprofitable or new firms but don't have much relevance for a mature, profitable business.

In my world, it comes down to the fact that there are three main methods, with comparable sales used as a sanity check. Research business valuations and you'll find a lot of appraisers talking about how there's as much art as science to it (and they're right).

Capitalization of earnings

For a small or mid-sized business, what are the most valid methodologies? Return on investment or capitalization of earnings is always at the top of the list. Any buyer wants a rate of return commensurate with the perceived risk of the business. This is why larger companies will sell for a higher multiple than smaller ones, all other factors being equal. There is less perceived risk.

In simple terms, the return on the investment is reflected in the pricing of the business. If the buyer desires, or demands, a return of 20% based on historical earnings, then he or she will pay five times earnings for the business.

THE IRS METHOD

As you might suppose, a method with the initials IRS in it will tend to lead to higher values, as the IRS often gets involved with gift and estate tax issues and wants a high value so there is more tax to collect. In simple terms (and you can easily do an Internet search to get more detailed information on this), the ongoing cost of the company's assets is deducted from earnings, and a multiple is applied. This becomes the value of the goodwill and it is added to the value of the assets. Here's an example:

Earnings—$500,000

Assets—$400,000

Cost of funds—10% (or an annual cost of $40,000 for the use of these assets)

Goodwill ratings—four (or 25% desired rate of return)

Profit	$500,000
Cost of assets	-$40,000
Net	$460,000
Multiple	4
Goodwill ($460,000X4)	$1,840,000
Value of assets	$400,000
Value of assets and goodwill	$2,240,000

You can see that the rate of return on this price is 22% or 12% less than the buyers desired 25% return on investment. That's why it's stated that this method gives high values. The values become more skewed (higher) when there are high asset values and low to average profits, as the following example shows.

> ## REAL LIFE STORY: COMMON SENSE SAYS WATCH OUT FOR WHAT DOESN'T MAKE SENSE
>
> *The firm being sold was a high inventory business. In fact, the amount of their inventory was many times higher than similar firms because of shipping, the number of product variables (size, color, etc.) and production lead times. Using the IRS method gave a value so high that no buyer would pay it. The return on investment would be way too low for this $5-10 million (sales) company.*
>
> *The fact was that the company was getting a very poor return on assets, and its value was about the total value of the assets because of this. In this case, growth was the answer. At twice its size, the firm projected it would need the same inventory, with a better inventory turn rate.*

DISCOUNTED FUTURE CASH FLOW

Personally, I think buyers and sellers should be very careful of this method or any variation of it. It's often said that buyers buy because of potential and pay based on history. This method determines a price based on future, projected earnings. I'm not alone with these thoughts. The SBA will not allow a valuation that uses projections of any type. The value has to be determined based on historical earnings.

Again in simple terms, the projected earnings have a discount rate applied to them to create a present value of those earnings. This sounds fine in theory, but just imagine the situation if someone bought a company in 2008 based on all the rosy projections floating around. Nobody imagined the great recession. As a seller, you don't want to be dragged into a lawsuit because you sold based on projections that didn't come true (whether it's the buyer's fault, the economy or anything else).

Real Life Stories: Watch out for agendas (again)

A client showed me two valuations done on his firm. The first was from a national, road-show company that sold incredibly expensive valuation reports and was known for inflated values in those reports. The value was so high that this owner just laughed because he knew that, even in his wildest dreams, no buyer would pay that amount. They got these high values by basing them on projected earnings.

The second valuation was from a very reputable regional CPA firm. They used the same method (discounted future earnings) and added in a residual value. This means that they projected the buyer would sell the business in five years; they discounted to a net present value the price the buyer would receive and added it to the current value (based on projections). In other words, pay the seller now for what you will sell it for in the future. Their value was even higher than the national firm's value.

Again, the risk is a future lawsuit if those projections don't materialize. This client was smart enough to know that he wouldn't buy his own business for these inflated prices and no sane buyer would either.

Goodwill ratings

I previously gave my definition of goodwill and the following is a standard form used by business appraisers to estimate the feelings of company owners or buyers on the goodwill of the firm. You can find it in many places (perhaps with some slight variations).

I instruct clients to "Rate your company or your target company and be honest." Give thought to each category listed below and put down the number you feel is most representative of the company's status. *Ratings do not need to be whole numbers and can range from 0 to 6 (for example, they could be 3.1, 4.7, 1.4 or 5.0).*

Give serious thought to your answers and justify them. Question why you chose a particular number rather than a higher or lower one. For example, if a rating is a 4, why is it not 4.5 or 5 and why is it not 3.5 or 3?

Please provide a brief explanation of why you chose each rating. Be skeptical of any ratings at the 5 or 6 level. It is highly unusual for a business to be at a 5 or 6 in any of these areas. A score at this level means your firm is in the "best-of-the-best" category. Provide **proof** of why you're at this level.

Alternatively, if you give a rating of 1 or 2 in any category, please give a brief explanation of why you don't think you're "up to speed" in that area.

Risk Rating _____

0 - Continuity of income is uncertain
3 - Steady income likely
6 - Growing income assured

Competitive Rating _____

0 - Highly competitive in unstable market
3 - Normal competitive conditions
6 - Little competition in market; high cost of entry

Industry Rating _____

0 - Declining industry
3 - Industry growing faster than inflation
6 - Dynamic industry; rapid growth likely

Company Rating _____

0 - Recent start up or not established
3 - Well established with satisfactory environment
6 - Long record of profitable operation and excellent reputation

Company Growth Rating _____

0 - Business has been declining
3 - Steady growth, slightly faster than inflation
6 - Dynamic growth rate

Desirability Rating _____

0 - No "prestige" status; rough, dirty, undesirable work
3 - Respected type of business in good environment
6 - Great demand by people desiring to own this type of business

TOTAL RATING _____

These ratings serve two purposes. First, they give insight into the buyer's and the seller's feelings about the company, its future and the risk involved.

Second, in the IRS valuation method, the average of these ratings is often used along with a desired rate of return. For example, if the average is 4.3 it translates into a 23% desired ROI.

REAL LIFE STORY: HUMAN NATURE GETS IN THE WAY SOMETIMES

The two owners, one buying the shares of the other, each filled out this rating form. The buyer's ratings averaged between 2 and 3. The selling partner's ratings were one 4 and five 6s.

Of course both were wrong, and in this case the buyer was closer to reality. For example, both buyer and seller told me that the industry was not growing very much, and their growth was at the expense of competitors. Yet the selling partner gave "Industry Rating" a 6, "Dynamic industry; rapid growth likely." I think he (actually both of them) was trying to influence me.

THE BALANCE SHEET

I mentioned previously an operator who, as a buyer, had a newfound appreciation for balance sheets. While it's true that most deals have a price (and value) based more on cash flow than on the assets, don't ignore the balance sheet. In these days of complicated accelerated depreciation, it pays to have a CPA unravel the balance sheet.

A company with very low assets will tend to sell for a lower multiple of earnings than a company with a lot of assets, all other things being equal. There is a feeling of safety with assets and less goodwill. Remember, from the Five C's of Banking, one of them is collateral.

My first look at a balance sheet is to see what the quick ratio situation is. The quick ratio is cash and equivalents and accounts receivable versus current liabilities. I take it one step further and look at the quick assets to all liabilities. In other words, if the business sold, could the seller pay off his or her debts from the current cash and receivables? This is often a deal point, especially if the seller owes more than they can pay off from their assets.

REAL LIFE STORY: THE MORE INFORMATION THE BETTER

The owner had an accounting background, and for that reason he didn't just show me a balance sheet, which had assets after depreciation of under $50,000. He had a list of assets with cost, date of purchase, depreciation, estimated useful life and his estimate of the current fair market value. The current value of assets was about $750,000 (of which a bank may use half towards collateral). This shows how Section 179, immediate write off of assets purchased, and other techniques can skew a balance sheet and why I recommend an accountant undo the depreciation schedules to get a true current market value.

A trend in 2011-12 is for working capital to, more and more, stay in the company. For larger deals this has always been true and it is now working its way down the deal size ladder. Sellers' can't build a company with an involved balance sheet and expect to unravel it at time of selling (or at the time of valuation). In simple terms, as in my story, buyers should have an appreciation for the balance sheet and sellers should realize that buyers, bankers and appraisers will.

TERMS AND DEAL STRUCTURE

In the book, *Transaction Patters*, by Toby Tatum (RDS Associates, 2000), Mr. Tatum states that, "Acquisitions, which were financed by the seller, sold for a 15% (median) higher price than all-cash transactions. The average down payment was 37%. This difference is more pronounced if we compare the all-cash transaction to those selling with seller financing of 70% or more. In these deals, the median sale price was 27% higher price than all-cash transactions."

I will offer the disclaimer that his study came primarily from Biz-Comps, a database of done deals, and BizComps is dominated by small deals. But still, the bottom line is: finance a little, get a higher price; finance a lot, get even more.

Terms won't influence a valuation but they will influence the price. As a buyer, you need to look at the whole package including your capabilities, cash at closing, and net after tax, and try to understand what the seller needs in cash. In 2012, and in preceding years, interest rates have been at all-time lows. In 2009, one seller went to his buyer, whom he felt was the right person to take the business to the next level (he was right) and renegotiated to carry a larger note. His note was at six percent interest and he said he couldn't come close to that with bank.

When it comes to structure, your CPA earns their fee. Their job is to keep both parties out of trouble, which means that the seller gets as much of the price as possible at capital gains tax rates versus ordinary income rates, and the buyer gets as large a write-off as possible. In an asset purchase, this means not having any depreciation recapture (putting a value of the assets above what they are on your books) because this is taxed as ordinary income. Again, both parties should consult their CPA in advance and at the time of the deal.

Realize that for the seller, "It's not what you get, it's what you keep." Price, terms, structure and conditions all play a part in this. While this is technically not part of the valuation process, it is part of the pricing process, and they are closely connected.

REAL LIFE STORY: IT'S WHAT YOU CAN DO WITH THE COMPANY THAT INFLUENCES (YOUR) PRICE

Pricing and value are often different in real life. One of my clients, Craig, knew what he could do with the target company. We were in the same ballpark on price when he said, "I don't care if I pay X or X plus $100,000. I want this company because I know how much I can improve it and grow it."

Price, like beauty, is in the eye of the beholder.

MYTHS OF BUSINESS VALUATION

Here are some myths of valuation and pricing I've come up with over the years. Some of these are a bit tongue-in-cheek. Most aren't. They are all worth paying attention to.

The "rule of thumb" says my business is worth "X." Rules of thumb are just that, and nothing more. They give an indication but do not substitute for a valuation. Use them for quick comparisons only. Here's a big reason why: often, a rule of thumb is an average. If one company sells for 2X revenue and another for 1X revenue, the rule may state that companies in that industry sell for 1.5X revenue (a simple average). If you use this rule, you could tremendously short change yourself.

I'm going to sell my small, privately owned company for the same price to earnings (P-E) ratio as a large, publicly traded company sells for. This is not valid for at least two reasons. Public company P-E ratios are based on after-tax profit. Private companies are valued based on pre-tax profit. One reason for this is that small business owners have access to a wide variety of tax avoidance strategies. Second, as stated previously, the larger the firm, the less perceived risk and the higher the multiple.

Owner's compensation is profit. Profit is what is left after allowing for fair market compensation for doing the job of company president. Note all my definitions on different ways to calculate cash flow (EBITDA, SDE, profit, etc.).

I deserve something for my sweat equity. There is no such thing as sweat equity. Sorry, but no sane person is going to overpay for a business just because you put in a lot of effort to get it where it is. Profit over a manager's fair market salary is your payment for sweat equity.

The business is worth the current market value of the assets. I've had buyers tell me they won't pay for blue sky (goodwill), and my response is then the probably won't buy a business because more businesses are valued based on cash flow. I've also had naïve CPAs tell their clients nobody will pay more than book value for their company.

My business is worth the assets plus a multiple of earnings. Businesses are valued on either their assets *or* on their earnings. <u>Not both</u>. Your business is not worth a multiple of earnings plus the essential assets of the business because this "method" values those assets twice. The assets are worth the greater of what they will earn or what they can be sold for. (Non-essential assets such as cash or accounts receivable can be valued separately and added to the firm's value.)

REAL LIFE STORY: TAKE ANY ADVANTAGE YOU CAN GET

The seller's team made a mistake. They agreed to a (fair) price with the inventory pegged to the amount on the balance sheet at the time of the offer. This happened to be a time of unusually high inventory. By the time the deal closed the $2.5 million dollar price with $1.1 million dollars of inventory was $1.9 million with $500,000 of inventory. The $1.1 million dollar level was truly a bump on the chart of rolling inventory values, and the buyer got a heck of a deal.

There is a value to the cash I pocket (without reporting on my taxes). If you're willing to cheat the IRS, how much trust should a business buyer have in you? If you're skimming, you've already been paid by not paying taxes. This does not just pertain to small retail and restaurant businesses. Remember my previous example of an eight figure sales company whose owner sold scrap on the side for six figures a year and didn't report it.

POINTS TO PONDER:

1. Business valuations are part art and part science. The art comes from experience, from knowing what the information really means.

2. Profits are the driving force behind a high value (and selling price).

3. Much of what you've heard about what a company is worth isn't true. That can hurt you if you have a strong company.

The price needs to cover the personal and business debt I owe. Back in the early 90's a seller informed me that he set the price by adding the business debt, personal debt and the price of a new RV. Stop laughing. I'm serious. In 2011 I heard a similar story from the owner of a multi-million dollar sales business (which was struggling).

The potential of this business is great. In fact, you, as a new owner, should do much better than I've done with my 20 years of experience. Therefore, I want you to pay me for the future profits I haven't been able to generate.

The losses and my reduced salary over the last three years are a fluke. Just look at the profit eight years ago. (See the previous paragraph on potential.) In 2011 the owner of a business told me what he wanted. I told him I thought he'd be lucky to get half of what he wanted and he said his rationale was that in 2006-07 he made a lot of money and that business would be back to that level in another year or two, so he should get paid based on that profit level.

VALUATION STANDARDS

While many people who do business valuations are not certified or a member of a valuation professional group, they should adhere to the standards that industry groups have. Here are the standards from two groups: the National Association of Certified Valuators and Analysts (www.nacva.com) and the Institute of Business Appraisers (www.go-iba.org).

FROM THE INSTITUTE OF BUSINESS APPRAISERS

1. Nonadvocacy is considered to be a mandatory standard of appraisal.

2. The essence of business appraisal is a supportable opinion.

3. The appraiser's procedures and conclusions must permit a disinterested party to replicate the appraisal process.

4. The appraiser's duty is to inquire about information that appears to be incomplete or inaccurate.

5. When the appraiser is denied access to data considered essential to a proper appraisal, the appraiser should not proceed with the assignment.

FROM THE NATIONAL ASSOCIATION OF CERTIFIED VALUATORS AND ANALYSTS

GENERAL AND ETHICAL STANDARDS

A member shall perform professional services in compliance with the following principles:

1. INTEGRITY AND OBJECTIVITY A member shall remain objective, maintain professional integrity, shall not knowingly misrepresent facts, or subrogate judgment to others. The member must not act in a manner that is misleading or fraudulent.

2. PROFESSIONAL COMPETENCE A member shall only accept engagements the member can reasonably expect to complete with a high degree of professional competence. If a member lacks the knowledge and/or experience to complete such engagements with a high degree of professional competence, the member is not precluded from performing such engagements. In such instance, the member must take steps necessary to gain such expertise through additional research and/or consultation with other professionals believed to have such knowledge and/or experience prior to completion of such engagements.

3. DUE PROFESSIONAL CARE A member must exercise due professional care in the performance of services, including completing sufficient research and obtaining adequate documentation.

4. UNDERSTANDINGS AND COMMUNICATIONS WITH CLIENTS A member shall establish with the client a written or oral understanding of the nature, scope, and limitations of services to be performed and the responsibilities of the parties. If circumstances encountered during the engagement

require a significant change in these understandings, the member shall notify the client. A member shall inform the client of conflicts of interest, significant reservations concerning the scope or benefits of the engagement, and significant engagement findings or events.

E. PLANNING AND SUPERVISION A member shall adequately plan and supervise the performance of services.

F. SUFFICIENT RELEVANT DATA A member shall obtain sufficient relevant data to afford a reasonable basis for conclusions, recommendations, or positions.

G. CONFIDENTIALITY Unless required to do so by competent legal authority, a member shall not disclose any confidential client information to a third party without first obtaining the express consent of the client.

H. ACTS DISCREDITABLE A member shall not commit any act discreditable to the profession.

I. CLIENT INTEREST A member shall serve the client interest by seeking to accomplish the objectives established with the client, while maintaining integrity and objectivity.

J. FINANCIAL INTEREST A member shall not express a Conclusion of Value or a Calculated Value unless the member and the member's firm state either of the following:

"I (We) have no financial interest or contemplated financial interest in the subject of this report"; or

"I (We) have a (specify) financial interest or contemplated financial interest in the subject of this report."

Action points

* Realize it's what the seller keeps that matters.

* Valuation is as much art as science.

* Know the value ranges; they really do matter.

* Understand the different terms for cash flow. For example, it's suicide to use a multiple of profit on seller's discretionary earnings.

* Pay attention to the goodwill ratings and the non-financial factors.

* Know what's included in the deal. Is it just essential assets or are you getting cash, receivables, payables, etc.

* The myths of business valuation will crop up. Be ready for them.

* Use common sense.

* Understand it is very important to realize that growth matters. As a private equity group manager told me, "If we pay 7X (EBITDA) and the company grows like we want, it's a great deal. If we pay 4X and it doesn't grow it's a horrible deal."

~ 8 ~

LET'S COMPROMISE AND DO IT MY WAY

Let's keep in mind that for every seller it is of prime importance to remember (and this bears regular repeating), "It's not what you get; it's what you keep." Business buyers should always keep this in mind, as the seller's advisors will (eventually) bring up this subject. A price that is high but includes double taxation (C corp), depreciation recapture, ordinary income tax rates versus capital gains rates and similar is not a deal that stands a good chance of closing.

We've already covered the differences between a stock and asset transaction, so we won't cover that here. There are three basic components to every deal:

1. Price
2. Terms
3. Conditions

WHAT COMES FIRST?

When I ask audiences what are the top three factors to getting a deal done I get the usual answers of price, terms, down payment, etc. However, the top three factors have nothing to do with price, cash, terms or anything related to the structure of the deal. If the top factors are not present you won't get close to dealing with them anyway.

MOTIVATION

The key of keys, the reason of all reasons, and the basis for any deal happening is motivation. Without a motivated buyer and seller there will never be a deal. "Paying me three times what my business is worth" does not make a motivated seller. On a 1-10 scale with 10 being the highest motivation, getting paid a lot is a 1. A 10 is when the seller experiences one of the three D's of motivation: divorce, death or disability. Somewhere in between, usually when the seller is a 6to 9, is where deals get done. Typical reasons include burnout, retirement, boredom and stress because the business has grown beyond the owner's skill level. It could be they are now managing, not doing (the making of, selling or delivering their product of service), and they don't like managing.

Buyers have motivations also and it's not just, "I want to own a business." Their current job may be a big hurt in their life. They hate their boss, they have peaked on the corporate ladder or they face a transfer and uprooting of the family. Their motivation may be the lack of a job and poor prospects of finding one (that can pay them their worth). There may also be reasons why a particular business increases their motivation. It's called opportunity, like when a buyer bought a company because he saw how he could improve customer service, sales and the use of technology in that company. In two years his sales and profits doubled.

Strategic buyers (other companies in the same or a similar industry) have different motivations. As previously discussed, they may want to acquire a firm to build a bigger sales base to cover their overhead, to tap into new customers or to expand their product mix.

In any event, the smart buyer fans the flames of why the seller wants to sell. They ask questions that reinforce what the seller says they want to do. If the seller says they want to do a lot more fly-fishing post-sale, the buyer should, every so often, ask where they will fish, reinforce how much fun fishing is, etc. On the flip side, the savvy seller paints a picture of the buyer running the business, controlling their future and improving their lifestyle.

RELATIONSHIP

What I just described in the previous paragraph happens because of relationship. A buyer and seller must like, if not love, each other. Both are taking a big risk. The buyer is putting down a lot of money and the seller is getting a portion of the price paid over time. There had better be some mutual admiration, trust and respect.

This is something I preach to my clients (and suspect a few of them get sick of hearing it). And it's true. Every so often I will hear about a first meeting between buyer and seller where they spent 80% of the time talking about life, not the business. Life in this case could mean golf, fishing, business philosophy, family or just about anything. My reaction is that they are on the right track. It doesn't guarantee a deal (the business may not be any good or the buyer's skills don't qualify him or her to buy it) but it assures they will proceed.

The business buyer who sits down with the seller and says, "Show me the numbers" will struggle to buy a company. The buyer or seller who grills the other party right from the start will have a tough time doing a deal.

As a former client once said, which has been reinforced by many, "I would never buy from or sell to someone I don't like."

EDUCATION

Education means both parties must understand there is a process to follow (and they must follow it). It's tough for some (especially buyers) to go slowly and be methodical. They want to jump in headfirst, ASAP. The simple version of the process is relationship building, initial analysis, financing alternatives, deal structure and due diligence (by both sides).

Due diligence is the process of proving what has been previously stated. It is where the buyer wants to confirm or prove what they've been told. It is not a time for discovery or surprises. When buyers get into great detail before a deal is struck they can waste a lot of time and raise the suspicions of the seller (who doesn't want to disclose secrets without a deal). At the same time, the seller needs to check out the buyer, not just their financial statement.

Both parties also have to realize there is always some give and take or no deal will happen. They have to understand there is always buyer and seller remorse. And when they are inexperienced they tend to look at every little bump or request as a major deal disrupter.

We've covered pricing and valuation in Chapter Seven, and part of the educational process is for both parties to understand the basic parameters of where deals happen.

PRICE

In Chapter Seven we covered ranges of value and pricing and we've discussed Toby Tatum's studies and the influence cash can have on a deal.

One of the toughest parts of the business buying process is to get the seller to realize what a fair price (and terms) is. The first step is to ask. I always try to ask that question when I screen a business. Sometimes the owner has an answer, sometimes they don't and sometimes they won't admit it. No matter what, start the process of getting the seller's pricing thoughts out sooner versus later.

Whether he or she has a price in mind or not, realize that there's a good chance the owner read in the Wall Street Journal or a similar publication that a business in his or her industry sold for nine times EBITDA. No matter that it was a $400 million in sales company; they only remember the nine times multiple.

So, you have to do some educating and get these points across to him or her (and the following assumes a financial buyer who needs profit and cash flow).

1. The business must pay for itself out of its profits. It doesn't matter if the payments go to the seller, the bank or the buyer's savings account, the business must pay for itself.

2. The rough price range is 3-5 times profits (less for retail) after fair market management/owner salary.

3. Where the price falls in that range, or if it even makes it into that range, is determined by the non-financial factors such as employees, landlord, suppliers, customers, management team, competition, etc.

The sooner these points are made, the sooner you can get on to other matters like due diligence or pursuing other opportunities.

Let's say the owner says he or she has no idea what the price should be. You might say:

"I'm like most buyers in that I'm a financial buyer. That means I need a salary to live on and profits to pay for the business and build equity. Most buyers are looking for a rate of return of 20-35% on their investment. Appraisers agree with this range and done deal statistics support this. This means a buyer will want to pay 3-5 times profits, after a fair market owner salary, for a small business. The profits must cover the payments, whether they go to you, the bank or back into my savings account to provide me with a return on my investment.

"Where the price will be within that range, or if it even makes it into that range, is determined by the non-financial factors like customer relations, customer concentration, employee abilities and loyalty, the lease and more.

"Does this make sense?"

Caveats: if you are considering a retail business, use the range of 2-4 times profits (a 25-50% ROI). If you are looking at a larger business, adjust accordingly, as per the chart from the Rob Slee book. Keep in mind that Mr. Slee used EBITDA and I'm referring to net profit or free cash flow.

YOUR OFFER

The following, and perhaps more, should be in your offer or Letter of Intent (to purchase), also known as an LOI. There are two philosophies on LOIs. One is that they should be general and friendly, and that the details will be worked out and put in the Purchase and Sale Agreement (PSA). The other is that the LOI should be as definitive as possible, be written in more formal legal language and that there will be very little discussion on the way to the PSA. Both methods work. It depends on the buyer, seller, their relationship and how the respective attorneys like to handle this.

As you review the following, realize that if you're proceeding via the latter, more formal method, you'll be expanding the verbiage. For example, instead of simply saying you will have the opportunity to survey customers, you will get into detail about how you will do that (customer satisfaction survey or reference check), who will do it (you, an advisor, etc.) and when it will be done (after all other due diligence is done, at any time, etc.)

TERMS

Terms and conditions have a lot of crossover. What may be a term to one person is a condition to another. For example, you may think the non-compete agreement is a term of the deal. Another person in the same position may think it's a condition. Don't get hung up on this and realize there are a lot of interchangeable parts in these next two sections. It really doesn't matter what category these are in, as long as you cover what is necessary.

One of the areas of crossover between price and terms is the need to understand exactly what is being sold. It's wise for every buyer to ask the seller to list all the assets they don't plan on including in the deal and figure the buyer gets everything else. This could be a personal vehicle, office furnishings, the family heirloom desk, a laptop computer, etc.

It's also wise to discuss how much working capital will be left in the business. Sellers should have an understanding of what the adequate working capital needs are and buyers should confirm this with their own analysis.

Here's a list of common deal terms, with some comments on each.

How are you buying—is it going to be an asset or stock sale, or both? (See Chapter Five regarding a duel sale.)

Who is the buyer—is it you as an individual, your corporation, LLC or partnership? Often this is left as a variable by saying, "I, my LLC or corporation intend to buy the (assets or stock) of XYZ corporation under the following terms and conditions."

Down payment—an offer should specify how much cash the seller is to receive at closing. To a seller, it shouldn't matter if it comes from the bank or you.

Seller note(s)—common information here is the amount of the note, the terms, the interest rate, whether there's a prepayment penalty and, if there's a bank loan, that the note will be subordinated to the bank's loan (the bank will provide subordination language and make sure your attorney reviews it thoroughly and understands subordination agreements because some banks will try to put in very restrictive language). If it's an interest only loan for a specific time period, mention that. If there are seasonal variations in payments, mention them. Finally, what is the security to the seller? Usually it's a position on the businesses assets (behind the bank) and a personal guarantee.

What is being sold—more specifically, what is not being sold? Make sure this section is specific, to avoid future arguments.

Non-compete—often my clients leave this pretty general at this time and note that the attorneys will work out the specific language. They will include common wording (agreed upon in advance) that says something like, "Seller will not compete in the XXX industry or service customers anywhere within Y miles of the current location(s) for a period of Z years." Get your attorney's input on this as every state has different enforcement policies on non-competes. What a buyer is really interested in is a non-solicitation clause (the seller can't be selling similar products or services) in any market the business is active in. A seller of a business with all local customers in Washington who is moving to Florida may not be a threat if he or she starts a new business, assuming it's with local, relationship based customers. If the firm sells via the Internet, this should be covered, as no matter where a new business is, it's in competition.

Contract transfers—the sale must include the transfer of all contracts, on terms acceptable to the buyer.

Training—Specify the training to be provided and over what time. This may be considered together with transition support; it depends on the company and the deal. Realize that any money allocated to training in the asset allocation is ordinary income for the seller and deductible to the buyer in the year paid.

Transition support—most buyers assume they will need a lot more transition than they do. Most sellers want to be out of there in 30 days. For most small businesses a good starting point is 90 days, up to 30 hours per week, in-person, by phone and email, all at the buyer's discretion. Following that, add another 90 days for phone and email support. Rarely is this abused. In fact, most sellers want to make sure the buyer gets off to a good start.

REAL LIFE STORY: YOU DON'T NEED THE SELLER FOR TOO LONG

The buyer said he wanted the seller around for one year to provide transition support. I told him he wouldn't get that and wouldn't need it. We settled on 90 days and about one year later the buyer said, "You hit the nail squarely on the head on the transition issue. I was so glad on day 91 he wasn't coming in."

Closing date—an offer should include a tentative closing date and state that both parties will make a best effort to close by that date. Sometimes an attorney will add language that changes conditions if the closing isn't done by this date, but often both parties want the deal and don't worry about that.

Escrow—small, micro-business, deals often have escrow to keep the buyer from getting buyer remorse and bolting. I rarely see escrow on deals from $500,000 to $10 million. I was involved with one recently, which was a little more than $3 million, when the seller brought in an advisor who was used to working on $300,000 deals. He insisted on escrow and we agreed as long as the terms were very loose (not onerous to the buyer).

Asset values—if there are assets that could have fluctuating values, it's wise to peg them to the value on the balance sheet as of a specific date. Inventory should be usable and salable and valued at the lower of cost or market (which may be different from what is on the balance sheet, especially if there is a lot of old inventory and adjustments have not been made). For fixed assets, like machinery and vehicles, the actual value may not be very important. What is important is that the buyer understands the condition of the equipment and the replacements needed (and when they are needed). If working capital is included, it should be specified.

Work in progress—if there is work in progress, whether on the balance sheet or not, it needs to be pegged to a certain date. This may be called the sales pipeline in some situations. The buyer is buying an ongoing business with a pipeline of orders, jobs in progress, etc.

REAL LIFE STORY: THE SELLER NEEDS TO MAINTAIN THE STATUS QUO

The pipeline or work in progress is important. A seller sat in a meeting with the buyer and when asked about the pipeline of orders and current jobs, he told the buyer that it would be as full as possible. He said that when he bought the company the seller accelerated as many jobs as possible so they shipped before closing. This left the buyer with an empty pipeline, no accounts receivable and very tight working capital. He went on to say that he wouldn't do that to his buyer.

There are other items that occasionally need to be mentioned in your offer. They include insurance coverage, deferred revenue, work-in-progress, off balance sheet items, prepaid expenses and more, as the situation dictates.

CONDITIONS

Conditions are factors tied to the closing of the deal but usually aren't part of the compensation from the buyer to the seller and the value transferred from the seller to the buyer. Think of conditions as a checklist of things that have to be completed to get the deal done.

Ongoing confidentiality—this is self-explanatory; both parties need to share information only with professional advisors and other relevant deal participants.

Environmental—if land is part of the deal every buyer will be getting at least a Phase one environmental study done. If land is not part of the deal, but there could be repercussions, you'll want warranties and representations from the seller that they are responsible for any hazardous material cleanup, fines, etc. However, the biggest issue may be any disruption to the business, so make sure your attorney knows how to cover this in the agreement. Don't just think gas stations or printers. Any business with vehicles, heavy equipment or if the business simply services equipment with hydraulics or oil can have environmental issues.

Employees—it should be stated that the buyer will interview at least the management team and key employees before closing. This is usually the last item of due diligence and, as previously stated, if the seller won't allow this, walk away from the deal. Employment agreements, with key people, may also be a condition of closing; work with the seller and your attorney on this.

Customer interviews—make sure you have the right to blindly survey the customers to see what they think of the company. As with employees, if you aren't allowed to do this before closing, walk away.

Erosion clause—an erosion clause comes into play if there's extremely high customer concentration or even high industry concentration. It's covered more in the following chapters on due diligence and doesn't come up too often.

Financing—it's important to state that the closing is contingent on financing acceptable to the buyer (usually this means bank approval for the acquisition loan, but it could include other financing sources).

Advisor approval—make sure there is a clause that states your advisors must approve the due diligence. This goes both ways; the seller will want his or her advisors to approve due diligence on you.

Lease—you must be able to get a lease that is satisfactory to your lender and you.

No adverse change—the offer should state that there are to be no material adverse changes in the business. This could include customer relationships, vendors, key employees, the financial performance or something else.

Capital Expenditures—have a clause that states there are no anticipated capital expenditures or, if there are, it states what they are and when they will happen. If anything material arises, you need to be notified and made part of the decision.

Non-solicitation—the seller is not to solicit or talk to other buyers for at least 60 days.

Expenses—note that each party is responsible for their own advisors and other expenses. One exception to this is if an outside escrow attorney is used it is common to split that cost 50-50.

Non-binding versus binding—your offer will state that it is non-binding. However, work with your attorney because you want to make sure that the confidentiality clause and the non-solicitation clauses (and maybe others) are binding.

Changes—all changes need to be in writing.

Purchase and Sale Agreement—state that the PSA will cover all details not spelled out in the LOI.

PRESENTING YOUR OFFER

I'm a big believer in making offers in person. This is an emotional issue for all involved and it's much more personal and easier to get to any possible roadblocks when you're face-to-face. This doesn't mean the LOI is brought to a meeting, it means you sit down with the seller and discuss your offer, your rationale and reinforce why you want the company (and reinforce his or her hot buttons for selling).

I prefer to use a simple term sheet. My version is in Appendix XXX and is nothing more than a table in Word that covers the main issues (price, terms, working capital, assets, etc.). I also prefer that the meeting start with a blank form that you fill in as you go through the offer. When sellers have been very casual my clients and I have done it on a legal pad.

The goal is to have all parties comfortable. This is not large corporate M&A; it's a life-changing event for buyer and seller.

Once in agreement on the main points you will tell the seller that you will memorialize it in the form of an LOI (a written offer). This is where you want to make sure your attorney advises you on what you're submitting.

REAL LIFE STORY: MANAGE YOUR RISKS

It can pay to take a risk. Tom's seller was in a dispute with the firm that licensed the product they made. The seller, after many years of doing business, didn't see why he still had to pay the licensing fees. The owner of the patent didn't agree. Tom wasn't sure where it stood, but he knew the seller was bullheaded, the seller felt he was right and would win on any settlement. The seller offered to take the first $30,000 of risk and we countered by saying Tom would take the first $30,000. As the seller thought the licensing fees were unjust he went for this. What did Tom get? Emotionally, he got incredible peace of mind; he knew his downside. Financially, he came out at least $50,000 ahead because the back-licensing fees were at least $80,000.

NEGOTIATIONS

Any flow chart of the business buying process will have negotiations and other steps in the process listed in order. They have to be when in writing. In the real world all the steps (except search at the beginning and closing at the end) are mixed up and done concurrently.

You actually start negotiations with the first contact and definitely with the first meeting. Both sides are positioning and posturing. The first real occurrence of this is when your advisor or you ask the seller, "What do you think a fair price for your business is?" or, "Do you have a price in mind?"

In chapter three I told a story about a newsletter that questioned if business brokers should ask more than what they expect to actually get (the answer they gave was yes, to allow for negotiating). This newsletter also stated, emphatically, that asking too high a price will cause buyers not to be interested because they'll feel it's too far a gap between reality and the asking price.

REAL LIFE STORY: DON'T TRY TO LOW-BALL YOUR OFFER

It applies on the other end also. A buyer lost a deal he very much coveted because he low-balled an offer. He started at about $6 million; the deal was put on hold for some outside factors and when it got back on track the offer mysteriously dropped to about $5 million.

The rationale was that sales over the last few months weren't at the same pace as earlier in the year, even though the company always had dramatic differences in month-to-month sales because of spikes caused by irregular big orders. The seller took it as an affront and decided not to even discuss the offer with the buyer.

When informed that the seller said, "There's nothing to discuss" the buyer went ballistic and after calming down said that this was just a number from which to start negotiating. However, his tactic didn't work; he lost the deal.

It is a game and when playing the game you must pay attention to the little things and all the details. It's important that you create an understanding that when an agreement is reached negotiations are over. Too many sellers keep asking for more and more and more. Usually it's just naiveté about the process, but sometimes it's ego or simply needing to feel they got the best of the deal or got the last word in. That's why you have to pay attention to the details and get them in writing.

RELATIONSHIPS WILL PAY OFF

I stress relationships and joke that my clients get sick of hearing me talk about the power of the relationship between buyer and seller. In Chapter Two I told the story of Jim Bernard, who stated how he would never do a transaction with someone he didn't like.

During negotiations is when good relationships pay off. Rather than write theory about this I'm going to give you a dozen examples of how strong relationships sealed the deal and got more favorable terms.

1. Bill and the two sellers (business partners) hit it off like long lost friends. They joked, laughed and just had a good time

together. The reason for the sale was that sellers were burned out. Actually, they were fried and just going through the motions. They liked Bill so much that when they gave us their asking price we later looked at each other and asked ourselves, "What should we negotiate on? It sure won't be the price!"

2. The seller and Matt didn't seem like they would be natural friends, but Matt has a way of making everybody feel at ease and welcome. In this case he welcomed the seller's expertise and asked him a lot of questions about how things were done in the industry. As with most people, the seller loved talking about his business, how he had grown it and some of his secrets to success. Before we even had made an offer he took Matt to the office and introduced him to his management team as the next owner of the company (they already knew he was selling).

3. William was a very capable engineer and businessperson who had a laidback, easy-going style. The sellers (husband and wife) had started the business and grown it to the point that it was too big for them to manage (mainly because they were doers, not managers). They liked William so much that they offered to carry a larger note than what was in his offer. They told him they liked him, felt he was right for their business and they didn't know anywhere else they could get 5-6% on their money.

4. I was in a room with my client Bill, the two sellers (business partners) and the sellers' advisor. There already was a solid relationship and this meeting was setting it in concrete. It was probably the fifth meeting Bill had with the sellers and the third to discuss some of the loose ends before a deal was formalized. I hadn't said a word in at least an hour and neither had the sellers' advisor. He passed one of his business cards to me and on the back he had written, "Never get in the way of a deal in the process of happening." Final negotiations were easy because both sides knew it was a good fit. In

fact, the sellers financed a larger portion than expected and made no argument about the working capital requirements to be left in the company.

5. Ken's deal almost collapsed when the elderly owner said he didn't want Ken to take over a business whose sales had been declining every year. He cared that much about Ken. Ken was able to convince him that he had the right energy, skills and knowledge of the situation to make it work and showed him how he would do it. This was another case of not having to negotiate the price, as what was offered was more than fair. The deal closed, Ken was right and the firm grew almost immediately.

6. Tom's acquisition was a broker-listed business, and the broker and I had an excellent relationship. I knew a little about the business and told the broker that Tom was his buyer. Upon meeting Tom he agreed and the first meeting with the seller went fantastic. The broker then called me and said he would introduce the seller to a couple other buyers but would make sure none of them were a good match for the business (he needed to show he marketed the company). This is where it gets interesting. Tom and the seller went to a trade show around Labor Day and were scheduled to close October 31. About this time we noticed that sales were declining month-to-month, and further investigation showed the order pipeline almost empty. The seller said that he couldn't sell the business to Tom in this condition (Tom said to me that he couldn't buy it in this condition). The seller had been distracted by a start-up he was involved with and told Tom he knew what to do, to be patient and he'd get it back to where it was. He then hired Tom on a very lucrative consulting contract, just so he wouldn't lose Tom as his buyer. The deal closed a few months later.

7. The seller had two qualified buyer groups and he liked both of them. Both did a good job with the relationship building,

but one group talked a lot about growth while the other group focused on the downside. When it came time to make an offer the seller got what he expected; a full price offer from one and a deeply discounted offer from the other group, with other conditions that screamed, "We're scared." A good relationship isn't worth much if your strategy and offer is to be defensive. Sellers want to see optimism.

8. Bob was about 33 years old and passionate about owning a business. The sellers were in their 60s and their kids were not interested in the family business. They saw Bob as the "son" who would take over their legacy. It worked out well, as the price was fair, they offered 75% seller financing and later helped Bob finance some future growth and real estate purchases. I've found that younger buyers will appeal more to sellers in their 60s or 70s than to someone in their 40s. The older people see themselves in the buyer. If you're in your 30s, use this to your advantage.

9. Again the sellers were in their 60s, their son worked for the business but they knew he was not the logical buyer for the company. Kim is a true sales and marketing expert and knew how to build trust. He did so slowly, and as he did he found that this sleepy little company had a lot of potential. This was still another case of not having to negotiate on price. I don't think we negotiated on too much of anything. They loved Kim and the asking price reflected this.

10. In Mark's case it was knowing who to build a relationship with. I've only worked on a handful of deals for distressed companies in my 20 years as a Business Buyer Advocate (and for good reason; they are highly risky). Mark knew the industry, he knew the company and he knew the problem and how to fix it. We also realized that the key relationship was not with the seller but with the bank. The bank became Mark's biggest ally, and every time the seller hesitated on the deal the bank "encouraged" him to move it along and get it sold.

11. Dick also knew whom to build relationships with. First it was the seller and he did a great job of it. Second it was with the bank because he was buying a company in an industry in which he had no related experience. Third, it was with an industry veteran who counseled him during the acquisition process and after he owned the company. Relationships aren't just with the seller, they're with everybody and, when done right they pay off big.

12. Finally, let me say there is always someone you can build a relationship with; you just don't want to do it like this client of mine did. This story was relayed in full in Chapter Two. The buyer went too fast into asking about the owner's "secret sauce" and the company's trade secrets. He luckily found a seller who also didn't care too much for relationships, but it took him way too long and we burned through way too many good businesses.

WIN-WIN DEALS

If you are in contentious negotiations, as we see in union-company situations or with sports stars and their teams, then you won't have a deal. That doesn't mean there won't be disagreements; they just can't be major. This is also where an intermediary earns their fee. If I, or others, can keep a deal on track with no bad blood between buyer and seller (usually over minutia) we've done our job.

In example four above, we can see that it's wise to not interrupt a deal waiting to happen. The bottom line was that the sellers were smart. They were taking a substantial note against the purchase price and were going to be active in the business for a while. They told their attorney they looked at it not so much as a sale but as getting a partner (albeit one who owes them a lot of money).

This gets emotional. Don't forget that. And it's emotional on both sides. You are making what is probably the largest investment of your life. The seller is parting with his or her "baby" and taking a note for part of the deal (hoping and praying that you'll pay).

Real Life Story: Emotional issues top the charts

A few logistical speed bumps came up in one deal. Nothing serious, just some procedural matters—the primary one being that the seller greatly feared the buyer backing out after the employees knew the business was being sold, and he wanted protection.

My client, the buyer, sent me a copy of an email he was going to send to the seller. It all made sense; it was very logical. However, I pointed out that because it was logical, it didn't address the seller's emotional needs. A simple change and agreement to a protection mechanism for the seller solved the potential problem.

So what is a win-win deal? Is it when both sides are equally happy? Is it when both sides are happy but also equally unhappy (feeling they gave away more than the other side)? In many deals I've had conversations with the buyer and seller and both tell me they are giving, giving and giving some more but the other side isn't giving anything.

Buyers look for a deal that has potential and adequate debt coverage. Sellers look for how much they'll keep after tax, the continuation of their company and how their employees and customers will be taken care of.

Ed's deal is a fitting summary of a win-win deal. The seller's asking price was at the high end of the fair range and the assets were fully depreciated. When the seller had bought the company the non-compete agreement was about 15% of the total price, so he expected it would be 15% on this deal also. Ed's offer did the following:

1. Gave the seller a price less than the asking price

2. Agreed to not mark up the asset values to fair market (no depreciation recapture at ordinary income rates for the seller)

3. Made the non-compete agreement a very reasonable amount ($50-75,000), not 15%, which would have been about $500,000 (non-competes are taxable as ordinary income to the seller)

4. Kept adequate working capital in the business

The seller was able to get a lower price but keep more. The buyer gave up a little in re-depreciation of the assets and most importantly, he got a deal.

In closing on negotiations, negotiations start once you meet the seller, they don't end until you've signed the agreements and if there's a solid relationship they go smoothly. You don't want your negotiations to be a made-for-TV movie or a case study on hardnosed negotiating tactics.

ACTION POINTS

* Test the seller's motivation and keep his or her motivation high.

* Develop and nurture a strong relationship with the seller.

* Be patient.

* Understand the parameters of pricing.

* Know what you are buying.

* Be specific on key points.

* Cover all possible contingencies.

* Present your offer in-person.

* Leverage your relationship with the seller.

* Ensure that, in the big picture, it's a win-win deal.

$-9-$

ARE YOU GOING TO BELIEVE ME OR YOUR LYING EYES?

Buyers get excited when they see areas in a company where they can add value. You will uncover areas you and your team can add value to as you prepare for a future exit. Business buyers, of all types and sizes, are an inquisitive lot (and should be). There's an old saying, "When I ask you what time it is, don't tell me how to build the watch." Buyers are the opposite; they want to know how to build the watch. They want to know about all the little things that make the business what it is and worth buying at a price the seller finds acceptable. In other words, buyers want to know about all of the things that give it a competitive advantage.

We are going to cover a more detailed examination of the non-financial factors, including:

1. General company strategy, operations and condition

2. Employees and management

3. Essential factors—customers and vendors

4. Not-as-essential factors—landlord, financing, advisors, technology

5. Sales and marketing

The above are the heart and soul of any business. Financial statements show where your company was at a particular time in history. The non-financial factors paint a picture of where the company's going, whether there's a good chance projections will be met and what the risks lurking under the surface of the financial statements are.

THE OWNERS

If there are multiple owners, find that out early in the process. Make sure that all the owners are onboard with the plan to sell the company. In Chapter Three I discussed the reasons why owners sell. A seller needs to be able to articulate this reason, especially if they don't have health reasons, aren't of retirement age or don't have another reason that automatically makes sense to you. Understand that if you don't buy 100% of the company you won't qualify for an SBA loan.

Also, what do you want the owner to do post-sale? Realize there is normally a transition period that he or she provides as part of the purchase of your goodwill. This is normally 60 days to six months, depending on the nature and complexity of the business. After transition, do you want the seller to be a consultant, an employee or an independent sales rep? Would this be full-time or part-time? Do you want him or her to walk away and not be involved (this is the most common)?

Ask if there are any other business interests that the seller is involved with, especially if they relate to this company. This could be another business that shares expenses, uses employees or shares facilities. This could also be partial ownership in a customer or vendor business (rare, but it happens).

THE BUSINESS

A seller should feel that the more inquisitive the buyer, the better (especially once there is a signed letter of intent outlining price and terms). The best buyers, who became the best owners, are those who were inquisitive and wanted to understand the intricacies of what makes the business what it is.

Does the seller have a good answer, when asked what the nature of their business is? On the surface, the company may make, sell or service widgets. But those widgets solve a problem for somebody. They may be a vital component to an automobile, airplane, furnace or myriad of other things. It doesn't matter if what the firm does helps another business make their product better or if it sells to the end user who eats it, wears it, rides it, cooks with it, etc. You want to know why what they do is important.

Get the seller to go into detail about the main products or services (I will use the term product to cover product, service or a combination of the two). As you cover the potential for each product, don't be afraid to discuss the risks certain lines may face. Here's a start:

- Why do your customers buy?

- How does your product work?

- Why do you get the margins you get?

- How do you see the future unfolding?

You will buy a company because you like the direction of the business. History is important (and is the basis for the business's value), and yet a great history without a bright future means an unsalable business (or salable at a fire sale price). Imagine being in the year 2000 and hearing about a company's great success in selling floppy discs (as computers starting phasing out floppy disc drives).

The ability to grow a product line is important. Is there an in-house engineering or creative department? Is it market driven? Will new products come from acquiring another company? It's not just the answers that are important, it is also the fact that the owner has done his or her homework and has a handle on the strategies required.

Also ask about any limitations. This could be license agreements, copyrights, patents, tariffs or royalties (due the owner of certain intellectual property). Get a handle on the issue and the solution.

Every company has intellectual property, although we tend to think of it in terms of things like patents, software code and the like. A basic machine shop has a way of doing things that pleases their customers. So does an auto repair facility, a nursing home and a restaurant. My point is that every business has intangibles, whether copyrighted or patented or not, and that is part of their competitive advantage.

Your structure

The purpose of an org chart is to show responsibilities and relationships. This chart should show all the departments of a company. Not just for now but for where you want it to grow. For example, the following simple example shows a company with three basic divisions under the owner. I've not added levels under operations or finance and administration, but there definitely would be structures there also.

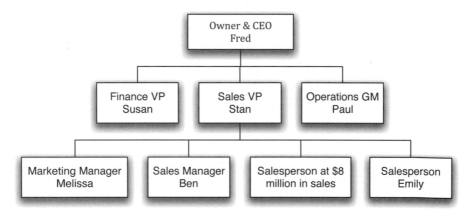

The above example is simplistic. Rather than detail everybody in this sample firm I want to make the point that as you plan you will have positions that are unfilled. In this example, the company is projecting they will need another salesperson when sales hit $8 million annually (which is called planning).

A long time ago I read that a good strategy for an org chart is to have a box for everything that gets done in the business. If you have 20 employees and 35 tasks (boxes on the chart) it's okay. Some people will be in multiple boxes. The smaller the business is the more likelihood of this. In fact, with a young and growing company, the owner's name will be in a lot of boxes. Your job, whether you have five or 50 employees, is to remove your name from as many boxes as possible. This adds great value to your firm.

On the flip side, are there any positions that could be combined or eliminated? Sometimes as a company grows they are able to hire more capable employees and managers and, for example, three highly qualified people may be able to get the results it previously took four, less qualified people, to achieve.

Does the company have woman-minority status? If the seller is male, is the company in his wife's name to get the woman-minority status? This may be an issue when selling if you can't maintain this status, which gives the firm an advantage.

THE COMPANY AND ITS POLICIES

People—This has to do with requirements, not capabilities. While not a pressing issue, you will want to know if there is a human resources policy and if the company is current on all regulatory matters for its size. An employee policies and procedures manual is something all firms should have (to varying degrees of detail, based on size).

Have they articulated a vacation and sick pay policy? Are these policies competitive or rich? Do they allow carryover of vacation from year to year? (Remember the example in the previous chapter where it cost the seller $100,000 to pay off all the accrued vacation time.) If it's a union shop, what are the advantages of being union (many buyers have non-union as one of their top criteria)?

Who does what—Technically, this is part of human resources. There should be job descriptions for each employee, employee bios and performance reviews. You will want to know if the current employees and management are capable of driving future growth.

Benefits—We don't know what our politicians are going to do. They have changed the rules on pensions and benefit plans numerous times, so check to see if the firm has a reasonable benefit plan that is ERISA compliant. Is there a retirement plan and if not, why not?

One issue that can become sticky is an annual bonus program. Sellers look at bonus plans as optional compensation. Once given, and continued from year to year, employees consider it part of their expected compensation. I've heard sellers say that the annual bonus is really profit (on which to base the price), because the bonuses don't have to be given.

Pretend you are working at the company. Would you want one of the buyer's first decisions to be not paying the annual bonus?

Insurance—Compile a list of all the insurance coverages, which are mandated, the agents, the annual cost of each and the last time the policies were reviewed. Insurance needs are constantly changing. Disaster planning is coming into vogue and part of it involves insurance.

Intellectual property and related—Make sure all the trademarks, copyrights and similar are properly registered and displayed. If the firm has or grants any license agreements, make sure they are in order and current. The same goes for any incoming or outgoing royalties.

REAL LIFE STORY: PLAY FAIR OR IT HURTS

The company made parts based on Boeing designs, and their license agreement required them to pay Boeing a small percentage of all sales as a royalty. A buyer got a very good deal because the seller was not in compliance on the license agreement, meaning he was overdue on the royalty payments and their accounting for the royalties was so poor that Boeing suspected fraud. Boeing strongly encouraged the transaction because they knew he would be in compliance.

Accounts and assets—Get a list of all assets that require titles, have liens, etc. Also have a list of all accounts that will need to be changed. This includes, but is not limited to, utilities, Internet hosting, cell phones, janitorial, copier, FedEx and the Post Office.

If there are any off balance sheet items such as copier leases, yellow page advertising or any vehicle or equipment leases, get that information sooner not later.

Government regulations—If you even think the company needs licenses, permits or has a hazardous material issue, make sure they are compliant. Does the government require at least one employee to have a certification? For example, in Washington State, any company providing low or high voltage electrical services must have a licensed administrator on the payroll.

Recordkeeping—Are there any recordkeeping systems besides what's in accounting? This could be for personnel, production, quality assurance, complaints or tracking marketing efforts. How is this documented? How often do they produce these reports (and the financial statements)? Is it timely information that provides value?

Litigation—Has the business ever been involved in a lawsuit? If so, what was the nature and outcome of each major case? Get a description of any legal action that might be threatened or pending against the company.

Capital expenditures—Often there is a focus on depreciation and the use of the pure accounting definition that states that depreciation a non-cash item that adds to annual cash flow. More important, much more important, is to know what amount of annual capital spending is required to allow the business to remain competitive. With ever-changing tax laws, this is the number you should focus on—not what was written off or when it was written off, but what you will need to spend your first year or two.

EMERGENCY PLANNING

The chances of small businesses—fewer than 20 employees for sure—having any kind of disaster plan or emergency planning mechanisms are slim to none. Now, this is not something that should slow up a deal, because most small businesses never face this situation. However, if you find that the company has done something in this area, it's a sign of forethought and adds another weight to the positive side of the "should I or shouldn't I buy this business" balance scale.

This is not my field, so here's a guest article from my friend Dan Weedin on the subject.

MANAGING THE GAME:
DISASTER PLANNING FOR SMALL BUSINESS

By Dan Weedin, CIC, CRM

I coached high school basketball for six years. One thing I can tell you is that the hardest part of the entire job is game management.

The game is very fast-paced with big momentum swings, snap decisions, consequences from your players the other team, and the officials. Fans have an agenda as they sit in the stands hollering at you, the kids, and the referees. And through all the chaos, the head coach must remain calm, clear thinking, and visionary.

You don't have to be a high school basketball coach to deal with "game management." As a small business owner or executive, you have to manage your own game on a daily basis. The similarities are endless...

1. **The coach**. That's you. The buck stops with you. You have to anticipate crisis, react and respond, and amid chaos, make decisions that impact you, your company, your employees, their families, and your supply chain. No pressure.

2. **The players**. Those are your employees. Employees bring human emotions, baggage, talents, and challenges to the "game."

3. **The officials**. You may have regulatory agencies that keep tabs on you. The consequences of being out of compliance are costly, especially if a disaster occurs.

4. **The Fans**. You have key stakeholders in your business, just like coaches do in the stands. Your supply chain includes customers, prospects, vendors, suppliers, investors, and employee families. They are sitting in "the stands" watching your every move with their own personal agendas.

"Disaster" and "crisis" occur many times in a basketball game. A coach needs to be prepared, and must prepare his or her players to respond under pressure. In the same way, as a small business owner you will encounter crisis every year. In many cases, it's not a fire or flooded server room. It might be losing a key employee, a downturn in the economy, an injured employee, or damage to your reputation from someone Tweeting!

Any coach worth his salt prepares for crisis. The same is true for any small business owner, entrepreneur, or executive. Allow me to give you my three-point play for managing your game…

POINT 1 – KNOW YOUR VULNERABILITIES

If I'm a poor shooting team, I know that having a bad shooting night is a possibility and could lose me a game. My response to that is being a great defensive team to keep me in the game as long as possible. What are your vulnerabilities?

If you're in the contracting business, it's employees being injured on the job site. If you're a hospital, you're concerned about disease control. If you're a professional service provider, you are vulnerable to poor quality work and service. If you own any business, cyber liability is the new menace that you should be scared of. Regardless of what industry you're in, you have vulnerabilities to disaster. In my experience, small business owners do a poor job of identifying their risks. Here's how you fix that…

Take two hours one day and reserve it for a vulnerability analysis. Bring in key team members and discuss those areas of concern for each department. Ask these questions…

1. What can disrupt or suspend our operations?

2. What can damage our reputation?

3. What keeps me up at night?

Brainstorm a list and then triage them. Put the bleeders (life and death) at the top and put the sprained ankles (annoyances) on the bottom. Make sure you get a critical mass of input. You want this list to be deep and wide. This isn't a time to be shy. In order to properly prepare and be ready to respond, you must be aware.

POINT 2 – IMPLEMENT A COMMUNICATION PLAN

My communication plan as a coach was varied. I used hand signals with my point guard to relay messages. I used code words that were unique to our team. And, in times of momentum swings, I used time outs to get everyone on the same page.

The majority of small businesses do not have an effective communication plan. I know this because I've dealt with hundreds and very few have any protocol or process written down, and even if they do it's not communicated to all employees (ironic, huh).

A well thought out and implemented communication plan is crucial to disaster response. Without it, nobody knows who is in charge (what if you're gone when the disaster strikes); what to do; where to go; or how to respond in the best interest of everyone. The consequences are that it exacerbates the original disaster and turns it into a bigger crisis. Here's how to fix that...

1. Write out a crisis response plan. Take what you learned from the vulnerability analysis and write out how you want your team to respond in case it happens. *Most disasters don't require a different response!* If you put together a process, any disaster will be fall into it. Consider it a "plug and play" format.

2. Get help. Ask trusted advisors like attorneys, CPAs, insurance agents, and consultants to review it and add their ideas.

3. Then by all means – COMMUNICATE it with your employees. Have them sign off that they read it. Make it accessible so if there is a disaster, they don't have to search for the plan. This ends up being the most critical step in this process.

POINT 3 – PRACTICE, PRACTICE, PRACTICE

Every day, I ran a drill called "situations." I created end of game situations and we ran through them. We may not ever encounter that specific situation; however if we did we knew what to do. And, most importantly we trained our brains to think clearly and respond to any situation.

This is your fire drill. Find your most critical vulnerabilities—your bleeders—and practice how you respond. I run Corporate War Games and Table Top exercises for my clients to simulate situations. The only way you know if your plan works, if your insurance works, and if your team works is to test them under a simulated fire. You don't want to have them "practice" when it really counts. Mistakes made there can be devastating. Make them in practice so you can learn, adjust, and perfect.

FINAL THOUGHT

No world-class athlete of any sport is without at least one coach. Most have multiple coaches. The very best business people in their fields have executive coaches and mentors. What about you? Your plate is already pretty full with what you do on a daily basis. Trying to understand risk, crisis, and opportunities that arise out of them is challenging without help. Find a professional to help you through the process. It might be your agent or broker, or it might be a consultant. Regardless, trying to win this game on your own might have terrible consequences, because you didn't know what you were doing. Great coaches employ great coaches to guide them. You should, too.

Managing your business risk is like managing a basketball game. You have to be savvy and cool under pressure. You must display confidence and trust. And, you need to be ready and prepared to respond to anything.

Are you ready to play ball?

© 2012 Dan Weedin. All Rights Reserved
Dan Weedin, CIC CRM is a Seattle-based insurance and risk management consultant who turns his clients risk into rewards. He helps his clients save money, time, and frustration on their business insurance. He doesn't sell insurance, nor does he ever accept fees or commissions from agents or insurers. He's an advocate for his clients and helps them make smarter decisions on risk. He also facilitates testing on crisis resiliency through Corporate War Games and Table Top Exercises.

To learn more about Dan and how he dramatically improves his client's condition, visit his web site at www.DanWeedin.com. You can also reach him by phone at (360) 271-1592 or by e-mail at dan@ danweedin.com.

CUSTOMERS AND VENDORS

There is no better place to concentrate your investigative efforts than with customers, one reason being that what you find out here spills over and makes the employees look good (or not good) and productive, and can increase margins and create a partnership (with the customers) that will impress buyers.

REAL LIFE STORY: INGRAIN YOURSELF INTO YOUR CUSTOMERS' BUSINESS

Creating a partnership with your customers can be huge. It can be important but shouldn't become dominating. Mark had what I called a symbiotic relationship with his top customer. This customer accounted for 50% or more of his sales, and at the same time, Mark's company was the only company that could make the key components for this customer's end product.

This was definitely a good news—bad news situation. They needed each other and were truly strategic partners.

YOUR CUSTOMERS

When asked, "Who are your customers?" what is the seller's answer? Is the answer that we sell to the aerospace industry, the pharmaceutical industry, female's age 30-70 or similar? Or do you give company names, like we sell to Boeing, Chevron, Costco or Honeywell?

As a small business, they may sell to huge companies. However, in reality they sell to a division or department of those large companies, and do so because the company solves a problem for them. Drilling down further, they sell to people in those departments. The company can make the part the customer needs cheaper than they can internally or can provide the service more efficiently than they can, without distracting them from their core business. When anybody, including your seller or you post-sale, asks about customers, the answer should be focused like this:

"We sell to (fill in an industry or company) because we help them (fill in the actual problem)."

So, who are the firm's customers and what are the trends in this customer group? Why do they buy from this company at a price that allows you to make a profit (this is the competitive advantage)? The answers to these questions are as important as the answer to the question, "Why are you selling?"

REAL LIFE STORY: HUGE RED FLAG: "YOU CAN'T TALK TO THE CUSTOMERS"

The buyer will remain nameless for obvious reasons. We were one month away from closing, due diligence, financing and the legal work was all proceeding nicely when it came time to talk to the company's customers (we proposed a customer satisfaction survey done by the buyer and me).

The owners (husband and wife) said, "Absolutely not." She told the buyer that it was a competitive industry, the relationships were so important that they had to be handled post-sale and any whiff of a change might spook some of the customers. These reasons by themselves should have given the buyer concern.

The seller's advisors understood the buyer's position, that he needed to talk to the customers, but couldn't convince the seller to change. The buyer's attorney and I both told him to put the deal on hold until he could talk to the customers. Our client said no and that he really trusted the seller on this, so all would be okay.

The post-mortem was that the sellers had a lot to fear. The number one customer, about 20% of annual sales, was extremely unhappy with the company. They had been loyal customers for years and felt that, because of the high cost of converting to a competitor's product, the company was gouging them on every little thing (treating them like a money faucet, not like a partner).

At the time of due diligence and the sale this customer had their board-room set up as a "test kitchen" with all of the competitor's products being tested, doing trial runs, etc. They did not include their current provider's products in this test. They wanted a divorce. (The seller didn't know about the "test kitchen" but did know the customer was furious with them.)

Losing 20% of your business has a major impact, and it caused buyer and seller time and legal fees and led to a restructuring of the deal. I mention elsewhere that some seller's will take as much cash as possible because of something they know. It's rare; in almost 20 years I've only had two or three clients find out about something deceptive like this. These sellers knew that if a buyer talked to the customer the deal was either dead or the price would severely drop. And, once it was out that the customer was unhappy, it would have to be disclosed to future buyers, and when the customer left the value of the business would be cut in half.

Why do your customers buy from you? What are their top considerations?

- Price
- Quality
- Service
- Availability
- Sales
- Engineering
- Credit term
- Right of return
- Technology

EXAMPLE & APPLICATION:

There's an old business adage that says: "We can offer the best in price, quality or service. Take two of the three. It's impossible to offer all three and stay in business." It's true, if customers (or you with your suppliers) want the best quality and the best service you have to pay for it.

Many years ago we took our kids to Venice Beach while in the Los Angeles area for a baseball tournament. Everybody got tee shirts—cheap tee shirts (like three for $10). After a handful of times through the wash machine we found out why they were so cheap. You get what you pay for.

CUSTOMER CONCENTRATION

Business is constantly moving and changing. A previous example explained how one company's top customer was always too high a percentage of sales, but it was never the same top customer. Concentration is where all customer due diligence will start. Every buyer will want to know this, and fairly soon in the process.

Once you have a signed non-disclosure agreement, ask for a customer list. It's okay if the list, showing annual sales volumes, is *without* the customer names. You'll get a list of customers with names after you have signed a letter of intent, with an agreed upon price and terms.

What are the red flags? Any customer over 10% is considered a red flag. In some cases it could be 5%, especially if there is industry concentration (more on this shortly). Statistics from RMA, the IRS and an old article in Inc. Magazine state that the average profit for small businesses is 7-10%. Lose a customer that is 12% of your business, and assuming you have a 50% gross profit margin, that 7-10% bottom line just turned into 1-4%. The seller may easily survive and bring it back, but what about you, with acquisition debt payments? You're now in a negative cash flow position, the bank is worried and their risk just multiplied.

What should you do if there is high customer concentration? Ask for some type of erosion clause. In simple terms, an erosion clause will state that if certain (named) customers stop doing business with the company with no-fault to the buyer (for example, the customer is purchased and the acquiring company has their own trusted supplier), that the price is reduced, payments to you are delayed or some other action based on your exact situation.

A seller will be thinking about how hard it could be to prove that losing a customer was not because of the buyer's actions, and this is a very legitimate thought. The seller can respond in one of three ways to this:

1. Get yourself out of this situation by reducing your customer concentration.

2. If you think the buyer can't handle the business and its customer relationships, then don't sell to that particular buyer.

3. Put in monitoring clauses for you to be actively checking on the business and its customer relationships.

REAL LIFE STORY: HIGH CUSTOMER CONCENTRATION CAN DEVASTATE YOUR COMPANY

I received a call from a desperate owner and I wish I could have helped him. His firm, doing about $10 million in annual sales, needed an investment ASAP, as they were about to close their doors. He was a specialty sub-contractor in the health food and supplement industry, with one customer accounting for about 60% of annual sales.

The two companies had grown together. He told me the customer started with him and did $100,000 of business their first year. He felt a certain loyalty to them and thought it was reciprocal. It was reciprocal until the customer hired a new CEO who had a friend with a competing manufacturing operation. They changed vendors almost immediately, leading to this owner's desperation.

One area often overlooked is industry concentration. While not as important as customer diversification, it is wise to sell into numerous and as diverse as possible industries. Industries can have wild swings. We all saw this with construction starting in 2008, and it surprised a lot of people.

I worked on two deals in 2006 that were related to commercial construction. All research, done by buyers and sellers, indicated that commercial construction in Seattle would be strong for at least five years. We all know what happened. If you can show industry diversification, and how you achieved it, the perception of your business's quality will improve.

REAL LIFE STORY: INDUSTRY CONCENTRATION CAN ALSO HURT YOU

Dave's purchase and sale agreement had an erosion clause for a top customer that was too high a percentage of annual sales. He asked for, and eventually got, a clause that said if this top customer went away or reduced their purchases by a certain amount the deal changed.

What wasn't present was anything regarding the industry concentration. There was a super high industry concentration, with two industries accounting for almost 80% of his sales. When the Great Recession hit in 2008, both of these industries collapsed (something that had never happened before). The erosion clause took effect, and helped Dave a lot, but he was still hurt because of the industry concentration issue.

Again, the best way to avoid an industry erosion clause, or even the thought of it, is for the seller to diversify the industry base and for you to do the same ASAP post-sale.

CUSTOMER SATISFACTION

Have any major customers left over the last two years? If so, why did they leave? Are you satisfied with this answer?

Why do customers leave? If they leave over price it will require different actions than if it's over service, overall value or a poor relationship. Most business-to-business sales are relationship based. The salesperson creates a bond with the customer that you hope makes it a partnership to solve the customers problems. Here is a three-step process for internal customer due diligence.

1. Have the salespeople, including the owner, rank, on a 1-10 scale with one being horrible and 10 being fantastic, how they feel about their relationships with every customer they work with (or every repeat customer or customer with annual volume over a certain amount). Then have them rank, on the same scale, how they feel the company's relationship is with all the other customers (those the other salespeople service)

   Realize that, unless you have specific insights into customer relationships, you should probably discount each rank by one or two points. It's just human nature to think relationships are better than they are.

   Next, have each salesperson describe, in writing, their general perception of each major customer's satisfaction with your firm, its products, service and value. Do they know of any customers putting your business "out to bid?" Are any planning to leave?

2. Ask for one to three instances where the company really came through for a customer (and especially when the customer let you know it). Stories tell the truth, and you should like nothing more than to hear success stories

   At the same time, ask about a time they let a customer down (hopefully this is a short list). Note how they handled it, especially if they went beyond a warranty. Hearing that they never let a customer down or had product, service or relationship problems does not sound plausible.

3. Finally, conduct a customer satisfaction survey. I always assist buyer clients on this (and when they do it they use my company name for creditability). You may have a specific area of interest based on what you do that will supplement the usual topics. I concentrate on:

   • Product

   • Service

   • Support

   • Delivery

- Timeliness
- Admin (billing and ordering)
- Employees

I ask the customer to rank each category on a 1-10 scale and then follow up by asking what the company can do better, whether there are any other services they would like to see offered and if there is anything upcoming that will cause them to not do business at the same level or greater. We can add to this the categories from above on why customers buy from the company. We can ask for the top three reasons they do business with the firm. The bottom line is that we want to know where the company shines and if there are any areas where they don't shine (as much as everybody would like to).

The suggestions can be very insightful, although I must say that when doing this for mature, profitable companies it is rare to get rankings below a seven or to hear anything bad. Taking care of customers is something you'd expect profitable companies to do well. Often the greatest value is when customers mention other areas in which they'd like to do business with the company. I recall one case where the customer, after saying what a great company it was (my client's company), told me, "I'm giving them a low score in the service area." I asked why and the response was, "The last time their guy was out here he was 15 minutes late." That sounds like a pretty good review to me.

REAL LIFE STORY: CUSTOMER CONTACT IS THE KEY

Kyle's acquisition was a decades old company, with an elderly owner, that was coasting. He brought in an old friend to head up his marketing efforts and six months after closing I was talking to him and asked how the marketing was going. His response was, "It's amazing what happens when you actually pick up the phone and call your customers."

This is the kind of opportunity buyers are looking for. Kyle paid less for the business than he would have if the seller had not been just taking orders (versus reaching out and helping his customers).

Sales process

Buyers are often only mildly interested in the sales process (mildly compared to their interest in concentration, satisfaction, etc.). Often this comes down to the fit between buyer and seller. If it's a sales organization and the owner needs to understand sales, sales management and motivation, they are probably not going to sell to an industrial engineer. Or, if they sell via inside salespeople and you want an outside-sales-based model it might not be a good fit.

More important is the selling process, sales cycle and closing ratio. The latter is often the most important. We previously discussed management reports. The sales department is a natural place to make sure there is a good reporting system.

The life insurance industry started a tracking system in the first half of the 20th century. That model can be carried over to many other industries. They determined that successful agents needed to meet people, fact find, open cases, close and get referrals. Points were assigned to each and a certain minimum number of points per week led to being successful.

I used a similar system when helping our "Partner" On-Call Network franchisees and licensees get started, because in all businesses it comes down to the same thing—you have to have people entering your sales system, expressing interest and being asked to buy. Once in the system it is important to know the success or closing ratio (and how to improve it).

For a client selling commercial furnishings we created a reporting system that tracked activity based on how the prospective customer was generated. Their model included call-ins, referrals, repeat business and bids. Bids are a different animal than the others so we had different tracking and reporting systems. Here's the basic model of what we did to help the sales manager (who, like in many small businesses, was a great salesperson, the most qualified to be sales manager but not experienced or skilled in management).

1. Track prospects into the system (call-in, referral, repeat)

2. Count prospects who agreed to meet (after calling in)

3. Identify those who had a legitimate need and requested a proposal or bid

4. Accept bids

5. Successfully close

One final comment on this subject: if the company has contracts with its customers, make sure they stay in force after the sale. This can be a sticky issue, and could affect the structure of the sale (asset versus stock), and that could affect what you are willing to pay.

WHO DOES THE SELLING?

A sales consultant recently shared with me that his clients are scared when one or two top salespeople control the vast majority of the company's relationships and sales. Salesperson concentration can be almost as large an issue as customer concentration. This is a dependency and one that, if present, needs to be fixed.

As a business buyer, you know that if those customer relationships are with the seller (versus the sales staff) the relationship will be gone in 90 days. At least with the salespeople you know they will want to keep their jobs and hope you inject a spark of enthusiasm to grow the company (and their compensation).

When the owner controls and has tight relationships with the customers, they have created personal goodwill. You want the customers thinking of the company first, not any individual, as this creates company goodwill, which is much easier to transfer.

VENDORS

The seller is in the middle, between your vendors and your customers. While customers are the most important part of any business (along with employees), the importance and relationship with vendors is not far behind. Earlier I shared a story about a former client whom lost two top vendors, years apart. In both cases it put his income and business at risk.

What is the relationship with the vendors? Is it a partnership, or is the firm just a customer they sell to? At some point, before any deal closes, the seller will have to introduce you to the vendors, if for no other reason than that the vendor may want to approve credit. Is the seller confident enough in his or her vendor relationships to pick up the phone today, call the vendors and introduce you (or even to discuss sensitive supply issues)? If not, you need to find out why they have a hard time making that call.

How in tune with the vendors' situation is the seller? (One could easily flip this around and ask if the seller's customers are in tune with his or her situation.) Does the seller communicate with the vendor about any lines that might be discontinued, material pricing issues, any product changes they foresee and any changes to the way they do business?

Real Life Story: Supplier concentration can be a killer

John owns an import based distribution business. The company's primary vendor is in Asia and supplies 80% of their product. Due to the nature of their product, lead times and shipping, it typically takes three months from placing the order to delivery. In addition, John's business is very seasonal.

I'm sure you can see the risks here. A production delay, shipping problem or incorrect ordering could devastate this business. John has 20 plus years of industry experience and understands his model very well. A buyer might not be so comfortable.

Pragmatic vendor issues

How are prices set? Are they negotiated or off a price list? Are there quantity discounts that make it worthwhile to have high vendor concentration or should you pay a little more to have multiple suppliers? What's the right answer to one business may not be the right answer to another.

What about your credit terms? More importantly, what about the credit terms a new owner might get? If the seller is taking a discount for paying immediately, will you also be able to get the discount? Given your acquisition debt payments, these are important issues. The tighter the relationship with the vendors the better the terms you, the buyer, will receive.

Real Life Story: Don't let credit terms bite you

Desperation was in the tone of the voice on the other end of the phone call. Doug was less than a week from closing on an acquisition when he found out that the seller had no credit with his suppliers; he paid everything COD. Doug's cash flow model assumed he had an average of 30 days to pay his bills.

Was this sloppy due diligence? Of course it was. Doug was my client, so I simply asked him what the seller told him when he asked question 32 on the due diligence questionnaire (which was about credit terms). After hemming and hawing he admitted he hadn't asked it. This is what happens when a buyer gets buyer fever. They ignore common sense and don't want to ask all the questions they should ask.

Doug's sloppiness almost derailed his deal. After all the time and effort both sides put into this, not to mention the expense, it would have been devastating for the deal to collapse because of this, to both buyer and seller.

The company should have a choice of vendors, with competitive products and prices. This is the ideal situation. However, at all sizes of companies it is often a bottleneck, or dependency. Consider the 2011 Japan earthquake and tsunami and what it did to the automobile industry. Not only Japanese firms were affected; Ford had supply problems because of the quantity of parts thcy bought in Japan.

Boeing had massive issues with their 787 Dreamliner delivery schedule. A large percentage of the problems were because of the work outsourced to sub-contractors (a vendor of sorts, providing a completed section or part, not just materials).

THE OTHER NON-FINANCIAL FACTORS

LEASE

It doesn't seem possible, but the lease, or more importantly, the buyer's lease, is a critical factor in determining how much cash the seller will get at closing. Banks will not approve a loan for a term longer than the lease including options (the exceptions may be pure service businesses like consulting, training and similar). The bank does not want the buyer kicked out of their space in the middle of the loan.

Any smart buyer, whether getting a bank loan or not, will want lease protection. Earlier I shared a story of a client whose lack of a lease dramatically reduced the valuation. That story is important because it's expensive to move a business, especially if the move is unexpected.

REAL LIFE STORY: MOVING A BUSINESS IS VERY EXPENSIVE

Jerry's company made saw blades, and we were doing a national search for other saw blade manufacturers to acquire. Jerry's plan was to move some or all of the production into his facility, where he had excess capacity.

As part of the planning for this project, we talked about his factory, his lease and the capacity for growth. The bottom line was, this highly profitable company couldn't afford to move. The cost to move massive machinery, the improvements to any new space, the electrical power requirements and the disruption would devastate the bottom line. Jerry, and most other businesses in manufacturing, distribution and especially retail can't afford to move unless it's because of fast growth, and then it's still expensive and disruptive.

Buying and selling a business is a relationship business. The same is true regarding your landlord and your lease. Having a good relationship with your landlord will help your acquisition.

The condition of your local commercial real estate market may dictate what happens in this area. A strong market may make a landlord demand higher rent, a shorter term and more nebulous renewal options. While analyzing a company for a sale to the company's CEO, I reviewed the lease and its renewal terms. The lease stated that it could be renewed at the "then-fair market rental value." Not much protection to the leasee here, is there?

REAL LIFE STORY: ALWAYS PAY ATTENTION TO THE LEASE'S DETAILS

Tom owned a very successful auto body shop. He built a building as he grew and eventually sold the building, signing a long-term lease. Because he knew the building's quality he didn't worry about the lease or the clause that had him, the tenant, responsible for all repairs and maintenance.

Fast-forward 10 years. Tom is in the process of selling his business. There are some potential major issues with the building that will be a significant expense and the landlord won't consider a different lease. The buyer's real estate broker and attorney advised the buyer not to sign the lease he was offered.

As the lease was expiring, Tom realized he was in a no-win situation. He had to move the business before the sale. Nobody won. Tom had a large expense, the buyer had to create recognition for a new location and the landlord lost a good tenant.

Let's step back and take a big picture view of the space, your needs and future needs. You want to grow the business. Buyers don't buy businesses to keep them status quo. If you don't see growth possibilities or a specific area where you can add value (increasing sales and/or profit) you won't want the company.

The facilities are a big part of the company's growth potential. If the company is bursting at the seams, what are the buyer's options? If there are 20,000 square feet and the business needs 10,000 square feet, what does that mean (especially as you also have to make acquisition debt payments)? Can you add a second shift? Does a remote location make sense? What about zoning limitations? All of these will be of concern to a buyer so know the answers ahead of time.

As I am not a commercial real estate expert, I've asked Kevin Grossman (www.kevingrossman.com, kevin@kevingrossman.com), who is a tenant representative, to contribute on this subject in more detail. Here's what Kevin has to say.

TOP 4 KEYS TO MAKING SMART OFFICE LEASING DECISIONS

A business space lease is something you only have to deal with every few years – but of course it's important to your company so you want to make a good, informed decision. So what are the keys to making this decision, from the perspective of other business owners and people involved in many transactions? I've been representing tenants in leasing and buying properties for their business operations—office, high-tech and manufacturing space—and here's a "quick list" distilled from client feedback and experiences over the years.

- Remember the big picture—keep the deal and specific points of the deal in context of what your business needs are for its overall success.

- Approach it thoughtfully and with a good process in mind—this ensures you get the best deal in any given market environment for your firm.

- Use a team and tools to ensure you have the objective and subjective input you need to support your decision making process.

- Be sure the documentation reflects the deal you believe you've agreed to. The landlord may tell you the lease document is standard, but there is no standard, and to avoid potentially crippling problems it deserves the time and attention to get it right.

Keep the big picture in mind - all the way through

It's easy to get distracted by urgency and the many small but important details and time involved in going through the lease process. The best context for all this, keeping things in perspective, is to be clear going in what's important to your company and you going forward. Here are some of the top trouble spots to be aware of:

- It's about the future, not the past—what are your priorities and needs going forward?

- Marketing, branding and positioning in your marketplace may be impacted by your space.

- Recruitment and retention are often influenced by business space decisions.

- Logistics to clients, daily transportation, goods & supplies or the airport may be important.

- Environmental issues for an increasing number of companies are critical—air quality, waste stream management, energy efficiency of the building, access to services and mass transit.

- Financial ramifications—everyone focuses on the rate, but flexibility can be critical, as can the clause about assignment and subletting. It's a rude awakening if you want to bring in a partner or sell and you realize you've given your landlord the ability to approve or extract concessions from you to get your financing or sale transaction done.

Good process provides solid foundation

A good process produces consistently good results. Given the complexity of many deals, a thoughtful approach ensures you make a well-informed decision. A general framework should include:

- Clarify your needs and requirements

- Determination and preliminary assessment of options

- Request for proposal process for top contenders

- Keep a fallback until the end – you need it to not give up leverage

- Negotiate, clarify and systematically compare on an objective and subjective basis

- Document well

- Design and construction if part of the deal

- Move and celebrate

Use a good team and tools

It's not rocket science, but it is a set of skills and information that you don't deal with on a daily basis. It is in addition to all the other things you have on your plate running your business and you'll be spending a fair amount of time with who's representing you, so choosing a representative (broker that represents business tenants) that's a good fit for you and your firm's values. Some key elements and tools to consider include:

- When choosing someone to represent you, experience helping business tenants not landlords is critical. Representing landlords is a marketing job. Representing tenants is a service job and involves a broader, more technical skill set to do it right.

- Using net present value to critically evaluate the range of proposals you'll see. There will be variations in rate, operating expenses, how tenant improvements are handled, rate increases, the load factor, how efficient the space is for your specific needs, parking costs, moving and rent abatement, off hour use, how the space is measured, etc. A comprehensively designed NPV worksheet is invaluable in the negotiations and to help you in having an objective apples-to-apples assessment of alternatives.

- Team players—it's important that your tenant representative can work well with you of course, but also your CFO, operations manager, legal counsel and communicate well with your banker, the architect, contractor and building management team. All of these are important to getting the best decision and setting in place solid go-forward expectations and working relationships.

Documentation - a critical clarification process

After the months of getting to a deal you're good with, the deal isn't quite done yet. The lease document is like its own minefield just before the finish line. It's not uncommon for the lease and related addenda to be 40 pages, and if it's a sublease you have essentially two lease documents combined and your situation is guided by the most restrictive elements of either document. This is where your tenant broker and your attorney working well together is important to ensure you get what you've spent a lot of timing working toward. Some key points are:

- The work letter—the part of the document that spells out the improvements, who's doing what, who's responsible for the process, construction, what costs are the landlord's and what if any are the tenants responsibility.

- Who's signing—you personally? The Company? If it's the company, is there a guarantee? Is it a reasonable amount relative to the landlord's actual risks or for the entire lease obligation?

- Assignment is often glanced over but shouldn't be. If you want to partner up or merge or sell, many leases don't have any criteria or set a very low threshold at which the landlord has sole discretion to decide if they will allow an assignment or subletting. You don't want your business subject to arbitrary involvement by your landlord.

- Mechanisms for extensions, expansions, give-backs, determining market rent, and the timing of each of these are additional potentially critical issues to be aware of and understand—and to negotiate if the starting document is unreasonable.

- Don't get sucked into the "you can trust me" by the landlord regarding ambiguous language. The response I often use is "I'm sure that's true, but since we don't know if you'll still be the person we're dealing with we

have to make sure the document reflects what is reasonable and not rely on a verbal understanding".

- Of course you have to tailor the approach to the landlord—many are quite reasonable. Some you will need to
rely on your fallback to have the fortitude to hold firm on
some critical items (and of course stay reasonable yourself—keep the big picture context in mind).

Celebrate Completion!

This isn't one of the four keys, but I highly recommend that after
you've executed the lease (and the landlord has too) you should
do a provisional celebration. It is a long road to get to that point.
Then after you've moved in have a broad based, all hands celebration with your team and clients. Let your marketing folks
have a fun time with it. By that time you will have really earned
a party.

BANKING AND FINANCING

There is a very good chance you will get a bank loan to make the
acquisition. This will, most of the time, necessitate that you use their
acquisition-funding bank for all of your banking needs. That said, the
new bank doesn't have a relationship with the business. They don't have
the insights the current banker has and that means they will, at least at
first, play things, "by the book."

REAL LIFE STORY: BANKS LOVE GOOD CHARACTER

*The business was going through a transition with one of the three own-
ers, buying shares to get to a super-majority position. This might have
led to some issues with the bank because the departing shareholder
had a large personal net worth and was a co-guarantor on the line of
credit. However, it wasn't an issue at all because the bank "loved" the
buyer, who was the CEO and COO. They loved his management style,
attention to detail and work ethic. A new bank wouldn't have that history and would have stricter requirements.*

What does that mean to you? It means you need to work with the seller on:

- Billings
- Accounts receivable and their collections
- The use of lines of credit (does the seller use them and pay them off or constantly have an outstanding balance)
- Inventory management
- Quality and timely financial statements
- Refer back to Chapter Five for more information on banks and financing deals.

ADVISORS

In Chapter Three I provided a list of the most common advisors on a deal. Let's discuss how to best use those advisors and the importance of the seller's advisory team.

Attorney

It's important that your attorney has buy-sell transaction experience and second, they should have experience with deals in your size range. A Real Life Story in Chapter Three was about a client whose attorney provided overkill on a small business deal because his customary work was on middle market and international deals. The flip side of this is an attorney used to micro deals (a price of $250,000 +/-) who is employed on a $3-5 million dollar transaction. They'll be overwhelmed.

It's also important to not let the attorneys control the deal, get involved in deal negotiations (have them stick to legal points) or create one-sided contracts. I prefer attorneys who can honestly answer yes to the question, "Do you write agreements in a way that if you were on the receiving of the agreement you would find it to adequately protect both sides and not overly favor either party?" Getting documents done in this way will save time, money and energy while reducing everybody's angst.

CPA

CPA and taxes are terms that go together like bread and butter. Your CPA earns his or her fee by adequately protecting you from paying excessive taxes; federal, state and local, depending on where you live.

It's important that your CPA understands transaction tax law and how to structure the deal, especially if it's an asset purchase structure. However, there's more. For example, in Washington State we don't have a state income tax. However, there is a sales and use tax (about 9% at the time of this writing) that the buyer pays on furniture, fixtures, equipment and vehicles unless they are used to manufacture a product. The value of these tangible assets reported to the state may or may not be the same as in the deal's asset allocation or the same as what the county has valued it for personal-property tax. This is just one example of why it pays to have an experienced CPA and use them for what they are good at.

In addition, your CPA can do a mini-audit of the company's books (I've had some clients do this mini-audit themselves to get an understanding, and others have just turned it over to their accountant), review the current accounting system and set up your accounting system. Especially if you aren't strong on the financial side, utilize the skills of your CPA. Nowhere else in small business creates as much discomfort as the financial systems and statements and the worry that the accounting department isn't as capable as they should be. Accounting is similar to computers, and the old computer industry mantra of, "garbage in, garbage out" applies here too. When buying a company, make sure you start off correctly on the financial side.

Banker

Chapter Five covered banking and bankers extensively. To reiterate, make sure your bank has an appetite for acquisition loans and that you get to meet your business banker, if he or she is a different person than your acquisition loan person.

CFO

Finance people, like CFOs, tend to look into the future (CPAs tend to concentrate on the historical). If your target company has high working capital needs, or if you plan on fast growth or you want high-end management reports, you want a CFO on your team. These days there are a lot of choices for outsourced CFOs from large national companies to sole practitioners and many others in-between. Having great cash flow and working capital projections will endear you with your bank and save you a lot of worry.

Human Resources

The end of this chapter includes two essays from guest contributors on culture and HR. I've found that it's rare that you need an HR person before the deal closes, but if the company is large enough to require compliance on employee policies you're best off using an outsourced HR expert (versus someone in-house or doing it yourself).

Commercial Real Estate

Again, an expert has contributed on this subject. If you need a new lease it's well worth the money to retain an agent who can assist you in a market analysis, rate comparisons and lease terms.

Insurance

Many companies have standard insurance needs such as liability, business owner protection, vehicle coverage, etc. (in addition to medical and dental). If there are special coverages, it pays to get a good agent to review and recommend prior to closing. If it's a stock transaction you can usually take over the existing policies. If it's an asset transaction you will need to get new policies for your new legal entity. Make sure you are adequately covered and paying a fair premium. One client who had special liability needs saved 40% or over $8,000 and got a better policy by having it reviewed.

Importance of seller's advisors

REAL LIFE STORY: WATCH OUT FOR DO-IT-YOURSELFERS

Gary hated paying advisors. He did, however, hire a buy-sell consultant to guide him through the closing steps. At one point I asked this advisor, a very competent person, if Gary had shown the deal to his CPA. This was because the accountant's advice didn't seem to be relevant.

What Gary really hated was paying attorneys (he also didn't like them doing anything). He brought his attorney in late and then took him out of the loop. Because he didn't understand legal nuances we got delayed and he got frustrated over what he didn't fully understand.

> *I encourage the seller to have good counsel and use that counsel. Every attorney I know will say that it's much better to have a good attorney on the other side (versus one who's inexperienced or doesn't regularly do transaction work).*

TECHNOLOGY

Let's step back and be sure the seller can answer the question, "How does your business benefit from the technology in which you've invested?" Today, all businesses use technology (or should). Let's look at a few examples.

- Retail or restaurant—There are sophisticated point-of-sale systems that track just about everything the business needs. This can aid in inventory management, developing customer lists and tracking sales so the owner or manager knows how to plan staffing.

- Distribution—These days there are specialty software programs that provide so much more than a spreadsheet (which was a major productivity increase over paper lists). Bar codes and tracking chips can reduce labor even more.

- Manufacturing—One of the most important jobs in one of the dirtiest, most basic fabrication and machining businesses that I ever saw was the programming of the CNC equipment. In this business the best programmer was a key link in productivity.

- Service—In Chapter Four I shared a story of a buyer who turned the company's website into an ordering system, when it had been just a brochure. Staffing agencies have placing and scheduling software that saves time and reduces errors.

These are the topics about which you will be concerned. If the firm is not using technology effectively it may be an opportunity or a risk (plus a cost). Of course, you might not pay as much as if the technology is up to speed

There are three areas in which you need to keep current. They are hardware, software and the Internet.

Hardware is the most obvious. One company had a mix of old computers and an antiquated server (in 2010). Some were on Windows XP, some on Windows 98 and one was still on Windows 95. The buyer saw this as a capital investment and this factor was used in his negotiations. The small investment in hardware was well worth it.

Software is often in the background and it can make a difference. Make sure the seller knows its uses, that it's all up-to-date and legal. If there is proprietary software you want to know the costs to keep it current and increase its productivity factor. The seller should be able to explain why the company uses certain software (versus other types).

A website is a necessity for almost all businesses these days. Yes, there are a few that don't need or want one but they are the exception. You want to know who does the hosting, who maintains the website, what it costs, what domain names are registered, where they are registered and when any registrations expire. Security issues are at the top of the list on technology due diligence, especially if you deal with secure information. Get a good explanation of security protocols, protection software and firewalls, offsite access and anything else that could be an issue.

The bottom line is, if the systems are up-to-date, adequate for growth and the employees know how to be productive on them it's one item on the due diligence list you can cross off.

MARKETING

After the word "potential," the next most common word used by business sellers is marketing. It's used in the context of, "If a buyer knows anything about marketing there is so much potential in this business." Of course, they are implying that the buyer with marketing experience should pay them for all that potential (before it's realized).

What a buyer hears is, "They've tried every marketing technique known and sales are still where they are. How am I going to do better?"

On Amazon.com I searched on the word "marketing" and the results included over 100,000 books. One could spend a lifetime reading about marketing and how to do it better. You need to ask:

1.   What is your marketing strategy and its tactics?

2. Do you have an actual plan for point one; do you document what you do and then track results?

3. Do you have cost benefit metrics (i.e., what are the actual results from your marketing efforts)?

Marketing can be one important part of your competitive advantage. In the mid-90s, when I was active with my local Chamber of Commerce, I realized that when the Chamber held events there were two topics that put people in the seats. They were money and marketing, and I doubt if things have changed.

We're not going to discuss any marketing or advertising specifics. That is not the point of this book. The point is that if the seller can answer the above questions, he or she has just eased the mind of every buyer and made a deal easier to achieve.

EXAMPLE & APPLICATION

A simple breakeven analysis can be applied to marketing. Let's assume your contribution margin (sales less all variable costs) is 40%. Divide a new expense, a marketing campaign for example, by 40% to find the amount of new sales you need to make the campaign run at breakeven.

If you spend $10,000 on marketing, you need $25,000 of new, additional sales to reach breakeven on the campaign (10,000/.40). If sales increase by $100,000, you have $40,000 of additional contribution margin and the marketing program gave you a four to one return.

Of course, in real life, it's not usually this easy. Marketing efforts, other than direct response like coupons, aren't instantaneous, require repetition and may just be part of an overall sales strategy, along with other variables.

More important is to show what happened before you started any marketing campaign or what happens if you stop it. Most important is to show you have a handle on your marketing.

SALES

There are even more books on sales than on marketing! As you may know, most business owners, CEOs and managers will say that finding good salespeople, versus order takers, is one of the toughest parts of their business.

Tom Hopkins, in his classic book, *How to Master the Art of Selling* (Tom Hopkins International, 1980) starts the book by writing, "I learned a long time ago that selling is the highest paid hard work—and the lowest paid easy work—that I could find."

As with marketing, I am not going to discuss selling, sales strategies, closing techniques or anything else about sales strategy or tactics. What I'd like to convey are the important points you should be interested in, so you can be ready. Here are nine areas you should be able to discuss and there are probably more that are specific to the business or industry you are investigating.

- What is your typical sales cycle (from lead to sale)?

- Is there seasonality to your sales and what do you do to minimize it?

- Do you have a sales plan?

- Do you track all leads, where they come from, closing ratios (by salesperson) and other sales related information?

- Is there a contact management system (and do you use it)?

- Do you use this information to make meaningful projections?

- Do your salespeople have a handle on your customers, the relationships and how to find new customers?

- Is there a compensation plan for your salespeople that is win-win (see the example below)?

- Most importantly, do any of your salespeople control key accounts in a way that creates a dependency that may be disruptive if they or you leave?

Real Life Story: Get good salespeople and pay them well

My client had a convoluted sales compensation plan. The salespeople received a low base salary and bonuses (really a commission) when their monthly sales exceeded a benchmark amount. However, the bonuses kicked in before the company covered their base costs of employment.

For example, if it took $50,000 of monthly sales per person to cover their employment costs including salary, benefits, share of overhead and a target profit, the bonus started at $40,000. This meant the company was losing money on each salesperson unless their sales greatly exceeded $50,000.

One, of many, things we did was to redesign the compensation plan so the salespeople covered their total costs before getting a bonus.

Like marketing, sales has a lot of intangibles. Find out if there is a system and a process and learn how to manage them.

COMPETITION

"The company doesn't have any competition" will never impress a savvy buyer. Every business has competition and if it doesn't you should be worried. You don't want to be perceived as similar to the floppy disk industry in the early 2000s. Sure, there wasn't much competition, but that was when Apple, followed by PC manufacturers, stopped putting floppy drives in computers.

As a buyer, research the competition, which is easier to do these days than ever before. I've seen situations where buyers have known more about the competition than the owner.

This is where the term "competitive advantage" comes to the forefront. Be able to coherently explain what the firm's advantage is over the competitors and what advantages they may have over your (potential) company.

I have written numerous articles for and spoken at the national convention of the Non Ferrous Foundry Society, whose members are foundries that do materials other than steel (brass, gold, bronze, etc.). In researching the industry for my speech, I found out that these small U.S. based foundries have an advantage over China when it comes to prototypes, small runs, immediate needs and custom products. Chinese foundries have an advantage if it's large orders with a long lead-time.

The foundry industry has huge barriers to entry. Not every business or industry is so fortunate. It's incredibly easy to start a staffing agency, a janitorial business or a restaurant. However, in these industries, where there are constant startups and franchising (often the indication an industry has low barriers to entry) there are also large, dominant players. As with foundries, there are advantages for many different types of companies.

REAL LIFE STORY: BARRIERS TO ENTRY CAN CHANGE

When my children were active in youth sports, two or three large sporting goods firms in the Seattle area provided uniforms and equipment. A startup uniform company in our area started in the owner's garage for production and his basement for the office.

The competitive advantages were initially price and service. The price part was easy because they had almost no overhead. The service took time. I recall the owner went to many, many little league and soccer association board meetings to build relationships and demonstrate that his quality was the same as the big stores.

Fast forward a few years and this company now had a location in an industrial park (still no expensive retail space). His prices had increased but the company still maintained the relationships and kept their customers.

What are the barriers to entry in your industry? They could be capital requirements, licensing requirements (a specific certification for someone on the staff or FDA approval, for example), knowledge, geographic location or something else. No matter what they are, be able to articulate them.

The seller should be able to explain:

- Is there a threat from a large competitor, or is there a large competitor in your industry that can muscle smaller firms?

- Do your competitors or do you have a product advantage (or an engineering advantage)?

- Who has any production advantages?

- Are there any shipping advantages?

- Are there service and quality differences that are reflected in the price?

To summarize, know your future competition; is it friendly or cut-throat and how difficult is it to enter the industry? This is what you should know and a buyer will definitely want to know.

A company doing $5 million in sales had a handful of competitors, including one that was about 15 times their size. One of the competitor's employees accepted a job with the smaller firm, and the larger firm sued him. His new employer got caught in the middle and it cost them over $60,000.

One of the risks they identified in their business was the threat of another lawsuit from this large competitor. The competitor had a lot more capacity for legal bills, and as the smaller company gained market share there were constant hints of more lawsuits. This is the kind of thing that will scare many buyers.

THE PEOPLE

"I'm interested in your employees because, while, technically, I'm buying the business, what I'm really buying are the people who make the business what it is." A buyer said this to a seller, a seller who didn't understand why the buyer needed to talk to his employees before closing the deal.

Your people are your business; not much more can be said about their importance to any company. No matter how strong the product or service is the company's value is raised by its employees, as in the following examples.

1. The company may have invented a fantastic product and yet someone has to make that product.

2. Have the best service in town? It's because the people provide that service.

3. Is your customer base wider and deeper than your competitors? Most likely it's because the sales staff is great at generating new customers and maintaining solid customer relationships.

Let's focus on three areas. These areas, and their subsets, are the areas I have found buyers are the most interested in knowing about. Put time into learning about the employee structure, culture and systems.

1. The pragmatic, including what the employees do, what they're paid, etc.

2. The softer side, including teamwork, culture, delegation and similar

3. Compliance with rules, regulations and benefits

I am not anywhere close to an expert on human resources, its policies and requirements, so at the end of this chapter there is an essay by one of my guest contributors, Jack Goldberg, who is an expert.

EMPLOYEES SHOULD BE EMPLOYEES

Before we discuss the above topics, make sure that you are not breaking the law by treating people who should be employees as independent contractors. I know that the vast majority of the people reading will do the right thing. However, while writing this book, I've experienced two instances of companies either violating the statutes or operating in a very gray area. These experiences follow the quote of the IRS regulations on what determines if someone is an employee.

Here is a definition and example from the IRS website (www.irs.gov).

… Anyone who performs services for you is your employee *if you can control what will be done and how it will be done.* This is so even when you give the employee freedom of action. What matters is that you have the right to control the details of how the services are performed.

Example: Donna Lee is a salesperson employed on a full-time basis by Bob Blue, an auto dealer. She works 6 days a week, and is on duty in Bob's showroom on certain assigned days and times. She appraises trade-ins, but her appraisals are subject to the sales manager's approval. Lists of prospective customers belong to the dealer. She has to develop leads and report results to the sales manager. Because of her experience, she requires only minimal assistance in closing and financing sales and in other phases of her work. She is paid a commission and is eligible for prizes and bonuses offered by Bob. Bob also pays the cost of health insurance and group-term life insurance for Donna. Donna is an *employee* of Bob Blue.

One reason the federal government wants people to be classified as employees is that people working as independents have a higher rate of not reporting income (fraud is the term to use). State governments, whether your state has an income tax or not, want people to be covered by workers compensation insurance and unemployment insurance. Do it the right way, because it is a huge cost and disruption if you don't.

Example one: Jane worked for a small company that put on educational events. The company paid everybody as an independent contractor and she accepted this, even though she had been advised that she was an employee (the company told her what to do, where to do it and how to do it, and her work was reviewed by a supervisor).

Jane's supervisor got in a disagreement with the owner and was let go. One of her first stops was the State Unemployment Security office, where the supervisor was told she was a contractor and not eligible for benefits. This also triggered an investigation that caused the firm to be penalized and forced them to make everybody an employee.

The hassle and financial penalty caused the business to suffer, Jane's hours were reduced, she insisted on full-time work and was let go. She also was denied benefits by the State. As you can see, the employer and the employee were both hurt.

Example two: On the surface this was a very nice service business. They had a defensible niche (in what normally is a competitive industry), good margins and a motivated seller.

Upon initial review of the financial statements I read the cost of goods line items and said, "Oh, oh." Cost of goods sold was dominated by one line item, "Independent Contractor Expense" and was about 90% of the total cost of goods sold. In addition, the company provided the tools, supplies and vehicles for the contractors.

The first question I put on my list was to ask the owner if he had gotten an opinion from his CPA or attorney that this was an allowable independent contractor situation. (A quick note to a friend in the same industry, in another city, confirmed that these contractors really should be classified as employees).

If a CPA or attorney had indicated that this was allowable, it would give the buyer something to think about and cause him to get his own tax opinion on this. If they said no, or if the buyer's tax opinion was no, it created a huge dilemma. The tax burden for FICA, Medicare, unemployment and workers compensation would require an eight percent price increase to give the company the same net profit (assuming no customers left because of this). At current prices, profits would be reduced by 50% and that would kill any deal.

An even more troubling result could be that it puts the integrity of the seller into question.

CULTURE

Determining the culture in a small business is not that easy from the outside. Given that buyers are by nature skeptical, they will assume the company's culture is not good until shown otherwise. Here are three areas I have found buyers will want to know about and be able to investigate. As I am not a teamwork and culture specialist, I've included an essay from Libby Wagner in the next section (www.libbywagner.com, libby@libbywagner.com). Libby helps companies create a culture of profit.

If you watch sports at all, you inevitably hear commentators talk about team chemistry. Often the most talented team doesn't win the championship, or even the game, because the less talented team plays better together. In other words, they maximize the benefit of teamwork. You have to lead the effort to create teamwork.

There are teambuilding events like performing a charity event as a team, rock climbing or zip lining together. But the effect has to sustain itself past a few hours or a couple days. One of my clients companies has a history of an annual Christmas party where one of the bosses plays Monty Hall and they do a version of "Let's make a Deal." The employees all win and they love not only the gifts but also the atmosphere. Libby will share more on this; my point is that a buyer can sniff out problems in this area.

I've used the word dependency quite a few times in previous chapters. It is absolutely critical that you sniff out the most critical dependencies a firm has. The smaller the company, the greater the chance that operations, sales, accounting and more are dependent on the owner's involvement. I've seen companies with over 50 employees where the owner was the key cog in the operations, and I remember one company with 12 employees where we determined it was really an 11-person operation because the owner did almost nothing.

Delegating is not always easy, especially to a founder who knows the product or operations as well as anybody in the industry. It does take letting go. Before that it takes hiring the right people. Don't you want to hear that the company has great employees with a salary range at the high end? It's a lot better than determining the company has mediocre employees at the low end of the salary range (so productivity is low), isn't it?

I was taught that delegating has three components:

1. You (and your management team) must be willing to delegate. This is often the toughest element. It can be hard to let go, to let people stumble and bruise themselves (and hurt the company a little). But if you don't let them stumble and learn on small things, what happens when they are forced into dealing with big issues?

2. Your employees, at all levels, must be willing to accept delegation. Some people just don't want responsibility and they are easy to sort out. It's the people who do want to grow, advance and contribute that you want to nurture and train.

They will rise to the top, volunteer to take on projects and be willing to learn.

3. There must be a culture where delegation is acceptable. You may be willing to delegate, and some employees may be willing to accept delegation while others, usually not as capable, will not accept it and may actually sabotage it. Perhaps they are jealous they weren't delegated to or promoted. Perhaps they don't see where all the opportunities in the firm are. In any event, if you can make delegation acceptable it will impress your buyers (who all want to grow and use your team to do so).

REAL LIFE STORY: THE OWNER SETS THE TONE

Behind his back, employees referred to Rick's "drive-bys." He had a habit of hovering over an employee's desk or cubicle, fidgeting for a minute or two and then blurting out something like, "Don't worry about that, it's just my money" and stomping off. Nice culture of appreciation, isn't it?

Tom did things differently. He was a sales guy and knew he had to let his management team handle the operations, production and administration in his 80 people plus company. His six-person management team worked well together, they knew their roles and their employees loved them. I know firsthand because after I worked with this firm I had them do some work for me. What a difference when the employees, at all levels, are empowered and respected.

STRUCTURE

In the previous chapter I provided a small sample org chart. The important question is, what does it mean to you, the buyer? Most buyers will want to know there is a chain of command. It doesn't work when three managers can each give staff members instructions or assign tasks. This causes conflicting instructions or deadlines.

This is also important because you are interested in growth, and growth is easier to achieve if there is a proper structure and systems for getting work done. Some of the best buyers I've seen, whether I've been on the buy side or sell side, are those most interested in the company's people and their abilities.

REAL LIFE STORY: HIRE RIGHT AND LET THEM DO THEIR JOB

The owner, the owner's spouse and the COO all gave the accounting staff direction. The problem was that none of them understood finance or accounting very well. Compounding the problem was that the accounting department people were not qualified for the size to which the company had grown and nobody would stand up to management (out of both fear and uncertainty).

There were inadequate structure and delegating systems, and they had not hired the right people for the job. Because of these two factors they also had an inadequate financial system, so the accuracy of the financial reports was suspect.

Having a structure also contributes to your overall culture, as explained by Libby in the next section.

PEOPLE DUE DILIGENCE: HOW DO YOU KNOW IF A COMPANY HAS THE RIGHT CULTURE FOR PROFITABLE SUCCESS?

By Libby Wagner, www.libbywagner.com, 206-906-9203

Sometimes, business buyers make the mistake of looking only at the P & L or Balance Sheet when making a decision to buy a business. Certainly, looking at the financial picture, the business history, and the potential market are all important in the process of making the best decision for you. What buyers often overlook, however, is whether or not the organization can sustain a big change like a buy-out or owner transfer to keep things moving along toward profitability and growth, two characteristics that most want for business performance.

Organizational culture exists, and the question all business leaders should consider is whether this culture is *accidental* or *intentional*. Sometimes, especially with small to medium sized businesses, leaders or owners have created initial success with an entrepreneurial spirit and they haven't really taken time to articulate the important elements that they desire in their company culture. Or, they haven't created the systems and processes to support that positive, profit-building culture. If you are buying a business, you may want to make changes and create new ways of doing things, but make no mistake, there is a culture currently operating in this business and you will need to determine whether or not it is resilient enough to stay on track through the changes that will naturally occur with a business buy-out.

Here are three areas to examine and some questions to investigate before you buy:

1. What is the relationship like between the employees and the managers? Especially ask about the following:
    a. what's the level of trust—low, medium or high?
    b. how do employees receive feedback about work performance?
    c. can the employees clearly articulate the business mission and vision?
    d. what happens when things go wrong?

2. Look for indicators of "organizational drag," or those things that are the silent costs that erode profit margins and the bottom line. These may include:
    a. lowered performance
    b. interpersonal strife and conflict
    c. unresolved "history" or issues
    d. increased costs
    e. turnover in employees
    f. absenteeism or misuse of leave time (medical/personal)

    g. frequent miscommunication

    h. lower team function

    i. missed goals and deadlines

    j. missed opportunities for innovation and creativity

3. How are people recognized and rewarded for the following:
   a. consistent performance?
   b. above-and-beyond performance?
   c. long-term performance?

4. What is the current communication infrastructure?
   a. do supervisors and employees meet regularly for one-on-ones to discuss performance? (not resolve day-to-day issues, but specifically for performance)
   b. do the leaders have regular, systematic ways of updating the company, interacting with the workers and getting to know them?
   c. what systems are in place for encouraging transparency, i.e. "speaking the truth to the top?"
   d. how transparent are the decision-making processes?

Shifting in ownership or leadership is a significant change for any sized company and successful ones make sure that they manage the cultural elements in that change. In general, you cannot communicate too much, and investigating the items above will give you some indication of where you might want to focus your efforts to make sure you are supporting the best culture for profitable success!

*Libby Wagner is president of Libby Wagner & Associates and Influencing Options. Her book, **The Influencing Option: The Art of Building a Profit Culture in Business** helps leaders develop practical, immediately useable skills for leading high performing teams in the best environments to support high profits.*

PRAGMATIC STUFF

There is a three-legged stool regarding the retention of employees post-transaction. Everybody wants the employees to stay and everybody is fearful they will leave or be asked to leave.

- The seller wants his or her loyal people to keep their (good) jobs and have security.

- The buyer is buying the people and is afraid the employees will leave and disrupt the business.

- The employees are fearful of the buyer bringing in his or her own people

Of course, all are wrong in thinking that others want the employees to leave, because the people are the lifeblood of the business. So, let's look at what you should be interested in.

WHAT DO THE EMPLOYEES THINK ABOUT THE BUSINESS?

The larger the business the more a buyer will be interested in, and the more evidence there will be of structure and delegation. No matter what the size of your business, all buyers will be interested in, or should be interested in, what is in this section.

When discussing customers, I recommended a customer satisfaction survey and asking the employees to write out when the company really came through for a customer and when the company let a customer down. Apply the same type of questioning to the employees (better yet, have an outsider interview them). Ask yourself, what is the seller's relationship with the employees? More important, how would the employees describe their relationship with the seller (and the company in general)?

I've been involved in many employee interviews, both in individual and group settings. It's amazing how smart the employees usually are. Above, I gave the example of Mark and how the owner he acquired the business from didn't respect his managers' opinions or ideas. Unfortunately, that is all too common, although it usually comes from poor management skills (not knowing what to do) and not from being a control-freak or dictator.

The employees see things from a different perspective than an owner or buyer sees them, and that can be valuable. Below are some comments and ideas generated from three companies where I did one-on-one employee feedback interviews or facilitated group sessions. All were done without the owner present if it was the management team in the session or without the both the owner and the management team present if it was only the employees in the session.

- The owner is too nice, he can't say no to the customers and it spreads the company too thin.
- We don't get enough money upfront from customers and it causes cash flow issues.
- We wasted a lot of money and better communication would help.
- The company needs more key people and more supervision.
- This is a good place to work, we like the owners and hope they succeed and we can stay here.
- Define the role of the number two person; he is too scattered and doesn't have time to provide direction.
- Eliminate redundancies between departments (lead tracking, job tracking and some accounting functions were being done simultaneously in two departments).
- Establish stricter customer expectations.
- Increase lead times to reduce rework.
- Have more focused meetings and increase standardization (of processes).
- We "panic manage" too much.
- Increased and improved cross training will improve operations (reduce bottlenecks).
- Improve communication between departments.
- We don't know what the expectations are.
- There is a lack of teamwork, part of which is caused by a lack of briefings.
- Our laborers need more training.

REAL LIFE STORY: OWNERS PRESENCE CAN STIFLE INPUT

I promise complete anonymity when doing interviews. In other words, I will share with my client a summary of all comments and ideas but will not identify the employee if it is a criticism. I must appear to be very trustworthy (which I am) because employees really open up to me.

The trust factor is extremely important. During one group session the wife of the owner walked in about half way through the meeting. She worked in the accounting department, so technically she was an employee. Boy, did the atmosphere cool, and fast. The employees saw her as a spy not a co-employee who wanted to contribute, and their comments went from blunt to sanitized (reducing the effectiveness of the session).

One part of the exercise I've found critical is to ask the owner and management team what they think the employees will say and what issues the employees will say are important to improving the company. I tell the seller that when a buyer interviews their people, they won't be there. By doing these interviews, in advance of a sale, the seller will uncover areas they can improve before a buyer comes on the scene (which makes the buyer happy).

REAL LIFE STORY: MANAGEMENT AND STAFF HAVE DIFFERENT OPINIONS

We met with the management team or a manufacturing company and they identified eight areas they thought the employees would mention as needing attention. The managers ranked three as critical issues, three as needing work but not critical and two as "okay," meaning they might need some tweaking at the most.

The employees brought up 13 issues, eight being critical, three as not critical and two as "okay." The management team's issues were predominantly operations focused. Their list included more training on their job estimating system, more product training and better sched-uling. Overall the management team was right on about 50% of the employees' issues.

One of the areas management ranked as okay was communication. Of the employees' eight critical issues, five were related to communica-tion, with communication between departments on jobs given "super critical" status.

Things look different from the top. This management team not only missed the bulls-eye, they were barely on the target. Can you imagine a buyer finding out about this dysfunction during due diligence? Some would run, some would negotiate the price down and others, if they have team building skills, might see it as opportunity.

THE EMPLOYEES

You will want a list of employees, their total compensation, date of hire and title. How are compensation levels determined? Are they high, low or average for the industry and location? The most important reason for getting the information should be to know how to plan for growth and the cost of people in positions that will need to be expanded.

Here are three things to discuss with the seller regarding employees:

1. Don't let the seller give any indication there will be raises for all employees, whether they will come from you or the seller. One seller actually told the employees the buyer would be giving everybody a raise post-close. It sure shocked the buyer and almost derailed the deal.

2. If they give annual bonuses, and they've become routine and expected, include them in annual compensation figures. The last thing you want to do is cancel bonuses because they based the price on pre-bonus income levels.

3. Have the seller operate the business as if there was no deal in the works. This means hire as needed, promote as needed and perform as usual all other aspects affecting the employees.

All sellers should be able to describe, in detail, the availability of competent employees, especially at the management and key employee level. Also, it's important that they can share how they find people. It could range from Craig's list to retained searches and everything in-between. Here are three wide and varied examples. The higher the turnover rate the greater the interest in where they find people.

1. The majority of this manufacturing business's employees are machinists. As I write this, there is a tight market for good machinists and the future market is predicted to be even tighter. The company's average machinist age is about 55 and the owner is concerned that when this group starts retiring, replacements will be hard to find.

2. A testing laboratory hires scientists to run the tests. One might think the market for science majors would be tight but it isn't. There aren't a lot of science jobs if you don't have a PhD, and there is always an availability of technical people.

3. A friend owns a specialty pizza restaurant. While there's turnover of college students for the serving type jobs, he's got great longevity in the kitchen. It's a good place to work for a cook (this is not a menu driven restaurant that needs a chef), he pays a fair wage and there's a feeling of being part of team.

REAL LIFE STORY: WATCH OUT FOR HYPERBOLE

The memorandum describing the company for sale mentioned "unprecedented employee loyalty." We came to find out what the word unprecedented meant in this case was that there was 100% employee turnover in the preceding two years (20-30 employees) and the general manager was fired and replaced three months before the business was put on the market.

Are there employment agreements and non-compete agreements? Has your attorney recommended you have them, at least for management and salespeople? Realize that, in most states, a non-compete agreement can't prevent someone from earning a living in their field. It usually can prevent an ex-employee from contacting your customer or employees (to recruit them away). This is known as a non-solicit agreement and generally is the part that is enforceable. As with anything that has legal or tax ramifications, consult your attorney and CPA.

REAL LIFE STORY: DON'T BE OVERBEARING

We were two weeks away from closing when the deal almost collapsed. The seller was a small business. The buyer was a mid-market company that was buying service providers in their niches.

The buyer's president came in one day and said that all employees, yes, all employees, including laborers and clerical staff, would have to sign their standard employment and non-compete agreement. And, if any employees didn't sign the agreement and left employment, the deal would be reevaluated and in jeopardy. To make it more interesting, the agreements were very onerous (the seller's attorney said it was mostly unenforceable).

This deal was crucial to the seller. There weren't any financial buyers for this breakeven business and health issues necessitated a deal sooner versus later. One employee held out and wouldn't sign. After talking to the seller's attorney and getting a small bonus (call it a signing bonus although it was from the seller), she signed and the deal closed.

WHAT DOES EVERYBODY DO?

A question I ask every buyer is, "What do you want to do on a daily, weekly and monthly basis?"

A question I ask every seller is, "What do you do on a daily, weekly and monthly basis?"

After asking hundreds of business buyers this question I can state that at least 80% answer by saying they want to be involved with strategy, vision and planning. In addition they will also mention things based on their experience, whether it is marketing, finance and budgeting or sales.

The 20% that don't directly say strategy, vision or planning will describe their day or week in terms that translate to planning and strategy.

There has to be an overlap of at least 50-75% of what you want to do and what a seller does. A buyer who is a sales expert won't survive if the seller is a product engineer (and engineering is what the company needs from the owner) and vice versa.

An owner who spends most of his or her time being CEO and dealing with strategic issues is a more attractive acquisition candidate than if he or she is deeply involved in the day-to-day operations. Financial buyers can easily see themselves in a big-picture role and strategic buyers want a management team.

Equally important is to be able to go beyond job descriptions and discuss what the management team and employees do on a daily, weekly and monthly basis. Get the owner to share stories about what they do, as it is more memorable than reading a job description. How the team supports the owner is extremely important because as buyers plan for growth they will rely on the team as much or more than the seller does.

EMPLOYEE INTERVIEWS

As I think about all the deals with which I've been involved, I can only think of a handful that were unsuccessful, meaning the buyer struggled or failed. One was a company in the very fickle entertainment industry (the buyer knew the risks and was willing to roll the dice), a couple were for health reasons and two failures that rise to the top of the list had a common factor. In both case the seller would not let the buyer talk to the employees (or the customers in one case) before closing.

While this is a small sample size, it is interesting, and shows how a buyer can be persuaded to bypass a crucial element of due diligence when they have "buyer fever." Of course, given that it is rare that a seller will not hold a note for part of the price, it is not in the best interest of a seller to hide things from the buyer. Now, some sellers will be glad to get whatever cash they can if they truly believe the employees (or customers) will hurt if not kill their deal.

So, realize that you have to talk to the employees before closing. Understand that it generally is the last element of due diligence, because it is so crucial and delicate. The most common scenario is that you will sign off on all other areas of due diligence (financial and non-financial) before this happens. You may also have a signed purchase and sale agreement with one contingency—your interviewing of the employees (or certain employees).

REAL LIFE STORY: THERE ARE MANY WAYS TO GET A DEAL

Want to really get to know the employees? Do what Bob did; run the company for almost a year before closing on the deal. Of course there's a caveat; the company was not doing well, the owner was not active and there was no way a deal would happen until the business was fixed. This is a special situation, but it does happen. If you're looking to minimize risk, find a fixer upper that you like and do what Bob did, using the seller's checkbook (because he or she doesn't have any other options).

Let's conclude with a "who, what, where and when" for employee interviews (we already the why).

Who—the management team and key employees. This doesn't have to extend down to all employees, although I've seen situations where all the employees were brought together for a group meeting before closing to meet the buyer, share ideas and be assured their jobs were safe. Word travels fast. Once management meets the buyer the rest of the staff will know what's going on.

What—what will you ask them? Anything and everything may come up and the only restrictions the employees should have regarding their answers is to not give away any trade secrets. Your questions should concentrate on culture, growth and their ideas for improvement.

Where—a private room is a must; offsite will be best if the seller and you don't want the rest of the staff to know what's going on until the interviews are done.

When—this is THE MOST IMPORTANT part of employee interviews, which is why I'm repeating it. Employee interviews happen only after you have completed and checked off everything else on your due diligence list. This means you've approved due diligence on the financial statements, customers, have a new lease and checked out everything else. The only exception is if the seller has been very open and all the employees know about the sale. In that case, these interviews still come near the end but may not need to wait until all other due diligence items are satisfactorily completed.

Keep in mind that this is also the place where your employees will want to shine for their future boss.

BEING COMPLIANT WITH EMPLOYEE RULES AND REGULATIONS

Jack Goldberg is the CEO of Personnel Management Systems in Kirkland, WA (jack.goldberg@hrpmsi.com). His firm is one of the best human resource outsource firms in the Seattle area. This is an area in which I am not an expert and it is very, very important. There are too many rules, regulations and laws that can trip up any business if they are not followed correctly. Pay attention to what Jack writes in the following paragraphs and hope that your seller is paying attention his or her HR issues.

> This book would not be complete if there wasn't at least one section devoted to Human Resources. Business owners can spend considerable time and resources getting their business ready to sell but somehow fail to address this important area. This is ironic when you consider that for many businesses, payroll and employee benefits can be the first or second largest expense.

> This chapter is intended to get you to think about how to get this area of your business in shape – in shape and ready to sell.

> HR people often think about HR in two ways – *Compliance* and *Best Practices*. Sometimes Compliance is seen as "tactical HR" and Best Practices is seen as "strategic." These labels don't always hold up under every condition but they can be useful as we attempt to organize a rather diverse and in some ways, a complex part of running a company.

> Regardless if you are a buyer or seller, taking the time to think through the HR aspects of an organization can pay enormous

dividends. At a minimum, it can help eliminate possible deal breakers.

Compliance issues cover a whole host of topics. This list is intended to be somewhat generic, meaning there could be specific state or local issues that are not listed. And of course, there are most likely industry-specific issues that will need to be addressed.

COMPLIANCE

DOCUMENTATION

There is the required documentation that must be on hand for every employee. This includes current W-4 and I-9 forms. Each I-9 form must be completed correctly or you face thousands of dollars in possible fines if there is an audit. In some industries, audits occur quite frequently. I-9 forms that are not available - or completed incorrectly - raise a red flag of the possibility of illegal workers. Recently, in the process of selling his dry-cleaning business, a friend of mine discovered that several of his key employees were working illegally. Learning this at the point of sale created a huge obstacle for the buyer. I doubt anyone wants to purchase a company only to then have the employees hauled off and deported. Avoid all this by making sure you have legal employees and all the necessary documentation is in place for each employee.

UNEMPLOYMENT INSURANCE

Virtually all companies pay for and provide Unemployment Insurance for their employees. First, verify that this is in fact the case and that coverage is in place for employees in each state that the company has employees. Second, find out what the rate is. Rates are normally experience based, meaning a relatively high rate could indicate frequent layoffs and high employee turnover. A low relative rate would suggest a stable workforce, low turnover, and high retention.

Workers' Compensation

Like Unemployment Insurance, the rate or premium that a company pays for Workers' Comp has a lot to do with its experience. A company with a high relative rate may be suggestive of frequent employee accidents or an unsafe work environment. Make sure that coverage is in place for each state and get a copy of a claims experience report.

Employment Posters

It may sound silly, but states and the feds require that employers post certain notices. You should be able to see anywhere between 8 and 10 posters conspicuously displayed in a common area (e.g., lunchroom).

EEO-1 Report and/or Affirmative Action Plan

Companies with over 100 employees are required to complete an annual EEO-1 report. Companies with over 50 employees and government contracts (or they are sub- contractors to government contractors) are required to complete an Affirmative Action Plan (AAP) every year. Not having an AAP means the company is out of compliance with the requirements of the contract. The penalty can be severe and includes cancellation of the government contract(s). AAP preparation is a huge task. If a company says they have one, ask to see it. It should be several inches thick and weigh more than a couple of pounds!

Benefit Plan and Retirement Plan Administration

It is beyond the scope of this chapter to talk about all the requirements associated with administering a company's employee benefit plans. Competent advisors should be engaged to review all employee benefits plans for compliance. However, at the preliminary due diligence stage, some basic questions should be asked. For example, benefit eligibility (which employees get the coverage) should be clear, nondiscriminatory, and consistent with the carrier(s) contract. It is a red flag if eligibility appears to be arbitrary or discriminatory.

If the company has over 20 employees then it is COBRA eligible. The company should be able to demonstrate competent administration of this program. If not, the company could be exposing itself to huge liability. Part of the COBRA review should also include an audit of the procedure for adding and removing employees from the company benefit plans. More often than not we see sloppy administration in this area. Oftentimes, terminated employees are left on a plan and new employees are not added in a timely fashion.

An organization should also be able to generate plan descriptions and summary plan descriptions (SPD) for each health and welfare type plan.

Minor Work Permits

Many states require work permits for employees under the age of 18. There are very clear rules regarding what hours minors can work and what jobs they are allowed to perform. As with many other employment-related regulations, the penalties for non-compliance can be severe.

Wage and Hour Laws

Some people spend their entire professional careers just dealing with Wage and Hour laws. The area is complex and often counterintuitive. If there is one area of employment regulation that is going to be messed up, it will be this. At a minimum, a buyer should ask some basic questions and depending on the response proceed accordingly. For example, ask "how is overtime being tracked?" Be very afraid if the response is "everyone here is salaried" or "we don't pay overtime." Both of these responses indicate a poor understanding of the wage and hour laws and almost a guarantee that employees are being paid incorrectly. Also, be very leery of a company that can't explain how overtime is being calculated; how work time is being recorded; or if employees are taking regular rest and lunch breaks. If administrative employees are working from home or the word "comp time" comes up in your conversation, pay attention. These "buzz words" are indicative of potential problems that you don't want to inherit.

Harassment Training

Most savvy business owners understand the negative consequences associated with sexual harassment claims. And for good
reason, the subject is not something to be taken lightly. I would
"walk away" from any company where I witnessed a callous or
disrespectful attitude toward women or minorities or a workplace where "bullying" was an accepted part of the work culture.

Many states require annual harassment training.

Safety

Workplace safety is a necessary part of every work environment.
Certainly some industries involve work that is more dangerous
than others and will be subject to specific industry requirements
on which you should be well versed. Regardless, every company
should be able to demonstrate how they have created a safe
place to work. Depending on the situation, this may mean having a formal Accident Prevention Program, Material Safety Data
Sheets (MSDS), CPR training, personal protective equipment,
safety committees, etc. You should be able to review an OSHA
log (or equivalent) and notes from a safety committee meeting.

Employee versus Independent Contractor

It should come as no surprise that the states and the federal
government dislike when employers classify workers as Independent Contractors (1099ers) instead of employees. There are
many checklists and worksheets available to help a company
make a correct determination. A huge red flag should go up if it
looks like the determination is being made in an arbitrary or non-
objective fashion. If the decision to make an employee an Independent Contractor was done because it was "less expensive,"
"easier," or "the employee wanted it that way," it is most surely
being done incorrectly!

Best Practices

Along with compliance and tactical issues, HR people also care a
lot about what we call HR Best Practices. In other words, things

that aren't necessarily required by a law or regulation but are still good ideas. Perhaps they are a good idea because they reduce a company's liability or because they just make the company a better, more successful organization. Whether or not you are a buyer or seller, you should care about HR Best Practices. Good HR practices simply result in an overall better company. A company with poor HR practices is simply asking for trouble and certainly is not operating at its full potential.

Many topics fall into the HR Best Practices area. The list below is not exhaustive but should give you a "feel" for what is involved.

JOB DESCRIPTIONS

There is no law that says a company must have job descriptions, but most HR people view them as mission critical. Job descriptions are very useful tools when it comes to hiring, training, compensation, and performance reviews. Without job descriptions how does one know what the critical skills and experience are of a particular job? How do we know if an applicant is qualified? What is included in a training program? How do we figure out the market rate for compensation? And, what are the criteria by which we evaluate the employee's performance? All things that a well written job description can help us address.

WRITTEN HIRING PROCEDURES

Hiring high quality employees is important for virtually every organization. Before buying a company, I would want to know that some organized effort was being made to hire good people. Evidence of this, at least in part, would be a process that was written down and used. And it is probably always a good idea to review employee turnover data.

MANAGEMENT TRAINING

Along with quality and competent employees we want to see competent management. Is there any management training going on? Is the current management team comprised of just high performing employees who were promoted? How are management skills maintained and developed? Is there any depth on the bench to draw from?

EMPLOYEE HANDBOOK

Employee polices need to be written down. Lack of written policies is clear evidence of a poorly run, "shoot from the hip" company. Clearly articulated polices that are fairly administered are evidence of a professionally run company.

Well-written Employee Handbooks also substantially help a company follow the applicable employment regulations. This includes everything from administration of leave policies, insurance eligibility, vacation accruals, time keeping, attendance, harassment, etc.

PERSONNEL FILES

Before purchasing a company I would always look at the personnel files. Are there copies of performance reviews, disciplinary notices, employment applications, resumes, etc.? You can learn a lot about individual employees as well as the company's organizational skills by reviewing a few key employee files.

PERFORMANCE REVIEWS

Certainly not every company does regular performance reviews. However, they can be evidence of a strategic workforce. In other words, performance reviews can be used as a tool to help individuals within an organization move forward and achieve strategic goals. If an organization claims to have strategic goals, I would ask how individuals are measured consistent with these goals. Strategic goals without an employee component could be quite hollow and simply fancy words.

BENEFIT PLAN DESIGN AND COST

It goes without saying that employee benefit plans are costly. These costs however can be managed. Questions here should involve items such as "How has the plan been designed? What cost sharing is taking place? Is the plan competitive within the industry? Who is the broker and what services are they providing?" Strategic thinking means the benefit plan is a component of the overall employee compensation, and some real thought has been put into the "Whys" and "Hows."

COMPENSATION – WHAT PEOPLE ARE PAID

Too often we find that companies have no rhyme or reason as to how employees are paid. It almost seems random. A well-run company should be able to demonstrate that there is some structure, some rationale, to pay levels. There should be some attempt to ensure both internal equity (employees are being paid fairly compared to one another) and external equity (employees are being paid fairly compared to the outside labor market).

EMPLOYEE COMPLAINTS

Hopefully the Employee Handbook contained a section on how employee complaints are resolved. If nothing like this exists, then chances are employee problems are being resolved by government agencies (e.g., EEOC) or attorneys. Needless to say, this is not very strategic and demonstrates a lack of professional management or possibly even ambivalence. Ask about recent employee issues and how they were resolved.

TERMINATION

As with hiring, HR people want to see some written policies around terminations. Are people just "fired" or is there a "progressive disciplinary" approach? Terminations without good documentation oftentimes result in employment-related lawsuits. At a minimum they demonstrate poor management skills.

Reviewing several of the last terminations can provide good insight into the quality of the management team. Ask to see documentation, exit interviews, etc. This can be quite enlightening and a good way to "see inside the organization."

This is also probably a good time to ask the company if there is an Employment Practices Liability Insurance (EPLI) policy in place. If so, I would ask to review any claims.

CONFIDENTIALITY AND NON-COMPETE AGREEMENTS

Many companies have their employees sign Confidentiality and Non-compete Agreements. Unfortunately, many times, these are either poorly written or because of state laws, non-enforceable. If, as a buyer or a seller, you place value on these agreements then they all need to be reviewed by an employment attorney. Emphasis is on the word "all." I have found that in some cases these agreements have not been executed in a timely manner and/or modified on an individual employee level. If so, this may invalidate the agreement.

UNION ORGANIZING EFFORTS

If you are part of, or talking with, a company that has one or more labor unions representing employees, then a basic review of the applicable contract(s) is a good idea. A general understanding of "norms" for the industry will help you evaluate the competiveness of the contract. It is probably unrealistic to think that you will be able to "bust" or breakup the union. Instead you need to make sure you can work with the union and still be successful. Dig deeper if the company has a history where the employees have attempted to organize, even if unsuccessful.

Sometimes the "Human Resources" of a company are neglected during a due diligence process. Sometimes the "Human Resource" is viewed as commodity—static and easily replaced, much like the inventory in the warehouse. Individuals who have run companies know better. They know that the employees—the HR—can be the trickiest part. Successful HR can be the most difficult to measure and unfortunately the most volatile and expensive if something goes wrong. A thorough due diligence process will involve a comprehensive look at the tactical and the strategic—the Compliance and the Best Practices.

ACTION POINTS

* Have a due diligence plan (don't wing it).

* Concentrate on the non-financial factors (you've already reviewed the financials, as has your bank), especially the customers, vendors and employees.

* Plan for growth and the people that will be needed.

* Determine if the company and its people are ready for growth.

* Be thorough but not anal-retentive.

* Is the company prepared for emergencies?

* Don't talk to any customers without written permission from the seller.

* Realize that sales (revenue generation) is huge.

* Understand the difference between sales and marketing—both are important.

* Look for any dependencies; especially a dependency on the owner.

* Investigate the culture.

* Make sure the company is compliance with all human resource requirements.

There's a Wizard Behind the Green Curtain We're Closing!

The following is a document I give my clients when we start working together, even though much of it doesn't need to be done until two months prior to closing. This list was compiled by getting input from 8-10 clients who had closed on deals in the two years prior to when I wrote this. A lot of these items are the nagging, little administrivia things that drive many people nuts; but they must be done.

FINAL THINGS TO DO WHEN BUYING A BUSINESS

DETERMINE LEGAL STRUCTURE

Sole proprietor

Partnership

Corporation — C or S

LLC

Your attorney can guide you through this process. Make sure you check with your CPA to make sure entity type is the best for anticipated tax issues.

ADMINISTRATION MATTERS

Government

Federal & State registrations

County and City regulations

Pick your name and register it

State & local business licenses

Dept. of Revenue

EIN #

S Corporation election and filing

Haz Mat reports

Local permits & licensing

Confirm seller's existing corporation or LLC existence

Registered agents address

All tax forms, L&I, sales, unemployment, personal property, etc.

If asset purchase — dissolve seller's entity or have him/her relinquish trade name to you

Non-Government

Bank — deposits, credit card processing, lines of credit, etc.

Telephone — long distance, local, cell

Utilities

Internet, website, shippers (FedEx, UPS)

Copyrights, trademarks & other intellectual property — including trade name registration

Insurance — property, liability, vehicle, life (bank may require), health, disability, etc.

New business cards, stationary

Lease

Software licenses, passwords, etc.

– 10 – THERE'S A WIZARD BEHIND THE
GREEN CURTAIN WE'RE CLOSING!

277

Off balance sheet items like equipment leases, advertising contracts, etc.

Employment agreements/non-compete agreements, W-9s & W-4s

Contracts with vendors, customers, etc.

Vendor and customer lists including *all* contact information

Signage, printing, labels, etc.

Change vehicle registrations

FINANCIAL

Books and records—what system, who does it, does your CPA approve of it?

Vendor list—must you apply for credit?

Closing reports, liens, taxes due, etc.— Whoever closes your deal should handle all the details such as taxes due, forms due, lien filings, lien removals, etc.

Pro-rated expenses and revenues—including accounting for customer deposits for future work and the cash needed to fulfill such work.

Post-closing settlement date—usually 30-60 days after closing to reconcile normal business transactions that occur around and after closing.

Life insurance—this is a timely issue. Your bank or seller note may require it. It takes 6-8 weeks to get a policy issued so you must start early.

Disclaimer: The above is not a due diligence form. It supplements your due diligence forms. It is designed as a guide for the little things it takes to prepare for closing, get your entity off-the-ground and assure a smooth transition. It is not guaranteed to be all-inclusive (as all deals and situations are different). Items are not listed in any particular order. If you are unsure about the sequence of events, just call me. If you find anything missing, please let me know so I can add it to the list.

Timeline

Following is a sample closing timeline (provided originally by Diana Altchech with ACT Capital Advisors, Mercer Island, WA). Start filling in the tasks and dates once an offer is agreed to (at least verbally). Each deal is different, and this form is not meant to be all encompassing. It may represent tasks not required for your deal. Take note that getting life insurance takes six to eight weeks and will delay your deal if a policy is not in place (especially if there's a bank loan involved).

Sample Closing Timeline

Note that the target dates and checkmarks for completed tasks are for illustration purposes only. You will start off with blank columns. Also, while most of the tasks listed are common to all deals your deal may not have all of these tasks and may have some not listed her.

Done	Task	Target Date
√	Preliminary committal letter from bank	
√	LOI signed	March 31
√	All financial information (for bank) from seller team	Wednesday, April 6
√	Package to bank(s)	Monday, April 11
√	Buyer–seller meeting – initial due diligence	Friday, April 8
√	Bank package to credit department	Tuesday, April 12
	Due diligence- on-going	
√	Draft - legal documents – start of process	Thursday, April 14
√	Draft- promissory note/security agreement - start	Thursday, April 14
√	Meet landlord – discuss lease	Monday, April 18

Done	Task	Target Date
√	Bank review completed	April 27
√	Final committal letter from bank	April 29
	Buyer calls customers as "references"	
√	SBA request for transcript of tax returns	
	Order business valuation, home appraisal	May 10
	Seller signs 4506 for bank	May 9
	Landlord waiver draft language (by bank)	May 10
	Escrow agent alerted (by bank)	May 9
	Asset allocations from accountants	May 9 week
	Final draft-legal docs with any modifications	May 9 week
	Promissory Note Security agreement to bank	May 9 week
	Lease tentatively approved by both parties	May 9 week
√	Life insurance approved	May 9 week
	Business valuation returned Home appraisal returned	May 20
	Banks final documents ready	May23
	Buyer meets employees	May 24
	Final documents ready for signing (P&S, etc.) and signed	May 24
	All documents and escrow instructions to escrow agent	May 24
	Signing of subordinate agreement by sellers	May 24
	Buyer's money in escrow account	May 24
	Loan documents signed	May 24
	Signing of final documents & funding	Tuesday-May 31

The point of the written timeline is to organize the project and provide the lead times all parties will need to understand. I like to work backward. Determine an estimated closing date and then ask the bank, lawyers and others what kind of lead-time they need to meet that date. We then put their dates in the timeline to make it feasible (with a cushion in all areas).

THE BANK AND YOUR CLOSING

Notice that about two-thirds of the tasks involve the bank. If you're not going to use a bank for your deal many, but not all, of these tasks will be reduced or disappear. For now, let's assume there is a bank involved.

The bank controls the process, the timeline and the closing date; there's no way around it. Note that the timeline starts after you have a preliminary commitment letter from the bank and at least a verbal agreement on price, terms and conditions (or an LOI). Then your efforts are concentrated on the following areas:

- Getting the bank everything they need to give final and formal approval

- Having the lawyers draft and finalize the Purchase and Sale Agreement (PSA)*

- Getting all the administrivia mentioned in the closing check-list handled, including a lease or lease assignment, vendors, employment agreements, etc.

- Completing due diligence including talking to the customers and key employees

* I recommend that you have your attorney draft the PSA and related documents. It will cost you more but you will usually get a document with "Warranties and Representations" that will be fairer to both sides. If there's a note or a lease from the seller, it is the obligation of the seller and his or her attorney to provide you with the note and lease.

Your team's involvement

This is where your team gets active. Obviously your attorney takes the lead and the most active role. Make sure your attorney (and hopefully the seller's attorney) likes to draft and edit documents with the intent that the other side will find them fair. It's too easy, and I've seen too many instances, where one attorney wants 95% of the risk on the other side. This does nothing but increase legal bills, cause frustration on both sides, and delay the deal. Busy attorneys (who are also good) will avoid this, as they have many clients and just want to get the deal done.

Your CPA will need to work with the seller's CPA to determine the asset allocation. This is where they both earn their keep. You want as many write offs as possible, and the seller wants as low a tax bill as they can get. My experience is that the emphasis will be on depreciable assets, the non-compete agreement and the training allocation—the rest being current assets and goodwill. How retained debt fits into this is for your CPA to determine.

Your CPA may also help you with financial due diligence, spot-check audits, analyzing the accounting system, chart of accounts and other tactical accounting related matters. There is no set agenda here; part of it depends on your knowledge of accounting matters, and your willingness to do some of this work. I've had clients bring in their CPA for a few days to do it all and I've had others go in themselves to do mini-audits (compare bank statements to deposit books to the accounting entries and financial statements for particular months and do the same for expense tracking).

As mentioned in Chapter Three, other members of your team now may get involved. I've had clients whose team was their banker, lawyer, CPA and me, and others who used:

- A CFO to help with cash flow projections, budgets, etc.
- Human resource experts when there were employee issues that could be a problem
- Environmental consulting firms to do studies of the property
- Equipment experts to analyze the useful life of the machinery
- Commercial real estate agents to help with determining the fair market rent and to help with the lease

REAL LIFE STORY: DON'T SKIMP ON ADVICE; YOU GET WHAT YOU PAY FOR

Here's how not to use your team. My client was in the process of closing on a deal to buy a similar business in another geographic area. At the same time he was looking at another acquisition in a different state (for which he didn't hire me).

The attorney I recommended helped him with his Washington deal but wasn't licensed in the other state. He tried to help, but the other attorney not only came across as inexperienced in transactions but wouldn't even talk to the Washington attorney.

I later met with this owner and determined he didn't hire a CPA for the second transaction. And, his attorney truly didn't know deals. A big part of this deal was an earnout (percentage of sales over a number of years). It was structured to be goodwill, meaning a 15-year amortization. It should have been a royalty or similar to give the buyer an immediate write-off.

The bottom line was that with the payments to the seller, taxes on the profit and amortization of the goodwill he has extremely low cash flow from this deal. This will continue until his earnout payments are completed, at which time he'll have accelerated cash flow because of the amortization write-off and no payments to the seller. However, he needs the cash flow now, if for no other reason than to make him emotionally happy with the deal.

PURCHASE AND SALE AGREEMENT

This is the heart of all deals and by the time you arrive at this point there should be very little negotiating left to do. This doesn't mean negotiations are over; at the very least the attorneys may discuss warranties and representations. In simple layman terms, these are the clauses where both buyer and seller state that everything they have presented about the business or themselves is true and correct.

Most attorneys look for a fair divide within the reps and warranties clauses. Occasionally, you'll see an attorney who wants full protection

– 10 – There's a Wizard Behind the
Green Curtain We're Closing!

283

for their client and almost none for the other side. When it happens it's a pain; but it doesn't happen that often. This is why I ask attorneys to draft contracts that they would find fair if they were on the receiving end of said contract.

From a non-legal perspective, here are the most important items you should be concerned with.

As mentioned, the warranties and representations section is key. This is where both attorneys earn their fees. You want the seller to represent that what he or she has told you is true and correct. You also want to have some recourse if you find something that was materially misrepresented. Work closely with your attorney on this.

REAL LIFE STORY: CAN'T HIDE EVERYTHING

The buyer had acquired a computer store that assembled PC clones, did repairs and sold parts. While the business had a storefront, the bulk of the sales were to businesses and government.

About six months after closing, the owner looked at the morning paper and the headline said that his business was under investigation for selling black market Microsoft software. It seems the seller had received two "cease and desist" letters from Microsoft and not only did he ignore them for the most part, he didn't disclosed this to his broker or the buyer—even though he was directly asked the question, in writing, about potential litigation.

Because there was a strong purchase and sale agreement, a good attorney and a seller note (which gave him leverage over the seller), the buyer was able to survive this. In fact, a few months later the buyer said that the headlines were a boom to his business. People remembered the company name and forgot how and why they heard about the business.

The non-compete agreement, sometimes a separate document and sometimes a section in the contract, is also very important, especially if the seller is not at or beyond the typical retirement age. Some buyers want a long-term agreement that is very tight on what the seller can do and other buyers who don't care too much about the non-compete agreement. A big part of the decision is based on the relationship between buyer and seller.

Work with your attorney so it's realistic and enforceable. Realize you can have a lot stronger non-compete with the seller than with the employees. The seller is trading the value of the business in return for not competing with you. If the seller wants a very loose or short non-compete you might want to wonder why.

We've discussed asset allocation a few times previously and this is where it gets memorialized. Your CPA and the seller's CPA will work to find common ground. As stated, the biggest issue for the seller will be any possible taxation at ordinary income rates versus capital gains rates. The common culprits here are depreciation recapture, the value of the non-compete and the value of training (of you by the seller).

You will usually want to accelerate depreciation of the assets in lieu of the 15-year write-off for goodwill. Be sure to pay attention to all taxes. For example, in Washington, the fixed assets are subject to sales tax (at over 9%) if they are assets not used to manufacture a product. While in the long run it's better to pay the sales tax and re-depreciate, in the short run it can be a large hit to initial cash flow.

The signing of the agreement is not necessarily at closing. Many times the actual signing is a week or two in advance of closing and final papers and funding takes place at the closing. One huge reason for an advanced signing is that the seller wants the buyer to be fully committed before interviewing the employees. The agreement will have one contingency and that is the employee interviews and key employees' willingness to stay.

On the flip side, it is not uncommon to have the closing after the effective date, meaning the documents are backdated. This happens if it's close to the year, quarter or month end and it's just simpler to backdate than to prorate expenses like rent, payroll and similar and have double tax reporting for a short period.

Whether you sign in advance, on the date of closing or after (and backdate), expect that all the details won't be worked out at that time. You will most likely have a settlement date between 30 and 60 days after

– 10 – There's a Wizard Behind the
Green Curtain We're Closing!

285

closing. Some of your down payment will stay in escrow to cover any payables not recorded as of closing, uncollectable receivables or other costs that materialized.

Here are a few things that your attorney, the escrow agent or you will want to handle (in addition to what has already been mentioned).

- The titles for any registered assets (often vehicles)
- Confirming the amount and value of inventory
- Verification and inspection of all assets
- All notifications to government and non-government organizations
- Intellectual property filings
- All computer related licenses, warranties, passwords, etc.
- Off balance sheet items and renewals of things like advertising
- Realize that if you purchase assets the seller will retain their legal entity, bank accounts, tax ID number and similar. They will have to file all necessary tax forms, handle their portion of employee benefits, pension deposits and similar.

TRANSITION PLAN

The transition technically starts the day after closing. Realistically, it starts once you've both signed an LOI. Your due diligence is both confirmation, of what you've been told, cultural and operational insights and the start of your initial transition training.

As with anything in business, having a structured transition plan accelerates your success. Let's take a look at a sample transition plan. This plan is for a company that is a sales and service organization, so you'll have to adjust it if your business is in a different industry and you'll need to tweak it even if you're buying a sales and service company. Realize that you may want the seller out long before the official transition period ends. One client told his seller that the seller would be on call by phone after only one-week of personal training (the seller didn't mind at all).

TRAINING PLAN - TACTICAL

This is a sample only. Your plan may look nothing like this (it may be larger or smaller). This was for a sales, installation and service company.

The following table outlines a tactical training schedule of items to consider on a daily basis. Provide the seller with a condensed version and get him to agree to it. The 'Goals" indicate the important accomplishments that must occur for that week. Revise as necessary, beginning day one.

Month 1 Training Plan (Tactical)

	Sales	Operations	Accounting	HR	Goals
Week 1	Review basic sales strategy (leads, follow-up, etc.).	Listen to and begin answering phone calls.	Establish a new company in the accounting system.	Review any and all employee records.	By the end of week one I will have:
	Spend time with the sales people as they call on customers. How are leads generated? What is their style and approach?	Figure out the scheduling system. Determine how jobs are bid and how the software is used.	Sit with the bookkeeper to learn exactly what she does.	Download all information on company policies.	-A general understanding of how the sales process works in this business -Observed live sales calls
	Get up to speed on all products.	Visit a job in progress. Schedule time to spend with each technician.	Download all system documentation.	Ensure everyone is enrolled in new benefit plans as applicable.	-A general understanding of all products and services the business offers
	Need to schedule introductions to suppliers and 3M training.	Spend time with key people if available. Determine what type of network is set up, if any, and reconfigure if necessary.	Set up outside payroll services. Apply for fleet fuel cards/ company credit cards.	Gather remaining signatures needed for corporate docs.	-New accounting system is up and running -Established payroll procedures
	Visit a few local customers - don't plan the major sales training this week.	Establish a VPN to enable remote access for myself only.	Visit CPA to finalize company set-up.	Finalize team member assessments and their capabilities.	-Been introduced either by phone or in person to key stakeholders or have meetings scheduled
	Plan major sales calls for next week.	Get an electrical apprentice training certificate that allows me to work as an installer.	Ensure online bank account software and hardware for remote deposits is set up and working.	Ensure all licensing with state L&I/ Employment security is transferred.	Install a remote access system to allow me to access the system from home.

	Sales	Operations	Accounting	HR	Goals
Week 2	Week one of "hitting the streets" with the seller. Plan to be out in the field for M/W/F. Change days if necessary.	Create a "cheat sheet" to assist with taking phone calls. Document the types of calls that come in most often.	Company should be completely set up by now. Independently use the system software and run reports.	Evaluate the physical environment. Does anything need fixing? Do things need to be organized or cleaned?	Be able to intelligently discuss products and services with customers in person and on the phone.
	Document the processes. Pay close attention to training methods so we can replicate later.	Spend a full day on installations this week. Observe how technician engages the customer and how he closes the work order.	Start thinking about how much accounting work I can handle and what needs to be delegated or outsourced.		Understand what the installation process looks like and describe the steps in an install
	Make sure to get quick feedback at the end of each day. Plan for a complete review of the week with the seller either on Friday or Saturday.	Review results of initial customer service calls and plan another round of these calls in next 60 days.	Discuss with admin staff and document their tasks. Should have an understanding of how the AR/ AP process works. Accelerate billing process.	Start thinking about job descriptions for each position. Have key people document their activities.	Know exactly where I stand with respect to the accounting processes and procedures and what resources I need.
	On office days focus on other areas.	Inspect all vehicles and field equipment, if not already com-pleted.	Tie up any loose ends with bank-ing, accounting or corporate documents.	Observe and document the relationships between all employees with one other and custom-ers.	Corporate and finance docs should be mostly complete by this point.

– 10 – THERE'S A WIZARD BEHIND THE
GREEN CURTAIN WE'RE CLOSING!

289

	Sales	Operations	Accounting	HR	Goals
Week 3	Fieldwork M/W/F. Should be actively producing my own leads.	Visit a nearby job in progress.	Ensure new processes are working. Was everyone paid on time and correctly with first new payroll?	Begin to review HR software solutions. Is there a low cost service to maintain key records?	Fieldwork M/W/F. Should be actively producing my own leads.
	Monitor salesperson's performance during this time as well. Know what jobs he is working on.	Begin to document the workflow process and develop flow charts to outline the critical path.	Begin to review AR collections procedures. Can bookkeeper handle this adequately?	Start to document key items that should be addressed in an employee handbook/HR policy.	Visit a nearby job in progress.
	Continue to review goals of initial sales plan.	Start learning the basics of repairing the equipment.	Develop credit policies and procedures for new customers, if needed.	Review existing employee handbook for critical/legal items that should be addressed immediately.	Ensure new processes are working. Was everyone paid on time and correctly with first new payroll?
	Do I need some formal sales training to help sharpen my skills?	Review inventory control procedures. Are they acceptable?	Schedule meeting with banker to discuss first month numbers and determine right mix of products/services.	Continue to learn and understand key areas of the low-voltage/skilled electrical trade.	Review inventory control procedures. Are they acceptable?
	Where are you, marketing wise?	Start getting bids on website rebuild.	If accounting will be outsourced, start getting quotes or looking for part-time bookkeeper.	Determine whether we have the best benefit package for this size of business.	Continue to learn and understand key areas of the low-voltage/skilled electrical trade.

	Sales	Operations	Accounting	HR	Goals
Week 4	Fieldwork M/W/F. Should have a refined calling strategy by this point and possibly have a sale.	Perform another install; try to do one alone with tech supervision and sign-off.	At end of week review first month's numbers and assess them against prior plan.	Put together a first month summary (culture, politics, customer service, attitudes) and review with seller.	Fieldwork M/W/F. Should have a refined calling strategy by this point and possibly have a sale.
	Review performance at end of this week. Discuss with seller and begin planning for next month.	Review operating system performance for first month. Does this system meet my needs? Do I need to get a quote for an update?	Close month and develop financial forecast for next month.	Schedule one-on-one meetings with employees to discuss first month.	Review performance at end of this week. Discuss with seller and begin planning for next month.
	Develop a sales plan for the next 60 days.	Review and transfer any dealer contracts from seller to me.	Are the newly established processes/procedures working?	Schedule first meeting with advisors.	At end of week review first month's numbers and assess them against seller's prior plan.
	Review salesperson's performance for the month.	Review our vendor systems.			Close month and develop financial forecast for next month.

DUE DILIGENCE INTERVIEW QUESTIONS

Break the interview into two parts: with the seller, and without the seller. Meet each employee at a designated location, with the seller there. He or she introduces you and makes small talk for a few minutes and then start to build the relationship.

Introduction (Seller Present)

- **Situation:** Discuss a bit about how we got to this point. Inform the employee that we have reached an agreement

– 10 – There's a Wizard Behind the Green Curtain We're Closing!

291

and that you will be taking over the business. The seller will remain in place for a transitional period.

A good way to do this is to ask the employees to tell you their story, to tell you about their life, what they like to do, what they like about the company. Build the relationship with soft questions and they will expand on their own.

- **Your background:** Briefly discuss your background. Do not get too much into specifics—there is no need to sell anyone on your capabilities—the seller should do that. Explain to the employee that you're excited about the acquisition and want everyone to stay on board to help ensure a smooth transition.

- **His/her background:** Ask the employee to start with his/her background *before* coming to the company. This is particularly important if there are any family members staying on. Focus on the following:

  - Past employers – time there

  - Past positions – roles and responsibilities

  - Skills and/or licenses

  - Educational background

- **Current position:** Ask the employee to describe his/her current responsibilities at a daily/weekly/monthly level. Focus on:

  - Daily routines—what has to be done every single day? How much time is spent doing it?

  - Main responsibilities—get sufficient detail

  - Weekly reporting or milestones to track progress? Specific to sales—how do they manage their sales prospects? How do they track performance as per a monthly sales goal? Do they have an individual monthly production goal?

At this point, the seller should announce that he or she has to leave.

Interview questions (seller not present):

- What are your thoughts about the company? Where do you see opportunity?

- What are your thoughts about this transition? Is there anything you'd like me to know specifically?

- How have you liked working in the business so far?

- What would you change about the company if you could?

- What are the company's strengths?

- What are its weaknesses?

- Is there anything else you'd like to discuss? Questions? Concerns?

Ask other questions specific to the industry or company.

REAL LIFE STORY: THE EMPLOYEES HAVE GREAT INSIGHTS

As part of the transition the buyer had the management team complete a survey. It wasn't long, only about half a dozen questions. One of the questions asked what they thought was the company's greatest weakness. To a person, all the answers were a variation of this answer, "The company's greatest weakness just walked out the door."

The seller was controlling, knew everything better than anybody else and wasn't a team player. It wasn't any wonder that the buyer built great initial rapport by simply asking the employees for their input. (Asking the employees for their ideas on how to make the business better is a tried and true strategy that benefits every business buyer who does it.)

– 10 – There's a Wizard Behind the
Green Curtain We're Closing!

293

Do it again

When I started in this business in 1992, my friend and "Partner" On-Call Network president, Ted Leverette, had a saying regarding business buyers buying another company. It was: "You've proved you're a buyer. Other sellers will seek you out."

Skeptical at first, I've come to believe that line, not for everybody, but for enough people to lend validity to the statement. The best way to prove this is to give you six examples. All of the situations described below are small businesses, and four of the six took place in the first two years of new ownership.

1. Within 90 days of closing the buyer's CPA told him that now that he was an owner, an insider, they would give him access to deals in case he wanted to buy another business. Within two years of becoming an owner, the owner of a small firm that offered a product complementary to his approached him, because he wanted to retire, and he bought that company. Also within the first year his primary supplier told him that if he ever wanted to acquire his main competitor they would help him finance the deal. You see, the supplier did not supply the competitor and wanted their volume.

2. The story in Chapter Two about growing by acquisition happened in the first two years after the buyer closed on his deal. Recall that he bought a manufacturing business that made a product he distributed. The seller was a product guy, not a good businessperson. This made for a win-win deal. The buyer's benefits included higher margins, greater volume and proof he could buy and assimilate another company.

3. This buyer always kept his senses attuned to what was going on in his industry. Within a year or so of the acquisition he came across an elderly owner with medical problems whose business was close enough to be easily manageable and far enough away so they had completely different customer bases. He took over that business and then we started hunting for another one.

4. This owner had already made one small acquisition and we had done a search for others. A couple years after our search one of his suppliers introduced him to an owner whom wanted to retire and was in a different geographic area. He bought the business and set up a small distribution hub in the other location.

5. This owner made three acquisitions in a span of three years. One was a smaller direct competitor, another was a distinct product line and the third was a sales organization in a different part of the country.

6. In a very fragmented industry the buyer realized, as he was investigating the business he bought, that consolidation of very small players was a possibility. Within two to three years he made a few small acquisitions, mainly taking over customer lists. This was one reason his firm made the local Business Journal's list of fastest growing privately held companies.

To some, buying another company is the same as buying another piece of equipment. They look at it as a routine growth strategy. Earlier I stated that numerous studies say that 90% of people who say they are business buyers never buy a business. On the flip side, in my 2012 survey of business owners, 86% say they are open to acquiring another company if it is the right situation. That's 86%! That's a huge number, and while very few of them will actually buy another business, it tells us that, given the right situation, there is interest. Of course, just like when you buy your first business, the right situation will come along more frequently if you take charge and are proactive.

Realize that as a repeat buyer your market is smaller because of the industry you are in (assuming you want something related) and also ripe with opportunity because you don't have to buy a profitable business. It's a lot easier, and cheaper, to take over a mediocre operation in order to get their volume (with reduced overhead), employees, location or product line.

– 10 – There's a Wizard Behind the
Green Curtain We're Closing!

295

Action points

* Pay attention to the details. They will drive you nuts, but you can't ignore them.

* Create a timeline for all tasks that must be done before closing, together with their finish dates.

* Involve your bank and your team in the timeline.

* Know the difference between the legal and business issues in the Sale and Purchase Agreement.

* Have a transition plan, finalize it with the seller, stick to it and be as flexible as you need to be.

CLOSING

This book starts off with 10 reasons why you should consider buying a business. The book ends with a reference to the statistic that 90% of people who say they want to buy and own a business never do so. Those 10 reasons are pretty powerful and they do come with risk.

But what is risk? Is it riskier to buy a business or stay in your job where you may be unappreciated, treated like a number, not making enough money and just not happy? A friend recently told me he was going to "play hooky" and spend the day on the golf course. He used the old line that a bad day playing golf was better than a good day at work. I replied, "Then you probably have the wrong job." The look on his face told me my comment resonated.

Is it riskier to buy another business or keep your current business on its same stagnant place? When it comes time to sell, how do you justify a high price if there's no proven growth strategy and a culture of working easy? How do you keep the competition from zooming by you?

Follow the tips and strategies in this book and, again, returning to the beginning of the book, the preface in particular, the leap of faith you'll make will be off a chair not off a roof. Happy and successful leaping!

AFTERWORD

I hope the information in this book is helpful as you make your first purchase of a business or grow your company via a merger or acquisition. You can find additional how-to insight on my website: www. martinkaconsulting.com

CEO's say that the most pressing issue they face when trying to grow their company is implementing their strategy. If you really want to buy a business, please don't be the business buyer who never takes serious action, kicks a few obvious tires and then, two years later, tells all their friends it's impossible to find and buy a good business. Call or email mc today to discuss my services to help you locate, analyze and buy a mature, profitable and fairly priced business.

On another note, if you've read this book, find the subject of business buying and selling fascinating and yet are wondering if, when all is said and done, "Will I be able to pull the trigger?" don't just put this book on your bookshelf. Pick up the phone and call me or send me an email to find out how "Partner" On-Call Network (www.partneroncall. com) can license you in our systems, train you on how to be a Business Buyer Advocate and how to market your services so you can help clients.

You can email me at john@johnmartinka.com and call me at 425-576-1814.

Appendix A

Due-Diligence Questionnaire

Use this list judicially. If you are making an asset purchase you aren't buying the whole company (which is a stock sale) and you may not need many of the legal documents (check with your attorney). Trying to get all of this information will overwhelm any seller and the smaller the business the greater the chances of the seller being overwhelmed. The most important thing you can do is get the seller involved in conversations about the business and these topics. Just getting written answers won't help you nearly as much.

ESTABLISH RESPONSIBILITIES AND TIME LINE FIRST

LEGAL DOCUMENTS

In the corporation (or LLC) good standing?

Articles of incorporation

Foreign jurisdictions

Officers/Directors/Owners

Subsidiaries and/or affiliates

Special shareholder rights, i.e. preemptive rights or other agreements

Minutes of Board meetings (3 years)

By-laws

What capital has been invested or loaned to business?

How has company been capitalized until now?

COMPANY'S BUSINESS

Describe the nature of the business

Describe each line of products and services sold

Describe proposed emphasis and direction of business

Is there an intention to widen the range of products and services sold?

Are there any limitations to products, tariffs, licenses, copyrights, etc?

Intellectual property ⬜ trademarks, trade names, copyrights, patents, software, trade secrets, other

The method of sales, contracts with suppliers

Contracts with other companies, etc.

Are subcontractors used and for what?

Are there any long-term contracts with subcontractors, etc.?

A list of competitors and a description of their products

What do you know about the competitors financing & technical resources?

What is the ease or difficulty to enter this business? IN DETAIL

Copies of technical information, trade marks, trade names, copy rights, licenses

Copies of any major contracts

Description of distribution channels

INDUSTRY GROWTH

What is the estimated growth rate of the industry in the next 5 years?

What factors will affect growth in the future?

Are prices, industry wide, stable or increasing?

MARKETING STRATEGY

What are the marketing objectives?

How will the objectives be implemented?

What marketing effort is required?

What expense is projected?

MARKETING PLAN

Who & how many people are involved in marketing?

What are historical sales increases/decreases by line (percentages)?

Sales projections by product, percentage of future revenue

PRODUCT PRICING

How are products and services priced?

Will there be any price changes in the future?

How does pricing compare with competitive and comparable products?

Review actual invoices with major customers (to check for discounts, special deals, etc.)

CUSTOMER ANALYSIS

Who are the customers?

What are the trends in this customer group?

Customer list by volume of sales (3 years)

What is the procedure to sell products and services?

Copies of all client agreements or contracts

What will be the determining factors to a buying decision?

Are sales controlled by a few high priced, well-connected salespeople?

FACILITIES REQUIRED

What facilities changes will be required in the future, size, description? Technology requirements, hardware, software, licensing agreements, etc.

EMPLOYEES

List of Officers & Directors (and key employees)

Resumes officers & Directors (and key employees)

List of all employees, salary, date of hire and title

Copies of employment agreements

Employee turnover, out of ordinary?

Compensation schedule for owners, officers and key employees (including bonus plan)

DUE-DILIGENCE LIST

List of shareholders & percentage ownership

Company's Attorney, CPA, insurance broker, health insurance broker, etc.

Company's Bank & statements, deposit books, check register, QuickBooks file, etc.

Environmental reports

Employee manuals

Copies of company leases

List of all major assets ☐ current, at fair market value

Brochures and other marketing materials

Financial statements last five (5) years

Financial Statements, monthly for 1-2 years

Accounts receivable aging report

List of all debts and liabilities

Copies of the last Five (5) years federal income tax returns (4506 with IRS if needed)

Copies of 3-5 years state sales and other state tax returns

Copies of all agreements, loan agreements, notes, pledge agreements and security

Copies of all profit sharing or deferred compensation plans

Business Plan

Litigation history and anticipated (both ways), court search

Insurance coverage, any changes, etc.

Liens (equipment, tax, etc.)

Off balance sheet items, vacation, sick pay, etc. and proprietary information such as drawings, reverse engineered and manufactured parts, etc.

Copyright 2001-2012 John Martinka, all rights reserved

Appendix B

DEAL TERMS

Structure	Asset or stock sale
Price	
Down Payment	Cash to seller at closing
Terms	Make sure you put in the disclaimer that it's subject to bank approval and conditions
Earnout	
Accounts Receivable	
Accounts Payable	
Cash accounts	
Prepaid expenses	
Vehicles	

Other liabilities	
Equipment	Get a list of assets not included and get it early; make sure to cover leased equipment, often office equipment
Space	Can the lease be assigned, will there be a new lease to the buyer, etc.?
Transition	Spell out the in-person time, phone and email time and end date
Inventory	Make sure it's usable and salable
Employee agreements	It is often best to go with what the seller is doing in this area
Insurance	In an asset sale the buyer will need new liability type policies and medical will usually only require paperwork to change
Non-compete	Make sure your attorney is fine with terms and get his or her approval early
Contracts	Vendors, customers, sub-contractors, etc.
Deferred revenue	This has to be covered with adequate cash or AR as it's work the buyer will do
Other conditions	Hazardous materials, off balance sheet items, license agreements, etc.

ABOUT THE AUTHOR

John Martinka is known as *The Escape Artist*™ because of the work he does helping executives escape the corporate world by buying the right business the right way. John has 20 years of business experience as a Business Buyer Advocate®, was a co-founder of "Partner" On-Call Network and has helped over 100 clients successfully navigate the treacherous waters of a buy-sell transaction. He was awarded "Board Approval" in Business Acquisitions & Sales by the Society for Advancement of Consulting℠ LLC. Since 2005 John has lead a team of Rotarians and students on international trips to work in schools in Turkey, Slovakia and Antigua. They have installed thousands of computers, distributed illustrated dictionaries to 7,500 3rd grade students and much more to improve education in those countries.